A/I
AFH9790

D1526208

THE POETICS OF DEATH

SUNY Series, The Margins of Literature
Mihai I. Spariosu, editor

THE POETICS OF DEATH

The Short Prose of Kleist and Balzac

Beatrice Martina Guenther

STATE UNIVERSITY OF NEW YORK PRESS

Cover: *Der Mönch am Meer,* by C. D. Friedrich,
© Bildarchiv Preussischer Kulturbesite, Berlin, 1996.

Published by
State University of New York Press, Albany

© 1996 State University of New York

All rights reserved

Printed in the United States of America

No part of this book may be used or reproduced
in any manner whatsoever without written permission.
No part of this book may be stored in a retrieval
system or transmitted in any form or by any means
including electronic, electrostatic, magnetic tape,
mechanical, photocopying, recording, or otherwise
without the prior permission in writing of the publisher.

For information, address State University of New York Press,
State University Plaza, Albany, N.Y., 12246

Production by Dana Foote
Marketing by Bernadette LaManna

Library of Congress Cataloging-in-Publication Data

Guenther, Beatrice Martina.
The poetics of death : the short prose of Kleist and Balzac /
Beatrice Martina Guenther.
p. cm. — (SUNY series, the margins of literature)
Includes bibliographical references and index.
ISBN 0–7914–3023–5 (hc : alk. paper). — ISBN 0–7914–3024–3 (pb : alk. paper)
1. Kleist, Heinrich von, 1777–1811—Criticism and interpretation.
2. Balzac, Honoré de, 1799–1850—Criticism and interpretation.
3. Literature, Comparative—German and French. 4. Literature, Comparative—French and German. 5. Death in literature. 6. Short story. I. Title. II. Series.
PT2379.Z5G77 1996
809.3'9354—dc20

95-52864
CIP

10 9 8 7 6 5 4 3 2 1

PT
2379
.Z5
G77
1996

*To the memory of my brother, Markus, and
to Gabriele and Christina*

CONTENTS

ACKNOWLEDGMENTS

This book has grown out of the dissertation I defended some years ago at Princeton University. I would first like to thank those individuals in the Departments of Comparative Literature, Romance Languages and Literatures, and Germanic Languages and Literatures at Princeton, who helped facilitate my research and writing. I would especially like to thank Victor Brombert, Walter Hinderer, Ora Avni, Sandra Berman, and Thomas Pavel, who each read the dissertation and supplied much-needed critiques and suggestions for its improvement.

I am also very grateful to my colleagues in the Department of Modern Languages and Literatures at the College of William and Mary who provided encouragement during the process of revising the manuscript. I am, in particular, indebted to Katherine Kulick, Martha Houle, and Eliza Nichols for their intellectual and moral support.

Special thanks also go to Mihai Spariosu, series editor, and to Stanley Corngold as well as to SUNY Press editors Carola Sautter, Dana Foote, and Kay Bolton; Kay Bolton's painstaking copyediting has especially been appreciated. I'd also like to add here that Karin Tiemann's proofreading of the copyedited manuscript was also of great help in this last stretch of reworking the manuscript.

On a personal note, both Wai-Yee Li and Patricia Rosenmeyer through their friendship and example of their scholarship impelled me to continue in my work on Balzac and Kleist. More recently, Nancy Michael and Gabriele, my sister, helped to provide new insights into the question(s) of literary criticism. Most importantly, however, I would like to thank my sister, Christina, who has been an inspiration to me for as long as I can remember.

Introduction

An Uneasy Alliance

Writing and Death

Literary representations of death do not necessarily conjure up images of pessimism and defeat. Traditionally, indeed, it is often the act of writing that is meant to challenge the finality of death. The written text is meant to outlive the writer; it will represent a faithful, perhaps immortal copy of its author. Montaigne, in his "Au lecteur" ["To the Reader"] for instance, describes very eloquently the testamentary function he bestows on his *Essais*:

> Je l'ay voué à la commodité particuliere de mes parens et amis: à ce que m'ayant perdu (ce qu'ils ont à faire bien tost) ils y puissent retrouver aucuns traits de mes conditions et humeurs, et que par ce moyen ils nourrissent plus entière et plus vifve la connoissance qu'ils ont eu de moy.[1]

> I have dedicated it to the particular convenience of my relatives and friends, in that having lost me (which they will have to do soon), they will be able to find there any traits of my conditions and humors, and that through these means, they [will] nourish more completely and more keenly the knowledge they have of me.[2]

We can note here: the essayistic self-description does not simply salvage the lost original. It also carries out a dynamic, supplementary function, granting readers a livelier knowledge of the deceased individual, one that is more accurate than any achieved through experience or personal interaction.

Montaigne's response to the threat of death, though creative, is not explicitly rebellious. He does not use the limit of death as a metaphor of anarchy in order to question the perfection or even primacy of the world at hand. In the case of Baudelaire, however, the transformation of death into a figure of artistic creativity seems simultaneously to challenge the authority of the preexisting world. Consider, for example, his lyrical text, "La Mort des artistes" ["The Death of Artists"]:

> C'est que la Mort, planant comme un soleil nouveau,
> Fera s'épanouir les fleurs de leur cerveau.[3]
>
> It is that Death, hovering like a new sun,
> Will make the flowers of their mind blossom.

"La Mort des artistes" follows two sonnets describing poetically the death of lovers and the death of the poor, both poems that disarm the anxiety of the poet, either by evoking the motif of resurrection through love or by conjuring up the misery of a pauper's existence, thereby heightening the desirability of death. In "La Mort des artistes," the defiantly jubilatory tone of the sonnet's last two lines masks the fact that here the poet confronts most directly the absurd finality of death, the "infernal desire" of the "grande Créature," a symbol that points presumably both to the world and its natural laws as well as to a "theological" universe. By appropriating the tension generated by the sense of impending death, by experiencing a death-induced, perhaps even mortal, creativity, the poetic persona is able to strike up a disrespectful, carnivalesque pose. He can counter the traditional "armature" of Authority with his own artistic edifice, his "étrange et sombre Capitole" [his "strange and somber Capitol"].[4]

Writing is not always represented as the force that might disarm death's sting, besides—as for Montaigne and Baudelaire—surpassing one's life experience. For Christa Wolf's all-seeing prophetess, Kassandra, it is the act of narration that leads directly to her own death: "Mit der Erzählung gehe ich in den Tod" ["With the tale do I go to face death"].[5] For Kassandra, knowledge and representation are inextricably fused. The gift of seeing and of telling forces her potentially to construct her own execution, at least to note and intensify the disturbing parallels between her act of telling and her act of dying.

> Werd ich, um mich nicht vor Angst zu winden, um nicht zu brüllen wie ein Tier—Werd ich denn bis zuletzt, bis jenes Beil—Werd ich denn noch, wenn schon mein Kopf, mein Hals—werd ich um des Bewußtseins willen bis zuletzt mich selber spalten, eh das Beil mich spaltet, werd ich—[6]
>
> Will I, in order not to writhe out of fear, in order not to bellow like an animal—will I then until the end, until that axe—will I then still, when my head already, when my neck—will I for the sake of conscience split myself until the end, before the axe splits me, will I—

Her destruction, which also marks the limit of her perceptive powers, robs her of her speech; it fills her sentences with hyphens and ellipses.[7] Moreover, Kassandra has no access to the consolation provided by Montaigne's sense of community. There will be no readers of her tale, she fears. Her testamentary text is doomed to fall into a void:

> Ich will Zeugin bleiben, auch wenn es keinen einzigen Menschen mehr geben wird, der mir mein Zeugnis abverlangt.[8]

> I want to remain a witness, even if there will no longer exist a single human being, who demands of me my testimony.

It is, finally, in the work of Franz Kafka that writing and death lose their adversative quality most clearly, indeed, where writing succumbs to the death drive. On the empirical level, Kafka describes how his writing taps his energy, in effect, fueling the process of dying by causing his life-affirming activities to atrophy. In 1914 Kafka describes his literary fate in his diary:

> Der Sinn für die Darstellung meines traumhaften innern Lebens hat alles andere ins Nebensächliche gerückt, und es ist in einer schrecklichen Weise verkümmert und hört nicht auf zu verkümmern. . . . Nun ist aber meine Kraft für jene Darstellung ganz unberechenbar . . . ich aber schwanke dort oben, es ist leider kein Tod, aber die ewigen Qualen des Sterbens.[9]

> The inclination to represent my dreamy inner life has moved all else into the periphery, and it has wasted away in a terrible way and does not cease to atrophy. . . . Now, however, my force for such representation is quite incalculable . . . but I fluctuate up there, it is unfortunately no death but the eternal agonies of dying.

The diary excerpt articulates quite a straightforward equation between writing and dying—an insight that is presented much more vividly during the scene of the officer's inscription/execution in Kafka's "In the Penal Colony." In the *Erzählung*, however, the scene that forces the reader to note how writing is mortal, seems to disclose more than the perception that the literary project consumes energy. In this text the officer symbolically submits to the writing principle or drive by placing himself literally under the harrow in order to be executed.[10] And once he yields to the authority of the "writing machine," Kafka's text becomes marked by the loss of clearly definable categories or boundaries. By becoming the victim of his own machine, for instance, the officer can no longer be evaluated—or, quite simply, "read." For instance, his fusion with the machine forces him to assume the simultaneous, normally mutually exclusive roles of tyrant and victim.

One can attempt—along with Gerhard Kurz—to interpret the officer's "punishment" as a sign of his essential (psychological) alienation from the death-bringing function of the machine.[11] But such an interpretation underplays the one constant in this text. Each character, by attempting to determine the status of the writing machine, ends up assuming a dual, rather contaminated role. The contamination of these roles can be easily described. The condemned man, for instance, experiences a curious transformation, easily leaving behind his exploited, passive stance in order to slip into the role of the executioner.[12] And the explorer fluctuates between acting as an unwitting observer and becoming the involuntary judge who turns violently on his would-be followers.[13] Most disturbing is the role of the New Commandant, since he seems—on the surface—to represent a milder, more equitable form of justice. And yet, he simply replaces the spectacle of the Harrow with a public, equally staged and, therefore, arbitrary spectacle of the judicial Conference. In effect, his judicial decisions seem to be as rigged as were the earlier, more violent displays of "justice" instituted by the Old Commandant. The officer argues:

> Ein flüchtiges, ein bloß unvorsichtiges Wort genügt. Es muß gar nicht Ihrer Überzeugung entsprechen, wenn es nur scheinbar seinem Wunsche entgegenkommt. Daß er Sie mit aller Schlauheit ausfragen wird, dessen bin ich gewiß.[14]

> A cursory, a simply careless word suffices. It need not even correspond to your beliefs, if it only complies even ostensibly with his will. That he will interrogate you with great cleverness, of that I am certain.

The writing machine is both the cause of the officer's death and the instrument that does precisely the opposite of establishing clearly defined categories, such as distinguishing justice from injustice. Indeed, in this text the act of "writing" hardly transforms the officer into a legible text—neither through his role within the *Erzählung* nor through his literal metamorphosis into a text. The explorer describes the face of the executed officer:

> Es war, wie es im Leben gewesen war; [kein Zeichen der versprochenen Erlösung war zu entdecken;] was alle anderen in der Maschine gefunden hatten, der Offizier fand es nicht; die Lippen waren fest zusammengedrückt, die Augen waren offen, hatten den Ausdruck des Lebens, der Blick war ruhig und überzeugt, durch die Stirn ging die Spitze des großen eisernen Stachels.[15]

> It was as it had been in life; [no sign of the promised redemption could be discovered;] that what all others had found in the machine, the officer did not find it; his lips were pressed together firmly, the eyes were open, had the expression of life, the glance was calm and

> devout [convinced of his convictions]; through the forehead went the tip of the big iron barb.

The officer's face remains impenetrable—devoid of (legible) meaning. And, equally troubling, not only does the act of "writing" undo the difference between justice and injustice. It even problematizes that most fundamental distinction of all: in this description the "expression of death" becomes indistinguishable from that of life.

Kafka's "In the Penal Colony" demonstrates more than the recognition that constructing literary or artistic images freezes vitality—robs the represented object of life. In Kafka's text, the conjunction of writing and death seems to bring about an epistemological crisis, where the work problematizes its own categories and thus, ultimately, its own legibility or the possibility of establishing where truth might lie. Here the anarchistic energy produced by the proximity of death is more radical than the poetic rebellion experienced by the lyrical persona in Baudelaire's sonnet. Rather than calling an external structure [like a theological universe] into question, Kafka's text subverts itself, constructing opposites only to expose that opposition as misleadingly false.[16]

Clearly, the anxiety surrounding death is one that marks the work of many writers, although the forms chosen to master or, at least, to represent that tension do not necessarily resemble one another. Wolf's iconic reenactment of death is as different from Baudelaire's antitheological challenge as Montaigne's validation of writing's supplementary force differs from Kafka's delegitimizing any one position—his staging of a death of "knowledge." Nonetheless, the juxtaposition of Montaigne with Baudelaire, Wolf, and Kafka should demonstrate that the act of writing cannot simply be interpreted as an antidote to the threat of death. In the case of Kafka, for instance, the project to write parallels or even recreates the experience of dying. We are not too far from the Platonic diatribe against writing described in the *Phaedrus*:

> By reason of your tender regard for the writing that is your offspring, [you] have declared the very opposite of its true effect. If men learn this, it will implant forgetfulness in their souls: they will cease to exercise memory because they rely on that which is written, calling things to remembrance no longer from within themselves, but by means of external marks; what you have discovered is a recipe not for memory, but for reminder.[17]

"Writing" as a subject for literary texts has its own tradition of imagery—and this is a rhetoric associated with loss rather than with immortality.

Indeed, we shall see later that for both Kleist and Balzac, writing's appeal to immortality seems to be overshadowed by the realization that writing exacts a price—the price of not experiencing or living fully. Kleist in his letters associates writing with a form of exile. And in his *Verlobung in Santo Domingo*, he uses the character of Toni—who belongs to no one ideological group or even community—as a parallel of the writer. Kleist demonstrates how his own artistic lucidity bars him from participating in society. Balzac, on the other hand, fears that, by writing, he is depleting or expending his vital forces. In *La Cousine Bette*, for example, he shows the (necessary) link between loss and artistic creativity by claiming that the artist must throw himself into the abyss in order to produce.

The link between writing and death brings one other connection to light. The writers mentioned do not all call the act of writing into question, once they reflect on the intersection of death and their craft, but their "metatextual awareness" does seem to be heightened. The limit of death seems to force a more explicit analysis of the process of writing. The writers consider the impact of their work on their readers or, more seriously, rearticulate the link between the written text and the subject it is meant to represent. For Montaigne, for instance, the text is so successful that it supplants the living original, whereas Baudelaire conjures up an alternative universe with his equation of death with a "new sun." The relation of the text to its supposed source is inverted. And in Christa Wolf's and Franz Kafka's works, by contrast, it is the texts that reveal their own inadequacy. The scene of death cannot be represented or translated into "meaning" or transcendence.

Although the four writers differ in their analysis of what effect (represented) death has upon their writing—bearing out Elizabeth Bronfen's and Sarah Goodwin's insight that the periodization of death seems to dissolve into an almost infinite diversity of emotions, relevant in all ages[18]—each author does seem to construct a "subversive" text. The conjunction of writing and death—besides highlighting or, finally, demystifying the creative act—leads in each case to a decidedly critical stance. The authority of the empirical world or, as in later works, even of the fictional universe is destabilized. The adequacy of either is implicitly or explicitly called into question.

METHODOLOGICAL REMARKS: DEATH AS A STRATEGY OF SUBVERSION

Three different questions emerge from the juxtaposition of Montaigne with Baudelaire, Wolf, and Kafka: an important starting point is the question of how Kleist and Balzac represent imagined scenes of death, how "death" is, in short, thematized in their short prose. And yet, since death transcends the limits of any poetic enterprise devoted to reflecting the world or experience, a second line of questioning imposes itself. Does the preoccupation with the scene of death lead to a problematic relation to literary language; does it lead to a construction of a new poetics? It is this second stage of the thesis that allows a *rap-*

prochement between more modern thinkers such as Lacan and Heidegger, who both reflect on the connections between death and language.

But the juxtaposition of the four authors also encourages—and this is the third strategy—the recognition that all writers cited, in addition to Balzac and Kleist, share a tinge of subversiveness that is not limited solely to the literary project. Since the writer's preoccupation with death seems to sharpen the critical tone of his or her work, it must be assumed that the representation of death brings with it a critical awareness that calls attention to the historical context in which the texts are being produced.

This third line of questioning, which turns around the issue of subversive narratives, raises pragmatic considerations. Even more importantly, however, it relies on the claim that the literary preoccupation with death can be linked with a "revolutionary" impulse. This assumption might appear to be a little hackneyed, especially if one takes into account the important critical work that has been devoted to Balzac's narratives. D. A. Miller's analysis of Balzacian fiction reinforces the impression "that the world is thoroughly traversed by techniques of power to which everything, anything gives hold."[19] For Miller, such an ideological underpinning thoroughly maintains the status quo and supports the policing function associated with socialization; this function, he claims, is carried out by narrative. And Richard Terdiman, along slightly different lines, notes how the Balzacian *roman d'éducation* both promises the reader or protagonist the power to manipulate the social codes necessary to succeed in the world and, by the same gesture, subordinates the would-be initiate to the system of socialization.[20] This domination of the *parvenu* by the social systems would lead, then, to the conclusion that at least Balzac's texts cannot be read as subversive.

These revisionings of an older (presumably discredited) understanding of narrative, which posits its anticonventional effects, seem to share the assumption that any possibility for subversion in fiction has disappeared. For instance, Roddey Reid's analysis of French families between 1750 and 1910 leads him to conclude that representations emphasizing transgression or lack as well as idealized scenes of restored family life "produced the desire for the normative conjugal family household."[21] Or, to return to D. A. Miller's study, the policing, conservative function in the novel can no longer be limited to representations of the police or the courts. Through scenes depicting the attempt "to educate, to cure, to produce, and to defend," the disciplinary power of narrative can be enacted and still remain invisible. It seems that the coercive power of discourse has become inescapable. Even resistance to disciplinary power only serves to reestablish its hold.[22]

My own analysis breaks with the notion that nineteenth-century narrative must by definition maintain the status quo, and this leads me to the second, more pragmatic point. My study locates strategies of subversion in Balzac's and Kleist's works, in part, by setting off their literary texts with their personal letters and nonfictional, even journalistic articles, in part, by showing how representations of death help to destabilize systems of knowledge and power in Kleist's and Balzac's fictions.

In the case of Kleist, both his letters and his essays point to the laying bare of his doubts concerning the possibility of atemporal knowledge and to his critique of the *Bildung* ideal of his time. The effect of this skepticism on his narratives can then be analyzed in terms of his attempts to find ultimately unsatisfying alternatives to the threat of an empty, meaningless sequence of events devoid of clearly discernible progress toward "truth."[23] In the *Comédie humaine*, by contrast, Balzac himself chooses to juxtapose his fictional narratives with playful scientific treatises, like the "Théorie de la démarche" ["Theory of the Gait/of Process"] in his *Etudes analytiques.* The comparison of his satirical "théorie" with his programmatic prefaces to his great literary project allows us to recognize that this author is perhaps less dazzled by the scientific advances than he claims to be.[24] His fascination with alternatives to clearly progressive scientific developments—such as his preoccupation with the "fragment" in *Louis Lambert*—can be subsumed under the heading of critical, if not subversive thinking, regardless of the decision concerning his political conservatism.

But Kleist and Balzac share more than an uneasiness with the conventional forms of knowledge of their time. By drawing on discursive forms other than their short prose, one can discover that Kleist and Balzac's subversive impulse includes a skeptical evaluation of contemporary events and figures. Despite the difference in their cultural conditioning, both share an obsession with the same strong historical figure—Napoleon Bonaparte—and both portray him negatively, albeit for almost contradictory reasons. Balzac includes several ambivalent images of Napoleon in his *Comédie humaine.* Perhaps the least ambivalent of them is Benassis, the altruistic, visionary "médecin de campagne" ["country doctor"] who is named by his admirers "le Napoléon de notre vallée" ["the Napoleon of our valley"][25] because of his devotion to the simple people of his district. Nonetheless, despite the agricultural and social successes resulting from his personalized and self-sacrificial guidance, in *Le Médecin de Campagne* (1832–33) the image of Napoleon remains a tarnished one—and not only because Benassis, like Napoleon, is burdened with a troubled emotional past. Benassis's story is framed by the story of a simple officer of Napoleon's army, who—along with his colleagues in the novel—has been abandoned by history. Indeed, the entire *Comédie humaine* contains images of individuals marginalized and destitute as a result of their devotion to "l'Homme": two of the more familiar examples are the baron Hulot of *La Cousine Bette* and the Colonel Chabert, although their social fall from grace is shared by the less well-known Bridau family in *La Rabouilleuse* and by the mother of Oscar Husson in *Un Début dans la vie*, to name just a few.

It has also been pointed out that Napoleon represented a rival for Balzac. Writing functioned as a compensatory activity for Balzac, meant to overshadow the more traditionally glorious career of the military. Nonetheless, the relatively scarce images of Napoleon in the *Comédie humaine* suffice to reveal that he represents a two-fold failure. Initially, he represented a new order—the possibility of introducing a powerful rupture into his time. But in the Balzacian accounts, he betrays that vision by adhering both to older Corsican codes of honor (a point that Balzac pursues in *La Vendetta*) as well as to monarchic forms. His subsequent defeat as Emperor—also evaluated in *La Vendetta*—adds to his initial failure to define a new political reality the recognition of the bankruptcy of older, more traditional forms. The flamboyant symbol of France's Empire conjures up for the writer Balzac, it seems, a troubling disillusionment with history understood both as traditional continuity and as rupture.

Kleist also identifies failure and loss with Napoleon, although in his case it is the failure of his own culture—its military weakness as well as the instability of its national identity—that is at stake. In his *Katechismus der Deutschen*, for instance, Kleist dramatizes how the military crisis highlights a fundamental question: "Wo finde ich es, dies Deutschland, von dem du sprichst, und wo liegt es?" ["Where will I find it, this Germany of which you speak, and where is it located?"].[26] Surprisingly, the political catechism ends with the speakers' decision to embrace complete cultural annihilation as the last-ditch resistance to Napoleon's invasion:

> Also auch, wenn alles unterginge, und kein Mensch, Weiber und Kinder mit eingerechnet, am Leben bliebe, würdest du den Kampf billigen?
>
> Allerdings, mein Vater.[27]

> Thus, also if everything were to be destroyed, and no human—women and children included—were to survive, would you condone the struggle?
>
> Certainly, my father.

Although Kleist's vehemence in his "Catechism" might seem to rule out the possibility of any ambivalence toward the French Emperor, he actually does consider the option of joining the "enemy" at a low point in his literary career. In 1803 Kleist writes to Ulrike, his half-sister:

> Ich habe die Hauptstadt dieses Landes verlassen, ich bin an seine Nordküste gewandert, ich werde französische Kriegsdienste nehmen, das Heer wird bald nach England hinüber rudern, unser aller Verderben lauert über den Meeren, ich frohlocke bei der Aussicht auf das unendlich-prächtige Grab.[28]

> I have left the capital city of this land; I have wandered along its northern coast; I will take upon myself French military service; the army will soon be rowing over to England; our peril lies in wait for all of us on the seas; I rejoice at the prospect of the infinite-splendid grave.

The letter follows Kleist's self-destructive act of burning his serious but unfinished tragedy: *Robert Guiskard.* The destruction of the text is accompanied by the decision to destroy the self—not only physically but also ideologically. The voluntary destruction of his cultural or national identity acts as a corollary to Kleist's gesture of literary "suicide."

The image of Napoleon in Kleist's writing is thus bound closely to the experience of dissolution. Whether Kleist perceives himself as mortal foe of Napoleon or as active (suicidal) participant in the Napoleonic army, a language of loss and death pervades his descriptions. Even the ultimate political resistance to Napoleon does not lead to a sharpening of national boundaries. The only identifying characteristic that emerges from the perceived threat to German identity lies—for Kleist—in the determination to renounce one's hold on circumstance and to die.

Through their preoccupation with Napoleon, Kleist and Balzac do share the same historical context despite the gap of twenty-two years that lies between them. That likeness should not be exaggerated, of course, since Kleist perceives Napoleon primarily as an historical, military force, whereas Balzac highlights the futility of change and progress represented by the initially glorious figure.[29] Nonetheless, both writers seem preoccupied with Napoleon as a symbol of their own "nation's" failure—as well as the ultimate futility of history—either by conjuring up the suicide of an entire culture or by pondering the annihilation of a construct named the "Empire." For both it is the literary preoccupation with depicting destruction that best translates their anxiety contained in the name "Napoleon," and both make use of the legendary figure in order to refuse to validate the present or a mythological (recent) past. In short, Balzac and Kleist—for almost diametrically opposite reasons—converge in their ambivalence toward the Emperor as emblem of an historical force and both do use him finally as a symbol of historical failure and pessimism rather than hope. Their subversive work can be read, in effect, as the revisioning, if not undermining, of their cultural legacy.

DEATH THEMATIZED

The historical context, in which Napoleon figures as only one salient example, provides one way of reflecting upon the concept of death, as it takes form in Balzac's and Kleist's discourses. Historical pessimism—or the fascination with cultural decline—can be read both as a form of resistance to contemporary and recent political practices besides conjuring up a set of images associated with death.

The second line of inquiry that underlies this study turns around the topic of death considered thematically. From a positivist standpoint, scenes of death abound in the works of both writers. One can easily picture the violent spectacles of murder in Kleist's short prose: fathers strangle their sons; images of bodies pierced by gunshot or plumed arrows are painstakingly described. These highly detailed physical scenes of Kleistian violence differ starkly from the more spiritual accounts of agony favored by Balzac. Although violence does erupt between parents and their children or between spouses in the *Comédie humaine*, Balzac is equally famous for his languishing aristocratic women. One need only consider Mme de Mortsauf, la Grenadière or even Honorine.

The thematic component of this study tends to emphasize more than the *kind* of death captured realistically in short narratives.[30] Instead, I pursue the narrative *function* of the scenes of death within the structure of a text. That narrative function has usually been summed up by the word *closure*. A scene of death, one argues, can usually be found to provide a necessary break, thus permitting an otherwise arbitrary ending to the plot. We are, for instance, quite familiar with the reshuffling of the narrative sequence in Tolstoy's *Death of Ivan Ilych*, which opens with a scene that temporally should follow the final chapter of the story.[31] The last word of the narrative—as a result of this reshuffling—is satisfying in its finality: "died."

A brief digression should foreground the limits of equating the function of (represented) death with closure as a "proper" ending. Even in a more conventional narrative like *Death of Ivan Ilych*, death takes on more complexity: Ivan Ilych's death is represented first and foremost as a *process*. Tolstoy faithfully notes the stages of *dying* experienced by Ivan—using the increasingly restricted mobility of his protagonist as a measure marking the proximity of the end. Ivan's confinement includes his bracketing out the world as he deliberately faces the wall and culminates in the celebrated image of the black sack—almost a psychic equivalent of the coffin.

> He felt that his agony was due to his being thrust into that black hole and still more to his not being able to get right into it. He was hindered from getting into it by his conviction that his life had been a good one. That very justification of his life held him fast. . . . Suddenly some force struck him in the chest and side, making it harder to breathe, and he fell through the hole and there at the bottom was a light.[32]

Curiously, the increased physical immobility of Ivan is attributed—at the climactic moment—not to his process of dying but to his perception of his past life. That reversal does not, of course, represent an unprepared authorial sleight of hand.

The moment of liberation experienced by Ivan explosively inverts the sequence of restrictions that actually constitutes the story of his life narrated (in capsular form) in the second and third chapters. Here we find in retrospect that every stage of social success in Ivan's life is depicted as the construction of new, isolating barriers. At the moment of complete mastery Ivan has effectively cloistered himself in his office. In short, the imagery of confinement used to depict Ivan's death is shown to have its roots in the life he has led.

The scene of death ultimately (and after a rereading) reverses the terms *life* and *death*. We notice the violence Ivan has imposed on his "authentic self" in order to develop socially and materially. Ivan dons a "harness" in his office, and his interactions with others are carefully devoid of spontaneity—contained by the bureaucratic forms.[33] We can thus see that the representation of death in the Russian narrative also draws from a subversive vein. Tolstoy carefully equates images of confinement with the experience of dying only to employ that rhetoric to critique an inauthentic, socially conditioned way of life. Ivan's social success is portrayed as a more intense form of self-betrayal—as the death-in-life of the individual within society.

Neither Balzac nor Kleist consistently place the scenes of death at the end of their narratives. In fact, both experiment with openings by representing an enigmatic scene of death at the beginning of their short text. A quick contrast of Kleist's "Der Zweikampf" ["The Dual"] and Balzac's *Louis Lambert* highlights how both writers use scenes of death to propel their stories forward. The death is a pretext; it initially provides the impetus needed to construct a "detective story," which for Kleist comes complete with a false but victimized suspect.

In "Zweikampf" the intrigue centers initially around the death that needs to be deciphered. And yet, the narrative focus of the plot shifts from identifying the wrongdoer to detailing the sufferings of the falsely accused protagonist. That shift draws attention away from the ethical aporia generated by the murder of the duke—the victim who is himself the source of rivalry and, ultimately, of violence. Gradually (although peripherally) it becomes clear that it is the duke's attempt to disinherit his brother's family that has precipitated the fatal attack.

The impossibility of distinguishing between the wrongdoers is dramatized by the central scene of the narrative: the verdict of guilt is essentially self-contradictory and therefore illegible. The defender of the (falsely accused) suspect is almost annihilated by the actual murderer only to regenerate while the murderer surprisingly wastes away after the duel. "Der Zweikampf" is indeed only one clear example of a pattern in Kleistian narrative. The scenes of death in "Der Findling" ["The Orphan"], "Das Erdbeben in Chili" ["Earthquake in Chili"], "Die heilige Cäcilie" ["Holy Cecilia"], and "Die Verlobung in Santo Domingo" ["The Engagement in Santo Domingo"], rather than resolving conflicts or enigmas, problematize clearcut distinctions between binary oppositions, showing up the essential similarities (even interchangeability) of supposedly opposed terms.

The "thematic" approach to representations of death leads to the recognition that "meaningful progress" is called into question by the narrative structures of Kleist and Balzac. Kleist uses the (uncontrollable) interchangeability of terms in order to question the viability of a "formation" (or Bildung) ideal that relies on the clear discernability of truth. In "Der Zweikampf," for instance, he undermines the imagery of "collecting a wealth of ideas"[34] by constituting a sequence of events that enhance self-doubt and finally lead to the willing renunciation of the self.

Although Balzac is usually associated with a masterful, progress-oriented narrative, one only has to conjure up Rastignac of *Le Père Goriot* to recognize the writer's deepseated ambivalence that can equate social success with power or wealth as well as with corruption and moral decline. Balzac uses a different critical tactic from Kleist, however, although it is again most discernible in a narrative that sets its goal on deciphering the "meaning" of a scene of death. In *Louis Lambert*, the narrator sets out to evaluate the life and death of his philosopher friend. He is left before the disjointed, captivating but mad pronouncements of his friend, unable to judge the validity of Louis's new philosophical form—a form that inherently denies the continuity of thought (and, by implication) of time. Louis's death thus marks his entry into atemporality—understood either to be the culmination of his "fragmentary" vision or the sign of its failure. The gradual fragmentation of the narrative, *Louis Lambert*—not to mention Balzac's particular fondness for shattering his short *récits* by introducing more and more complex narrative frames that supplant the "core story"—highlights both the opacity of the scenes of death and the inadequacy of progress-oriented, linguistically transparent forms.

We can note: my study of the narrative structures of Kleist's and Balzac's *oeuvres* has clearly been influenced by the deconstructive practice. That is to say, I demonstrate how the rhetoric of a text undoes—or at least problematizes—its own categories. Still, my concern in comparing the two writers is *not* to prove the futility of the literary enterprise. Such an approach—in contrast to mine—must emphasize, finally, the essential similarity between texts written by the same author or even the repetitive resemblance of all texts. My study works to throw into relief the historical particularity of a text's "unraveling" or destabilization. The concept of death—as it is defined and used in the texts—helps to ground, then, the rhetorical analysis.

Thus, by juxtaposing Kleist's and Balzac's preoccupations with Napoleon with their "thematic" or "structural" use of death scenes, one can note one primary cultural concern: how to define "progress"—either in moral or social and philosophical terms—and how to evaluate or even subvert that "progress." Whereas Kleist experiments with destabilizing traditionally binary oppositions or even with a "reverse Bildung," Balzac concentrates on narrative frames (reversing the relative significance of story and narrative context) or on stretching the concept of narrative sequence. Both strategies circle around the status and evaluation of the scenes of death thematized in the narrative. Both writers seem to belong, then, to the group of four authors ranging from Montaigne to Kafka, who each, in varying degrees, question or supplant dominant conventions of (both social and narrative) linearity and progress.

A NEW POETICS: THE LIMITS OF *MIMESIS*

The comparison of Kleist and Balzac does not limit itself, however, to noting that both writers confront the anxiety of death, even appropriate the subject by calling attention (through represented scenes of death) to the insufficiencies of key contemporary conventions. A third, perhaps even most challenging, problematic suggests itself: their own writing is not exempt from a different "threat of death" either—the death of meaning. Narrative fragmentation, which does pursue alternatives to social success also destabilizes the coherence and meaning(s) of the Balzacian text. Kleist's discovery of the interchangeability of contradictory ethical values also potentially equates the narrative sequences of his texts with empty, meaningless progression.

The task of representing death affects more than the coherence of any one given text. Fundamental assumptions *about* the literary project, that is "poetics"—as Todorov defines the term—also come under fire. Here is Todorov's definition from his *The Poetics of Prose:*

> First, poetics: What it studies is not poetry or literature but "poeticity" or "literariness." The individual work is not an ultimate goal for poetics; if it pauses over one work rather than another, it is because such a work reveals more distinctly the properties of literary discourse.[35]

And for both Kleist and Balzac the primary condition for a literary work is the assumption that the writer functions as a "secretary"—documenting social or political trends of his time. Representing the world by establishing criteria of psychological coherence or by supplying circumstantial data about context, whether this be spatial,[36] as for Balzac, or historical—shapes the poetics of both writers.

The representation of death is thus particularly critical for both writers' poetics, since it marks the moment in the text when language cannot capture the authenticity or accuracy of an experience. The personal experience of death cancels out the possibility of reportage or description. One might assume, then, that the representation of death automatically suspends temporarily the *mimetic* orientation of a literary project. Or, as in the case of Kafka, it is the unarticulable experience of death that ends up coloring the metatextual account of writing. The essential illegibility of the text, its resistance to symbolic meaning, allows Kafka to equate the process of writing with dying.

The epistemological aporias to be found in texts concerned with representing death vary, of course, especially in that they draw on aesthetic or even more broadly cultural debates generated by different historical contexts. Kleist's *Erzählungen* problematize the possibility of learning via a model or, indeed, the possibility of progress-oriented linearity. Balzac's short prose, on the other hand, fragments the text by highlighting and multiplying the narrative frame. In *Louis Lambert*, for instance, the omniscience, even the authorial control of the narrator often seem on the brink of slipping away. Although both writers explore the implications and contradictions associated with the concept of death in quite different ways, one can't help but notice a common denominator of their literary treatment: the fascination with modifying narrative convention, especially as this intersects with the mimetic project, not to mention the transmission of knowledge.

It is at this point that it seems pertinent to draw on an earlier literary example, where the preoccupation with death and the reworking of a continuous narrative form coincide. Besides providing several strategies for capturing ("personally experienced") scenes of death in language, Montaigne's *Essais* are key in highlighting one possible connection between discontinuity and the more general concept of mimesis. We might recall that his chief preoccupation in the *Essais* is to provide a monument of the self meant to overcome the finality of death. Still, the identity of the "self" is problematized through Montaigne's choice of vocabulary. Montaigne emphasizes, for instance, the truthfulness of the image distilling his "essential self":

> [///]Je m'estalle entier: c'est un *skeletos* où, d'une veuë, les veines, les muscles, les tendons paroissent, chaque piece en son siege. (II, 50)
>
> I display myself entirely: it is a *skeleton* where, at a glance, the veins, muscles, tendons appear, each element in its place.

The mirroring effect does not appear here to be complete, however. It is not the portrait of Montaigne that can be rediscovered; it is his outline, his skeleton. The choice of the word *skeletos* is in itself ambiguous. The term points both to the buried essence of the writer and to his projected absence. At least in Montaigne's time, a skeleton could only be seen once the living person had disappeared.

The curious simultaneity of presence and absence conjured up with this particular example of the mimetic project is extended in Montaigne's insistence on the authenticity of his thoughts noted down in their haphazard occurrence.

The text—in its discontinuous construction—faithfully reproduces the process of authorial thought.[37] Once that thought turns directly to its own disappearance, then, one could expect to discover total dissolution in the form of silence, a radical form of discontinuity.

Montaigne chooses a different rhetoric—that of loss over silence—in order to describe repeatedly his own diverse deaths. At first these descriptions of personal death seem to be double, experienced both as an event that is projected—still external to the self—and, surprisingly, as an already internalized happening. A closer look shows us that even the passages that seem to indicate Montaigne's preparation for his own death (as a future event) reveal a present iconic emptiness. This absence, which is made visible through rhetoric, is described as an oscillation, as the bracketing of a will: Montaigne is disenchanted with life but not yet eager to hasten his death. His judgment of his personal demise places him in a limbo of indecisiveness.[38] The evocation of limbo, usually equated with the state of being dead but describing here the passage from life to death, is repeated again and again. Even his "essais" are not firm, "almost self-effacing, barely indicated traces" [*montrés au doigt*] (III, 195–96). Life that stands in proximity to death becomes itself a form of death: "/// . . . je ne pense désormais qu'à finir; me deffois de toutes nouvelles esperances et entreprinses; prens mon dernier congé de tous les lieux que je laisse; et me depossede tous les jours de ce que j'ay" (II, 364) ["Henceforth I only think of finishing; I undo myself of all new hopes and undertakings; take my last leave of all the places I am quitting and dispossess myself everyday of what I have"]. At the farthest end of the imaginary, preparatory scale lies the consolation that this movement from life to death will not even be perceptible or especially distinguishable, since the transition will have been traced so often (if not completely) through the bladder-stone attacks, which Montaigne suffered from so frequently.[39]

The bladder-stone attacks (or his experience of being repeatedly and rudely awakened from sleep) take on the status of "practice" or little deaths in the *Essais.* In each case Montaigne deliberately suppresses sensation. He refuses to "savour" or fill the instant of expiration with descriptive images. And in the culmination of his personal death scenes, when he is almost killed in a collision of horses, we can find a rhetoric of absence used to mirror Montaigne's loss of selfhood:

> /C'eust esté sans mentir une mort bien heureuse; car la foiblesse de mon discours me gardoit d'en rien juger, et celle du corps d'en rien sentir. Je me laissoy couler si doucement et d'une facon si douce et si aisée que je ne sens guiere autre action moins poisante que celle-là estoit. (II, 47)
>
> This would have been without lying a very fortunate [happy] death; for the feebleness of my discourse kept me from judging any of it and

> [the weakness] of my body from feeling any of it. I let myself flow so gently and in such a sweet and easy manner that I hardly felt any other less burdensome action than that one.

Within the text the climax of death can only be portrayed as the moment of nonsensation and of nonjudgment, the absence of the self being represented through a rhetoric of negation. In other words, the mimesis of death becomes possible through the use of a double negative. The negative form of the signifier mirrors the negation of the signified.

This inverted mimetic structure (where a rhetoric of loss mirrors death) is maintained even when the status of writing is analyzed. Although the text is meant to have a testamentary function, it ends up mirroring the gradual dissolution of its writer. Since Montaigne himself is on the decline, his text must also bear the signs of fading.[40] Indeed, Montaigne's self-alienation from his own text takes several forms. A stranger, he claims, is more familiar with the *Essais*, since his [Montaigne's] recovery of the text only occurs through chance rather than through judgment (cf. I, 78–79). Even more radical is his relationship to other writers. The motion of forgetting, which allows the appropriation of ideas from other literary works, leads, finally, to the uprooting or displacement of his own text: "//Et suis si excellent en l'oubliance, que mes escrits mesmes et compositions, je ne les oublie pas moins que le reste" (II, 314) ["And (I) am so excellent in forgetting, that my writings themselves and compositions, I do not forget them any less than the rest"]. This forgetfulness causes a new barrier between Montaigne and the *Essais*, since he is even unauthorized to correct the text. He loses the dynamic interplay between his own work and himself:

> //En mes escris mesmes je ne retrouve pas tousjours l'air de ma premiere imagination; je sçay ce que j'ay voulu dire, et m'eschaude souvent à corriger et y mettre un nouveau sens, pour avoir perdu le premier, qui valloit mieux. (II, 231)

> Even in my writings I do not always rediscover the cast of my first imagination; I know what I wanted to say and often become heated in correcting and placing there a new meaning for having lost the first, which was worth more.

Later he even renounces the claim of correcting his text.

The rhetoric of loss that Montaigne sets in motion leads not only to the constantly repeated effacement of the literary work's author. If the writing self's only memory (of itself) resides in the written word and it becomes alienated even from this representative stronghold, then it is constantly losing itself. In effect, it is constantly dying.

It is through death—represented as the textual loss of self—that a new mimetic relation takes shape, one where textual discontinuity mirrors the discontinuity or radical absence of the object (here of Montaigne's "fictional" self). Thus the framework provided by mimesis is retained, but is transformed radically by the introduction of discontinuity as both the source and the direction of the mimetic project. And since the primacy of loss governs the triple relation between writer, text, and act of writing, it is quite in keeping with the movement of the text to find that the elusive phenomenon of death can be transformed into an image of literary fertility.

> //Puisque c'est le privilege de l'esprit de se r'avoir de la vieillesse, je luy conseille, autant que je puis, de le faire; qu'il verdisse, qu'il fleurisse ce pendant, s'il peut, comme le guy sur un arbre mort. (III, 59)

> Since it is the privilege of the mind to clear itself of age, I advise it as much as I can to do so; that it turn green, that it flourish, however, if it can, like the mistletoe on a dead tree.

For Montaigne, then, the discontinous structure of the *Essais* as well as the loss of authorial control staged in the text become some of the markers that help represent the event of death—at least tangentially. The crisis of mimesis, triggered by the anxiety over death, is circumvented by a rhetorical strategy that introduces diverse linguistic examples of loss in order to continue to "mirror" experience *via negationis.*

Montaigne's creative adaptation of the *imitatio* principle does not appear to be as accessible either to Kleist or to Balzac. For both the heightened awareness of death highlights an anxiety with the mimetic process that refuses to dissipate, although both writers interpret the threat of doubling (or representation) in very different ways. Kleist concerns himself primarily with the epistemological crisis—the circularity inherent in doubling—whereas Balzac's preoccupation manifests itself as an authorial obsession with originality and, by implication, autonomy.

The tradition of doubling—more familiarly, mimesis—has, of course, its own troubled history, starting with Plato. Philippe Lacoue-Labarthe clearly comments on the displacements in Plato's *Republic* and notes that the critique of mimesis is actually founded on the critique of the "mimetician," the tragic poet:

> Thaumaturgie anti-thaumaturgique (mise-en-abyme neutralisant le miroir), destinée à contenir le thaumaturge . . . qu'est le miméticien, à réduire son inquiétante et prodigieuse puissance, en *révélant* tout simplement qu'elle ne repose que sur un jeu de miroir(s) et qu'elle n'est rien—ou presque rien: un tour de passe-passe, une *Stellvertre-*

> *tung*, qui consiste à tout faire sans rien faire, à faire semblant de savoir tout faire quand on ne travaille pas et qu'on se contente d'imiter ou de "doubler" . . . en utilisant, pour "faire" illusion, une matière qui s'y prête à l'avance.[41]

> Anti-magical thaumaturgy (the *mise-en-abyme* neutralizing the mirror), destined to contain the magician . . . who is the mimetician, to reduce his troubling and prodigious power, by *revealing* quite simply that [this magic] only rests on a play of mirrors and that it is nothing—or almost nothing: a sleight of hand, a *Stellvertretung* [*representation*] that consists in doing all without doing anything, in appearing to know how to do all when one doesn't work and is content to imitate or to "double" . . . while using, in order to "create" an illusion, a material that lends itself in advance to this.

Lacoue-Labarthe notes the curious but revealing shift from the "mimetician" to the process (and product) of mimesis in *The Republic*, explaining it as an indirect strategy to discredit ultimately the "poet."[42] The threat of the "mimetician" lies in being able to assume or parrot certain (social) voices and, thereby, to unsettle the comforting hierarchy of differences in Plato's imagined republic. And Balzac does inherit this suspicion of mimesis as a socially chaotic force, which permits an indiscriminate, untraceable infiltration of the "upper classes," as noted by Prendergast in his analysis of *Splendeurs et misères des courtisanes*.[43]

One can easily point to moments in Balzac's corpus that highlight how he problematizes the mimetic principle. The "visionary" or "symbolic" component of his work has often been examined, even shown to be at odds with his project of reproducing a faithful image of nineteenth-century Paris, indeed France.[44] His own metatextual comments emphasize how multifaceted is his role as "secretary." He must first observe, actually take apart the object to be reproduced.[45] The relation between reflected object and reflecting language is thus unbalanced, since Balzac claims to be *shaping* the "model," more traditionally considered to be static and autonomous from the poet.

On the one hand, then, Balzac does not directly abandon the mimetic orientation of his literary work. And yet, although his poetic task continues ostensibly to be mimetic, he seems primarily concerned with *defining* his own "object," ultimately constituting the world he is supposedly imitating. The primacy of a preexisting but (paradoxically) never-before-perceptible world is not the only element to be called into question through this creative redefinition of mimesis. The possibility of maintaining (social) differences, once the code to mimicking them has been furnished, affects even the primacy of the authorial self—and this not only because of the repeated staging of the narrator's "dethroning," if not destruction, in Balzac's short narratives. After, all, the conditions that problematize determining difference include the category of "authorial difference" or originality.

We can conclude: the metatextual self-representation (in the "Avant-Propos") primarily shows cracks when the role of the author/narrator is to be identified. Not surprisingly, then, we find that the scenes of death in Balzac's short prose tend to turn less on the logical impossibility of *re*-presenting (or imitating) death in literature and more on the complex relation of narrator to his récit. The short texts tend to contain elaborate frames highlighting the narrator's role and the effect of his story on his listeners—but, equally significantly, on himself. Indeed, the predominant frame in the récits reinforces the impression that the narrator's autonomy is called into question by his own activity of narrating stories. That loss of autonomy goes beyond assuming the traits and thoughts of his fictional characters. The pattern in texts as disparate as *Sarrasine*, "Un drame au bord de la mer" ["A Drama at the Edge of the Sea"], *Louis Lambert*, and *Albert Savarus*, for instance, creates the impression that by telling a tale the speaker ends up reduplicating the textual experience.

In *Sarrasine*, as Roland Barthes points out, the narrator is affected by a symbolic castration. In "Un drame au bord de la mer" Louis writes about a family's destroyed future only to find his own energy and future endangered, whereas in *Louis Lambert* the narrator experiences a fragmentation of his style that mirrors his friend's form of madness, which he is supposedly documenting objectively. And in *Albert Savarus* the storyteller, who too transparently narrates his own story, literally becomes the protagonist of his reader's manipulations. Perhaps the most dramatic example of fatal narrative reduplication takes place in *Honorine*. There the narrator is so captivated by his own tale that, as we learn at the end, his own life takes on the outward (ultimately constricting) trappings of his story.

The crisis of mimesis that Balzac seems to associate with the representation of death does not appear to turn on a critique of language; it is highlighted chiefly by the relation between narrator and text. Even the characteristic fragmentation of Balzac's shorter texts—meant to forestall in part the limitations of more traditional models of progress and reduplication—tends to reinforce the relation of mirroring between frame and core story.

Kleist's *Erzählungen*, like Balzac's, are also marked by internal shattering. In Kleist's texts, although there is no frame, the structure of the *Erzählung* is usually made up of multiple perspectives on the same event—a trait that tends to add more rather than less opacity to the task of interpretation. This holds particularly true for "Die Heilige Cäcilie" and "Der Zweikampf"; still, the shifts in perspective are also noticeable in "Michael Kohlhaas" and "Die Verlobung in Santo Domingo." More importantly, however, for Kleist the mimetic crisis is very much bound up with the properties intrinsic to poetic language. In his letters, for instance, Kleist seems continuously troubled by the uncontrollable sequence of moments as signs both of life and death. And in a very late text, familiarly known as "Die Todeslitanei" ["The Death Liturgy"], the substitutions become so radical that no difference of meaning distinguishes one signifier from another. Each word in the prose poem, which is structured almost completely as a simple sequence of nouns, always signifies "Henriette," the woman with whom Kleist commits suicide. Such an extreme piece only extends Kleist's discovery in his *Erzählungen* of the ultimate interchangeability of radical opposites.

The poetic crisis for Kleist, as for Balzac, also does not lie directly in the impossibility of representing death. It seems to stem from his discovery of the "metaphorical" structure of language, where the substitution of terms cannot be controlled. This crisis originates in part from his rejection of the concept of Bildung [or formative education]—a rejection that is based on two insights. On the one hand, Kleist notes the subjectivity and, therefore, mortality of any truth. But equally important are his doubts concerning a sustainable, "binary" quality of any system attempting to follow or imitate a "model." The figure of mirroring leads simply to a reduplication of the subject who perceives the model. There can be no progress resulting from the imitation.

Kleist's critique of a metaphor based solely on the "mirror" becomes evident in a letter he writes to Wilhelmine von Zenge in November 1800. Here he describes the aesthetic viewer as a "dead" eye, whose perceptive abilities are indistinguishable from the surface ("Spiegelfläche") of the sea. The opposite alternative is hardly more satisfying. In the case of an actively critical viewer, such criticism reveals more about the spectator himself—and is therefore not sensitive to the specificity of the described world. A genuine interplay between two terms can never be maintained. As a result, with the inevitable obliteration of the subjective or the objective term, mimesis yields no new knowledge.

Kleist's narrative responses to the mimetic dilemma do not necessarily only repeat a message of futility. He explores, for instance, a poetics of music—emphasizing the movement of dynamic life—in order to counter the circularity of a poetics founded on a painterly model of mimesis. Especially "Das Bettelweib in Locarno" ["The Beggarwoman of Locarno"] can almost be read as a musical score, organized around the repetition of indecipherable groans that resist being attributed to one stable speaker. But in this short text—as in the more complex, ambiguous *Erzählungen* like "Die Heilige Cäcilie" ["Holy Cecilia"]—the poetic solutions are, at best, tenuous. Meaningful narrative sequences cannot be distinguished for long from the aimless series of substitutions that constituted Kleist's early voyages, or from the uncontrollable repetitions that structure "Das Bettelweib," and that later begin to dominate his experience of day-to-day living.[46]

Both Kleist and Balzac question the *adequacy* of mimesis much more overtly than Montaigne, who expands the concept of "mirroring" to incorporate what by rights should explode the binary structure: the unrepresentability of death. In contrast to the *Essais*, the works of the two nineteenth-century writers bear out Ronald Schleifer's insight that the incongruence between the concept and event of death occasions a multiplicity of approaches—"avoidance, repetition, metonymy, particularized descriptions of historical moments and events,"[47] among others. Kleist's and Balzac's doubting stance connects them much more closely to later writers like Kafka, whose poetics implicitly undermines even the authority of the writing project.

FINAL REMARKS

In all three stages of my study the term *death* remains a function rather than a carefully defined signifier. The representation of death tends to act as a threshold experience, a threshold that provides a vantage point onto the limitations and anxieties implicit in prevalent, historical ideas, in the particular structure of texts and even in the literary projects formulated metatextually by Kleist and Balzac. The reflections on "dying" lead here, in a sense, to a Heideggerian way of thinking—a *Sein-zum-Tode*—rather than to a contoured, clearly perceptible image of death. Heidegger himself defines the *Sein-zum-Tode* in the following terms:

> Die Charakteristik des existenzial entworfenen eigentlichen Seins zum Tode läßt sich dergestalt zusammen fassen: *Das Vorlaufen enthüllt dem Dasein die Verlorenheit in das Man-selbst und bringt es vor die Möglichkeit, auf die besorgende Fürsorge primär ungestützt, es selbst zu sein, selbst aber in der leidenschaftlichen, von den Illusionen des Man gelösten, faktischen, ihrer selbst gewissen und sich ängstenden FREIHEIT ZUM TODE.*[48]

> The characteristic of the existentially sketched out actual being to death can be summarized in such a way: *the Running Ahead [Projecting] reveals to Existence [Dasein] the loss of One-self and brings it before the possibility, primarily not propped up on the concerned [falsely] protective care of others, to be itself, itself however in the passionate, real FREEDOM TO DEATH, which is detached from the illusions of the social self, and which is certain of itself and anxious for itself.*

Although in this context we are not primarily concerned with authenticity or the existential self, Heidegger's formulation does help to accentuate how the preoccupation with death leads to a heightened critical awareness and sharper redefinition of projects. In Heidegger's formulation we might also notice that the specificity of the individual comes into focus more intensely. And, indeed, through the contrast of Kleist and Balzac I have tried to show that there is not one overriding representation of death. Through the comparison with other writers in this introduction I have tried to establish that, as a result of the anxiety with death (of the self as well as of meaning or truth), each writer attempts to define his or her own particular doubts about literary and epistemological goals.[49] It is appropriate, then, that we should turn first to Kleist's particular crisis, to the moment when he witnesses the "death of Truth."

Chapter One

Kleist's *Erzählungen*
The Crisis of Meaning

THE DEATH OF TRUTH

In March 1801 Kleist narrates the story of the death of truth to Wilhelmine von Zenge, his fiancée. The story he tells is not an allegorical death-bed scene. "Truth" does not figure as one of the characters, and there are no last words—sanctioned by impending death—that can be bequeathed to the mourning witness. The scene is framed by the public space of a silent grave, and it is precisely this silence of the aftermath that Kleist attempts to articulate in his letter to Wilhelmine:

> Wir können nicht entscheiden, ob das, was wir Wahrheit nennen, wahrhaft Wahrheit ist, oder ob es uns nur so scheint. Ist das letzte, so *ist* die Wahrheit, die wir hier sammeln, nach dem Tode nicht mehr—und alles Bestreben, ein Eigentum sich zu erwerben, das uns auch in das Grab folgt, ist vergeblich—-
>
> We cannot decide whether that which we call truth truly is truth or whether it only appears to be such. If the latter is the case, then the truth, which we gather here, *is* no longer after death—and all attempts to obtain a "property" that might follow us into the grave are futile.[1]

Kleist is attempting to describe his realization that there is no longer one Truth but many "subjective" truths, and this shift from the singular to many truths contributes to marking the scene of death. The inability of truth to lay claim to universality implies the loss of its immortality. In other words, Kleist does not so much stage the passage of an individual truth from life to death than the encounter of Truth with its own *mortality*.[2]

This strange reversal is not limited to the burial itself. It extends to the frame that narrates the event. Initially, it seems that the scene of death can be told only by the mourning bystander. Death "experienced," after all, defies its own representation. Nonetheless, the safe, marginal position that Kleist as narrator assumes, begins to be contaminated by the logic of his own account:

> Ich hatte schon als Knabe (mich dünkt am Rhein durch eine Schrift von Wieland) mir den Gedanken ausgeeignet, daß die Vervollkommnung der Zweck der Schöpfung wäre. Ich glaubte, daß wir einst nach dem Tode von der Stufe der Vervollkommnung, die wir auf diesem Sterne erreichten, auf einem anderen weiter fortschreiten würden, und daß wir den Schatz von Wahrheiten, den wir hier sammelten, auch dort einst brauchen könnten. (KB, 633)

> As a young boy (I believe, on the Rhine, through a work by Wieland), I had already worked out the thought that perfection was the purpose of creation. I believed that some day after death, [starting] from the stage of perfection we had reached on this star, we would develop on another, and [I believed] that the treasure of truths that we collected here would one day be useful there.

By *narrating* the death of Truth, Kleist is drawn to the realization that he himself experiences a form of death. The contamination that leads to his own symbolic death in this passage can be perceived especially clearly in the interplay of "sammeln" (the accumulation of treasure) and "folgen" (the treasure's continued company in the grave). As long as Kleist had believed that truths could be accumulated, this accumulation helped him to grasp death as a *stage* in a sequence. That sequence could be extended beyond the traditional definition of life to include life after death. In short, the accumulation of knowledge was to guarantee the coherence of a self; collected knowledge was to ensure the homogenous quality of the individual as s/he progressed through time, even past death.[3]

Losing his belief in the possible accumulation of an immortal knowledge not only endangers the future; it does not only suggest that Kleist's own death will be truly final. The crisis widens to include even the possibility of a meaningful sequence: so that Kleist is alienated even from his past, once he can no longer believe in a continuous quest that could link his young self as "Knabe" with an older, progressing one. He witnesses the loss of a thread that guarantees both his growth and his coherence, and so finds himself banished to the isolation of the present.

What can be the response to such a crisis, especially when the act of writing, formerly calculated to lead to increased wealth of knowledge (Kleist uses the word *reich* [KB, 505]) as well as Bildung, is radically undermined, because even the possibility of progress is deflated? Kleist's first response is paralysis. His will to read or to write is annihilated by nausea, and he equates his experience of a present, isolated in time, with suicide ["eine Verirrung . . . die vielleicht unwiderruflich wäre" (KB, 635) ("an aberration . . . that might perhaps be irrevocable")]. This irreversible act could equally well signify a rupture with Wilhelmine as suicide.

Still, there is a second alternative that he opposes to his brooding, to the stasis of pure reflection. In the same letter that dramatizes his crisis, Kleist asks Wilhelmine to allow him to travel, in order to replace the temporal deadlock with, at least, spatial displacement.

> Ich müßte, wenn ich zu Hause bliebe, die Hände in den Schoß legen, und denken. So will ich lieber spazieren gehen, und denken. Die Bewegung auf der Reise wird mir zuträglicher sein, als dieses Brüten auf einem Flecke. Ist es eine Verirrung, so läßt sie sich vergüten, und schützt mich vor einer andern, die vielleicht unwiderruflich wäre. (KB, 635)

> If I stayed at home, I would lay my hands in my lap and think. So, I prefer to go for a walk and to think. The movement on the trip will be more beneficial to me as opposed to brooding in one spot. If this is only an aberration, it can be redressed—and it protects me from another [error] that might be irrevocable.

With this temporary solution it might seem that Kleist overcomes his own death, that he simply replaces his temporal stasis with continuous movement through space. The spectre of death refuses to be banished, however, from his experience of traveling. The voyage he selects is an aimless wandering, and this choice seems to mirror his earlier realization that no meaning or coherence can be attributed to sequence. His initial disillusionment with progress is reaffirmed, in that his voyages remain ramblings, ungoverned by any organizing principle. More seriously: Kleist's travels seem to precipitate him into encounters with death, so that twice within a few months of his letter describing his disillusion with truth he is almost killed.

Although both events—the threat of being crushed by a wagon or drowning in a river—seem, on the surface, rather different experiences (KB, 666, 670), certain similarities are difficult to ignore. In the first experience Kleist finds himself being dragged at top speed ["spornstreichs"] through the town of Butzbach. Here the unbridled motion of the horses obliterates Kleist's will. What makes the experience especially upsetting, however, is the fact that the wild, directionless movement is brought about by a donkey's braying ["Eselsgeschrei"]. What appears to matter most, then, is not death but the arbitrary banality of the existence, not to mention the loss of control over the circumstances bringing it about.

The second brush with death occurs on the Rhine during a sudden storm that threatens to capsize Kleist, as he travels to Köln. Here, the concrete details of a watery death and of asphyxiation are swiftly glided over in Kleist's description; he quickly stresses that what matters is another kind of death—an abstract one:

> Ein jeder klammerte sich alle anderen vergessend an einen Balken an, ich selbst *mich* zu halten—Ach, es ist nichts ekelhafter, als diese Furcht vor dem Tode . . . Wer es [das Leben] mit Sorgfalt liebt, moralisch tot ist er schon, denn seine höchste Lebenskraft, nämlich es opfern zu können, modert, indessen er es pflegt. Und doch, o wie unbegreiflich ist der Wille, der über uns waltet. (KB, 670)
>
> Each one—forgetting everyone else—clung to a beam, even I to hold *myself*—Oh, there is nothing more nauseating than this fear of death. . . . Whoever loves it [life] with care, is already morally dead, since his highest life force, that is, to be able to sacrifice it, rots, while he nurtures it [life]. And yet, oh how incomprehensible is the will that reigns over us.

As in the Butzbach episode it is the loss of his will (and the contradiction in his desires) that mirror the movement without direction. Hence, by transfer, involuntary *motion* itself becomes the visible marker of death. Kleist's personal narratives gloss over the concrete details of a death in order to stress that *no* meaning can be imposed—even in retrospect—on the sequence of events. Most shocking to Kleist, when he seems to stand face to face with death, is that no voice replaces the absurd, unmotivated braying of the donkey. His dark, earthly life is an end unto itself; no invisible order governs it.

> Und an einem Eselsgeschrei hing ein Menschenleben? Und wenn es nun in dieser Minute geschlossen wäre, *darum* also hätte ich gelebt? *Das* hätte der Himmel mit diesem dunkeln, rätselhaften, irdischen Leben gewollt, und weiter nichts—? (KB, 666)
>
> And a human life would depend on a donkey's braying? And if it had come to a close in this minute, *that* is why I would have lived? That is what the heavens would have wanted with this dark, enigmatic, earthly life—and otherwise nothing?

The narratives of death in Kleist's letters reinforce the sense of a break between any sequence of events and any order of truth, for no sequence is genuinely coherent. Ironically, the voyage, which was a flight from living death, reminds him of his crisis; the motion produced through traveling itself becomes the signifier of death, of his obsession with it.

Clearly, then, the subject of death is central to Kleist's works, and indeed, this chapter will investigate the implications of both of Kleist's insights: his recognition that the subjectivity of "truth" implies all truths' mortality. For him, there can be no universals or absolutes. His second insight—the association of empty progression with an at least metaphoric experience of death—will be especially significant in his narratives "Die Heilige Cäcilie" and "Michael Kohlhaas," as well as in his drama, "Prinz Friedrich von Homburg." But before these insights can be pursued further, let us briefly consider an equally important corollary to Kleist's obsession with death, and that is, *how* death is to be represented through language at all.

NARRATIVE ENACTMENTS OF DEATH

What are the implications of a reversal, where the "detour" or "digression"—generally associated by Freud with the extension of life[4]—becomes so contaminated that it begins to represent the memory of death? Kleist's biography tells us only that the voyage begun in 1801 ends with a double and symbolic suicide: in 1803 he writes, "Der Himmel weiß . . . wie gern ich einen Blutstropfen aus meinem Herzen für jeden Buchstaben eines Briefes gäbe, der so anfangen könnte: mein Gedicht ist fertig" (KB, 735) ["Heaven knows how gladly I would give one drop of blood from my heart for each character of a letter that could begin in the following manner: my poem is finished"]. Within three weeks, however, Kleist burns most of his recently written manuscript (*Robert Guiskard*) and writes his half-sister, Ulrike, that he intends to throw himself into the infinite grave of Napoleon's army—and the sea. One can even cite Kleist's decision in 1811 to kill himself to show that the end of the voyage for him must be death.

Troubling as both the 1803 and the 1811 resolutions are, they do not explain what stands between the despair of the unproductive poet of 1803 and his *Michael Kohlhaas*, begun in 1804. Again, that unproductiveness seemed motivated less by the (perhaps only temporary) infertility of a poetic imagination than by a more far-reaching ideological dilemma. The crisis, which had even conjured up the writer's death symbolically through his act of narrating death, shakes the fundamental structure of literary language. Once Kleist has equated the flight *from* death (stasis and suicide) with the flight *towards* death, he has abandoned the self-evident metaphor of specularity as the trope governing the traditional laws of representation. The crisis of his faith in Bildung brings about an even more troubling suspension of the conventional laws keeping mimesis in play.

Within the context of a theory of representation, the equation of sequence with death contradicts the more usual mimetic relation based on the principle of *adequatio*.[5] In his book *Mimesis*, for instance, Erich Auerbach emphasizes that a binary structure is necessary to any mimetic construct.[6] "Representation" assumes an outside referent and a textual mirroring process, even if the rules governing this imitation resist codification. Even such "nonobjective" referents as consciousness still can be captured, mimetically, through the mediation of the random detail of everyday life.

Kleist's decision to represent death through its conventional opposite—movement—necessarily invalidates the more familiar logic of mirroring. Still, his response is hardly an arbitrary one. A traditional and masterful theory of representation makes no provision for limit-experiences, such as death, that are excluded from the sphere of everyday life. What, after all, *could* represent death adequately?

In a more philosophical context—in his comparison of the philosophy of death as it is set out by Heidegger and by Sartre—Henri Birault expresses most clearly the incompatibility of death and representation.

> L'idée de rencontrer la mort en chemin est une fleur de rhétorique, une image de style, car au moment où la rencontre s'effectue, il n'y a déjà plus qu'un seul personnage. Reprise par Sartre de l'argument antique: si je suis là, c'est que je ne suis pas mort; quand la mort me surprend, je suis mort: il n'y a donc plus personne pour être l'interlocuteur de cette rencontre.[7]

> The idea of meeting death along the way is a rhetorical flourish, a stylistic image. For the moment the meeting takes place, there is no longer but one single character. Repetition of the antique argument by Sartre: if I am there, that's because I'm not dead; when death surprises me, I am dead: there is thus no longer anybody who could be the interlocutor of this meeting.

Even if Birault's and, by implication, Sartre's reflections on death are anachronistic to Kleist's texts, the argument remains pertinent. From an empirical point of view, death can only be mirrored mimetically as silence, as a blank or, simply, as undifferentiation. Who is speaking, after all, when loss of life is being recorded?

To return to literary discourse: the effect of an obsession with death upon a writer's rhetoric will expose itself most obviously in scenes intent upon capturing the moment when life ends. Narrative descriptions of death do occur quite frequently in all of Kleist's short prose, not least in "Die Heilige Cäcilie oder die Gewalt der Musik" [Saint Cecile, or the Power/Violence of Music], written in 1810. Already the subtitle hints at a self-reflection that could highlight a connection between the unlikely pair: art and death. "Die Heilige

Cäcilie" marks a good place to begin in order to interpret a Kleistian "poetics of death," since the entire story is devoted to describing, then interpreting the spiritual and, finally, physical death of its main protagonists.

Three significant deaths take place in the story. One—that of the unknown "Oheim" [the uncle]—constitutes the accidental, unelaborated circumstance, which motivates the narrative. (It is because of the resulting inheritance that the main protagonists, four brothers, meet in Aachen at the time of the Catholic festival celebrating Saint Cecilia.) Their own, apparently simultaneous deaths are also described rather sketchily by an anonymous narrator:

> [. . .]die Söhne aber starben, im späten Alter, eines heitern und vergnügten Todes, nachdem sie noch einmal, ihrer Gewohnheit gemäß, das gloria in excelsis abgesungen hatten.[8]

> [. . .]the sons died, however, a bright and cheerful death at a ripe old age, after they had once again, as was their wont, sung the gloria in excelsis right through.

Similar to the death of Truth staged in Kleist's 1801 letter and to the poet's own empirical brushes with death, the actual description of the four brothers' end seems to cede to its rhetorical function in the text. If the Oheim's death set the story in motion, the brothers' death acts as a closure to the legend, setting a term to the transformation created by the miraculous, albeit violent, power of music.

Still, the representation of death is not quite unproblematic in this story. The narrator's description of the four brothers' loss of life as "heiter" [bright] and "vergnügt" [cheerful] creates a paradox for defining death in the text. Earlier, the punishment inflicted upon the brothers for their intention to reduce the cathedral of St. Cecilia to dust transformed them into "petrified stone." Their actions became silent and phantomlike, and the repeated reference to their barren ["öde"], cloisterlike life implies that a metaphorical death sentence is being documented in the text. What, indeed, can be both more alienating and deathlike than a ghostly ["geisterartig"] existence?

> Sie [die Vorsteher] setzten hinzu: "daß die Jünglinge, seit nun schon sechs Jahren, dies geisterartige Leben führten; daß sie wenig schliefen und wenig genössen; daß kein Laut über ihre Lippen käme." (C, 220)

> [The abbots] added that the youths had been leading this ghostly life for six years already; that they slept and enjoyed [ate] little; that no sound passed their lips.

The end of the legend—through its compressed reference to the joyful demise of the four brothers—functions much like the silent voice of Kleist's own near-death. Even though the brothers are liberated by death, their deathly existence has contributed rhetorically to the contamination of the two terms, *life* and *death.* In short: the ending does not shed light, retrospectively, on the sequence of the brothers' experiences. It simply adds one more enigma to the many questions that structure the entire narrative.

Similarly, the third form of dying—Schwester Antonia's death, described in greater detail—far from marking the meaningful culmination of lived experiences, also contributes to the empty progression in the text, to the unsatisfied quest for truth. The abbess remarks:

> Ja, Schwester Antonia würde ohnfehlbar selbst den Umstand, daß sie es nicht gewesen sei, die, auf so seltsame und befremdende Weise, auf dem Altan der Orgel erschien, bestätigt und bewahrheitet haben: wenn ihr gänzlich sinnberaubter Zustand erlaubt hätte, sie darum zu befragen, und die Kranke nicht noch am Abend desselben Tages, an dem Nervenfieber, an dem sie danieder lag, und welches früherhin gar nicht lebensgefährlich schien, verschieden wäre. (C, 227)

> Yes, Sister Antonia would doubtless have confirmed and verified the circumstance that it was not she who had appeared on the organ balcony in such a strange and alienating manner, if her totally unconscious state had permitted her to be questioned and if the evening of that selfsame day, the sick woman had not succumbed to the nervous fever which she was suffering from and that had formerly not even appeared to be life-threatening.

The representation of Antonia's death is doubly metonymic. The word *verscheiden,* although traditionally associated with death, points euphemistically to the metaphor of separation and traveling (*Abschied*), rather than insisting on the silence and nothingness of the event. The voyage that is evoked by the effaced, literal meaning of the metaphor *verscheiden* (and by the logic of the euphemism) does not only reveal the deflection implicit to language. The slipping motion is pertinent to the narrative structure of "Die Heilige Cäcilie" as a whole.

First, the signifier denoting one character, "Antonia," itself reveals a certain instability. The nun is found in an unconscious ["sinnberaubt"] state, a condition that results possibly from the doubling of her identity. While the ill nun is being watched by one of her relatives, the congregation simultaneously perceives her slightly pale, taciturn double. This double's refusal to explain her own miraculous recovery and Antonia's immediate death (precipitated, it seems, by the phenomenon of being duplicated) constitutes—on the level of narrative structure—another example of metonymic sliding. The promise of a stable interpretation, of the theoretical capability to uncover the true meaning of the occurrence, is split in two, leading to another quest. A new puzzle has been added to the initial, as yet unanswered, one. Antonia's death, far from acting as a locus of stable truth, only adds one more link to the chain of enigmas generated by the narrative.

The structure of this *Erzählung* bears the imprint of Kleist's crisis with the Bildungs model. It reinforces the impression that the existence of a sequence (and therefore of a continuous plot) cannot be equated with the unfolding of meaning. It is precisely the series of substitutions that contributes to the loss of meaning[9] and that uncovers the impossibility, even the futility, of a causal explanation.

In "Die Heilige Cäcilie" the narrative perspective shifts six times, although these changes don't complement one another. They function as obscured points of view that only add *more* enigmas to the text. A rhetoric of "slippage" [*glissement*] governs the sequence of events with no one perspective adequately filling in the gaps opened up by other commentaries. The rhetoric of slippage organizes the text, reenacting the crisis, in which the production of stable meaning is undermined.

"Die Heilige Cäcilie" begins with a reference to the tale's historical context. We are in the era of a new, Lutheran order, which vows the destruction of the more traditional Catholic Church. The advocates of the Reformation, who begin as strong centers of intentionality, are the four principal characters. Although they are strangers to Aachen, the four brothers' destructive impulse [to pillage a nearby Church] acts as a magnet, attracting numerous young adherents to the new doctrine.

The centerpiece of the legend—the miraculous conversion of the four young men—destabilizes the introductory section. As soon as they hear an unidentified piece of religious music, all four suddenly abandon their plan and, from that day onwards until their death, lead a cloisterlike life. The mysteriously feminine power of music undermines the four men's force and intentionality, and, significantly, this transformation is represented as a moment of death:

> Es regte sich, während der ganzen Darstellung, kein Odem in den Hallen und Bänken; besonders bei dem salve regina und noch mehr bei dem gloria in excelsis, war es, als ob die ganze Bevölkerung der Kirche tot sei. (C, 219)

> During the entire representation, no breath stirred in the halls and pews; especially during the salve regine and even more during the gloria in excelsis, it seemed as if the entire population within the church was dead.

Music has the power to kill metaphorically, either by petrifying or by possessing the listener. The possession, moreover, is expressed through a complete inversion of character. The four sons abandon their life-affirming nature in order to practice self-abnegation, and the culmination of this experience of being possessed (this death to the self) finds its expression in the four brothers being forced to repeat the melody of the mass at regular intervals. From the mouths of the four brothers the repetition of the melody—which had engulfed their identity—threatens to spill onto the external world; windows, supporting foundations of their building, even the "firmament" are shaken by their song. This moment is especially disturbing, since such a threat can blend the original destructive urge of the brothers and the violence of the music. It is hardly a coincidence that the word *Gewalt* (in the title) means both power and violence.

If loss of self is signified *through* Art (the singing) and also presented as a consequence of the music, how can the narrative explain the transformation? It is the four characters' mother who, by searching for her sons and their cure, structures the subsequent paragraphs. Her quest to discover the meaning of this transformation becomes the organizing principle of the text. Each of her four encounters—the unmediated presence of her insane sons; the discussion with Veit Gotthelf; the visit to the scene of her sons' spiritual death; and the final dialogue with the Abbess—repeats the quest for meaning, and reasserts the impossibility of such a reconstruction. Each explanation qualifies the preceding one, so that the event itself remains an absent center.

The displacement from scene to scene repeats the crisis of meaning. Both Gotthelf's and the Abbess's explanations begin under the sign of "Unbegreiflichkeit" [incomprehensibility]. The episode, they insist, eludes both the literal grasp and conceptualization ("der Begriff"). Gotthelf Veit begins by asserting the event's resistance to interpretation, only to end with the evocation of the insane asylum. His description focuses on the physicality of the rooms and walls of the asylum, so that the conjuring up of the physical building almost seems meant to deflect his anxiety. The brothers' repeated scenes of madness are contained, rhetorically at least, by the reference to the institution. The appeal to madness (and this is echoed by the narrator) supposedly is able to attribute an "inner" coherence to the affair ("innerer Zusammenhang der Sache," C, 224).[10]

The signifier "madness" only displaces the crisis of meaning, however. It represents primarily the desire for a solution, for boundaries, instead of endless sliding, and it does not provide a lucid interpretation of the enigma. An alternative to the diagnosis of madness is the appeal to a divine (Catholic) truth, which could replace the opaque label of insanity. During her dialogue with the four brothers' mother, the Abbess explains:

> Welcher Mittel er [Gott] sich dabei bedient, kann Euch, die Ihr eine Protestantin seid, gleichgültig sein: Ihr würdet auch das, was ich Euch darüber sagen könnte, schwerlich begreifen. Denn vernehmt, daß schlechterdings niemand weiß, wer eigentlich das Werk . . . da die

Bilderstürmerei über uns hereinbrechen sollte, ruhig auf dem Sitz der Orgel dirigiert habe. (C, 227)

Which methods [God] used, may remain indifferent to you, who are a Protestant. You would hardly understand what I could tell you about that. For hear that absolutely nobody knows who actually directed the work while sitting calmly on the organ bench . . . while the destruction [iconoclasm] was supposed to descend upon us.

A purely human account of a miracle, the Abbess asserts, can only lead to a conclusion of undecidability. Such an interpretation must submit to the limitations of Protestant subjectivity and, consequently, to the dead-end of "Unbegreiflichkeit" [incomprehensibility]. But through the appeal to divine grace, a logic based on "Mittel" (or pure human mediation) makes way for the miraculous figure of a saint's reincarnation. This stabilizing interpretation of the miracle is even supported by the Authority of the papal letter, where the spiritual force of Saint Cecilia is cited as the source of the miracle, which had saved the church. Most significantly, this image of resurrection can then be read as the key to solving all the enigmas in the narrative. The double existence of Antonia, the impact of the performance both on the performers and the audience, the immediate transformation of the brothers—all these elements become metaphors of a religious force and of God's purpose.

It is seductive to identify the Abbess's words as the story's stable center of meaning. Her account can obliterate the impression of an uncontrolled text, and this impression is especially strong in a work that seems to shift aimlessly by substituting one inadequate set of explanations for another. And yet, one must remember that the narrative appeal to different (subjective) opinions repeats iconically the enigmatic transformation of the brothers. So, the return to Catholic authority does not really manage to halt the endless slipping of the quest for an adequate explanation. There is a curious abundance of pastoral letters: the Abbess had previously had to call on the authority of the Archbishop of Trier, and the Archbishop's own certainty had, in turn, to be validated by the Pope. The Pope himself, we soon realize, also only stands in for a higher Authority, which would be *God's* Word.

The Catholic interpretation is unstable for another, even more compelling reason. The four brothers are the only visible signs of God's will—and yet, their integration into the Catholic order is interpreted as "madness" by the community. Even if the reader argues that the four have been punished with insanity for their misdeed, such a claim only succeeds in rendering innocuous the frightening proximity of Catholicism and madness.

The *mise en abyme* can also be rewritten as the contamination of the Catholic and Protestant positions. A traditionally Catholic interpretation can only appeal to a relation to truth that is mediated by the institution of the Church.

The four brothers may have abandoned the new theology, which claims that the individual's relation to God can be immediate. Still, in order to explain their reintegration into the Catholic faith, the brothers appeal, paradoxically, to their privileged, quite *subjective* knowledge. When accused of being insane, the brothers' response is a superior indifference:

> Die Vorsteher schlossen mit der Versicherung: . . . daß sie [die jungen Männer], wenn man sie für verrückt erklärte, mitleidig die Achseln zuckten, und daß sie schon mehr als einmal geäußert hätten: wenn die gute Stadt Aachen wüßte, was sie, so würde dieselbe ihre Geschäfte bei Seite legen, und sich gleichfalls, zur Absingung des gloria, um das Kruzifix des Herrn niederlassen. (C, 220)

> The abbots concluded with the affirmation . . . that they [the young men] shrugged their shoulders with pity when they were declared insane, and that they had expressed more than once: that if the good city of Aachen knew what they did, then the former would place its affairs aside and would also kneel down around the cross of the Lord to sing the gloria in its entirety.

Since their conversion is the only marker of the miracle, the irrepressible Protestant overtones of this change suggest that the Catholic explanation is not completely successful in imposing *one* code of values and meaning upon the story. Such an impression is only reinforced by the brothers' death, which is described as "heiter und vergnügt" [bright and cheerful], supporting the protagonists' own evaluation of their fate. Their death only contributes, then, to the confusion of the reader already perplexed by the conflicting interplay of various narrative perspectives.

The final narrative depiction of death only highlights the empty series of substitutions, which both structure the tale and undermine one another's finality. It is the empty progression of sequence—that ambiguous marker of death, which has implicitly unbalanced the (adequate) relation of the word to truth—that recurs insistently, and not only in "Die Heilige Cäcilie," as we shall see.

The dichotomy of Catholic and Protestant forms of truth in "Die Heilige Cäcilie" marks only one example of the epistemological dilemma underpinning Kleist's *Erzählungen* (short narratives).[11] What is presented as an unresolvable religious conflict—privileging no one position—can be detected equally well in the social antithesis of the revolutionary and the conservative positions. Even if, as in "Michael Kohlhaas," the confrontation between a "revolutionary" (Lutheran-based) and traditional (here: institutional) structure tends to undermine the more individualistic attitude (a stance, it seems, inherently more vulnerable to excess or madness), neither narrative—"Michael

Kohlhaas" or "Die Heilige Cäcilie"—is completely successful in reestablishing the primacy of stable, traditional, and enduring values.

The contamination of the two positions is impossible to avoid, as is apparent through the example of Luther's narrative function in "Michael Kohlhaas."[12] A brief summary might help here to throw the story's moral puzzle into relief. Upon travelling to Saxony with his horses, Kohlhaas, a relatively wealthy horse dealer, is mistreated by petty aristocrats in charge of levying tolls upon all travelling merchants. The narrative investigates Kohlhaas's increasingly violent claims for retribution, foregrounding him as a character who problematizes moral judgement; he is simultaneously the most righteous and the most terrible individual. Kohlhaas's insistence on his personal rights in the face of institutional corruption seems to place him firmly in Luther's camp. Surprisingly, that (of course fictional) character does not support Kohlhaas's attack on the institution. Still, even though Luther may urge Kohlhaas to submit to social order, to suffer injustice at the hands of the Law rather than to appropriate the role of an avenging angel, Luther's explicit conservatism does not transform him into a simple emblem of the institution. Luther, because he stands outside the political structure, takes up Kohlhaas's cause himself; he assumes, as it were, his position. The personal letter he writes on Kohlhaas's behalf counters the powerful letter of the Law, both by overtly attacking the Authority of the "Kurfürst" [Elector] and by deliberately redirecting (rewriting) the course of legal action:

> Am anderen Morgen erließ Luther ein Sendschreiben an den Kurfürsten von Sachsen, worin er nach einem bitteren Seitenblick auf die seine Person umgebenden Herren Hinz und Kunz, Kämmerer und Mundschenk von Tronka, welche die Klage, wie allgemein bekannt war, untergeschlagen hatten, dem Herrn, mit der Freimütigkeit, die ihm eigen war, eröffnete, daß bei so ärgerlichen Umständen, nichts anderes zu tun übrig sei, als den Vorschlag des Roßhändlers anzunehmen, und ihm des Vorgefallenen wegen, zur Erneuerung seines Prozesses, Amnestie zu erteilen.[13]

> The next morning, Luther issued a letter to the Elector of Saxonia, wherein, after [casting] a bitter glance at the men surrounding his person, Mr. Hinz and Kunz, Chamberlain and Cupbearer of Tronka, who had, as was generally known, suppressed the complaint, [Luther] disclosed to the [Elector] with the frankness that was particular to him, that under such annoying circumstances, nothing else could be done but—because of the events—to accept the suggestion of the horse dealer and to grant him amnesty until the review of his trial.

The effect of Luther's doctrines—both in "Michael Kohlhaas" and in "Die Heilige Cäcilie"—is quite ambivalent and helps to lay bare another manifestation of Kleist's troubling preoccupation with the coincidence of death and empty progression. Luther's duplicity, his double role as authority figure and insurrectionist, makes of him a particularly clear representative of the vacillation already noticed in "Die Heilige Cäcilie" and equally present in "Michael Kohlhaas." Because of his contribution to the text's undecidability—one that centers on how Kohlhaas can be both "der rechtschaffenste" [the most righteous] and "der entsetzlichste Mensch" [the most dreadful person]—Luther becomes one of the important figures to help explain the uneasy, endless series of substitutions that seem to characterize Kleist's narratives.

Luther's ambiguous role in the narrative seems especially pertinent, because his own work, *An den christlichen Adel deutscher Nation* [*To the Christian Nobility of the German Nation*], is reminiscent of the tone of Kohlhaas's mandates. Since both texts denounce the world through their appeal to Truth and Justice, Luther's self-justification and criticism of legal society is significant to our analysis of the crisis of Authority and meaning, so closely bound up with Kleist's obsession with death in his narratives—particularly as it is portrayed not only in "Die Heilige Cäcilie" but also especially in "Michael Kohlhaas."

The thrust of Luther's (historical) argument is aimed at equating the Pope with the Antichrist: in his letter Luther seems less concerned with modifying the religious hierarchy in Rome than with abolishing it completely. Luther justifies his appropriation of power on several grounds: as baptized Christians, all are equal; the different functions (*Ämter*) that priests, bishops, and the Pope assume are based on democratic choice and, therefore, cannot be considered absolute. Most compelling, however, is the reason Luther cites at the end of his letter:

> *Ich acht auch wohl, daß ich hoch gesungen hab', viel Dings für geben, das unmöglich wird angesehen, viel Stücke zu scharf angegriffen. Wie soll ich ihm aber thun? Ich bin es schuldig zu sagen.* Könnt ich, so wollt ich auch also thun. Es ist mir lieber, die Welt zürne mit mir, denn Gott; man wird mir ja nicht mehr denn das Leben können nehmen.[14]

> I do notice also that I have sung loudly, presented many things that will be considered impossible, attacked many aspects too sharply. How else should I act however? I am bound [indebted, guilty] to speak. If I could, I would also act this way. I prefer that the world be angry with me rather than God; one can do no more to me than to take my life.

For Luther denunciatory speech and writing is possible, precisely because the religious frame redefines the greatest threat to Man—death is replaced by the eternity of damnation. The religious frame supplies more; the threat of death (and, implicitly, of madness) can be repressed, because Luther does not question the equation of Scripture and divine will. Indeed, the written word becomes the new locus of God's Authority, and this mediation through Scripture makes unnecessary and corrupt any intervention of the religious hierarchy.

The significance of this shift is perceptible in many ways. It grounds Luther's own authority, by permitting him to perceive and then denounce the wrongs of the papal system. He attacks the Pope's monopoly of the Bible most vehemently, in particular, the Pope's appropriation of its interpretation. The papal law, prohibiting any personal readings of the Bible, is especially suspect according to Luther, because it suspends other Christians' ability to distinguish between right and wrong. Luther describes the importance of the Biblical text: "Wenn ich's nicht gelesen, wäre mir's unglaublich gewesen, daß der Teufel sollte zu Rom solche ungeschickte Dinge vorwenden und Anhang gewinnen"[15] ["Had I not read it, it would seem incredible to me that the devil should propose so many inappropriate things in Rome and win followers"].

Luther does not simply quote heavily from the Bible; he even constructs the first part of his denunciation by drawing on a biblical example, by comparing the arbitrary proliferation of papal laws to the walls of Jericho. The parallel between the walls of Jericho and the Pope's own paper walls makes two conclusions immediately compelling: the Pope is opposed to God; and his weapons are ineffectual because they are only documents. The scene of confrontation between the Pope and Luther is, then, from the start a metaphorical one. It takes place between two writers.

The second, longer section of *An den christlichen Adel deutscher Nation* [*To the Christian Nobility of the German Nation*] is devoted to the enumeration of religious, educational, and social reforms. This discussion allows Luther to equate the misuse of Law (its excessive proliferation) with greed, leading him to affirm at one point that it is no longer the Pope who legislates in Rome but instead a personified greed.[16] Each decision of the Pope, which introduces differences among Christians through the creation of saints, pilgrimages, or new religious orders, is unmasked by Luther as the desire to disrupt the uniformity of Christians in order to impose a logic of exchange and commerce onto the Christian world. This system of differences and substitutions, Luther argues, even threatens the status of language:

> Es kann dir weder Engel noch Pabst so viel geben, als dir Gott in deiner Pfarrei giebt; ja er verführet dich von den göttlichen Gaben, die du kaufen mußt, und giebt dir Blei um's Gold, Fell um's Fleisch, Schnur um den Beutel, Wachs um Honig, *Wort um's Gut, Buchstaben um den Geist,* wie du vor Augen siehst, und willst's dennoch nicht merken.[17]
>
> Neither angels nor the Pope can give you as much as God gives you in your parish; indeed, he leads you astray from the divine gifts that you

> must buy, and gives you lead for gold, fur for flesh, string for the bag, wax for honey, *words for the property [goods], letters for the spirit,* as you can see before your very eyes and still you do not want to notice it.

The disjunction of the word from the divine will is described through a language of finance, and a false exchange is the result of such a separation from God. The loss of the divine Spirit, indeed, of symbolic, in favor of metonymic, meaning seems to be the result of introducing laws common to the marketplace. Through the series of exchanges and substitutions only the valueless, meaningless letter remains. And although Luther carefully articulates that it is greed that has replaced the divine will as the foundation of papal law (thereby invalidating the Pope's prohibition), the confrontation he creates between two written laws already begins to be haunted by the spectre of endless exchange. By defining the danger of irresponsible law-giving as the series of escalating substitutions leading to the ever-increasing loss of value, he tacitly must admit the plurality of laws. The implication is: all written laws are potentially false. Luther may not problematize interpretation yet, because he does not here admit an involuntary difference between Scripture and the reading of Scripture. Still, once the equation between Scripture and interpretation can no longer be guaranteed, the replacement of one law by another can, theoretically, also no longer be controlled. Once again, a confrontation with death, with the death of meaning understood as empty progression, seems implicitly unavoidable.

The significance of the historical Luther to Kleist's poetics is especially visible in "Michael Kohlhaas." We have already noted Kleist's skepticism with the word and its conventional or fixed relation to meaning, an anxious skepticism that seemed to be generated by Kleist's confrontation with the loss of his former ideals, indeed with his own near-fatal brushes with death. Kleist's abstract experience of death was, of course, but a corollary of his discovery that even knowledge is mortal. This discovery, in turn, seems to influence Kleist's construction of his narratives, in particular, of "Die Heilige Cäcilie": the reader is effectively blocked from reconstructing *one* interpretation, since the text's meaning is divided up among several, conflicting perspectives.

In "Michael Kohlhaas" Kleist exploits the instability created by Luther's denunciation of the papal (false) Law in order to submit the Law of justice [and of writing] to a fundamental crisis. Most of the narrative is devoted to the dramatization of the written laws. Their description and subversion mark the central conflict of the *Erzählung.* Whereas, for Luther, the Bible and its writers had remained undefined and therefore seemed placed beyond the manipulation of human forces, Kleist is careful to unmask the written Law as a human construct. This is not only perceptible if we examine the familiar beginnings of the narrative. Kohlhaas's familiarity with the laws ["die landesherrlichen Verfügungen" (MK, 10)]; his possession of written proof that he has been wronged; and his formal complaint, which carefully follows the procedures of the law, only reaffirm the radical arbitrariness of the written word. Kleist's shifts in narrative perspective, his strategy to abandon the narration of Kohlhaas's experiences in order to focus on the meeting of Dresden's leaders, forces us to realize that the place of power is no absent, opaque locus from which "True Laws" can be dictated. The meeting between the elector and his councillors underlines how arbitrary power is, since here we must watch the actual drafting of a new law (Kohlhaas's amnesty)—one that can be used, one councillor suggests, as the (unjust) means to trick Kohlhaas into captivity.

Once the written word no longer is connected to a stable or just source in "Michael Kohlhaas," a series of substitutions results, which is reminiscent of the faulty, valueless exchanges that Luther had outlined in his critique of papal Rome. This instability is evident in the proliferation of the Kohlhaas Mandates, decrees which counter the official laws of Dresden. Although Kohlhaas argues that his written reforms will reinstate a system of proper exchanges (the substitution of gold for his mistreated horses, retribution for wrongs suffered), his attempt to impose this reform as the criterion distinguishing "good" individuals from enemies of his new state is immediately blocked by the example of the first "transgressor." The Mother Superior, aunt to "Junker Wenzel," violates the Law in ignorance of Kohlhaas's reforms and is, consequently, guilty and innocent at the same time.

The inadequacy inherent in written law is not only presented as the unbalanced relation between an experience and the evaluation of that experience. Kohlhaas's attempt to undo the corruption of Dresden laws only leads to greater injustice, culminating in his willful punishment of the innocent citizens of Leipzig. (Kohlhaas's oppressor—now cowering from the horse dealer's "righteous" persecution—is said to have sought refuge there; the rumor is soon unmasked as a ploy to throw Kohlhaas off balance in his pursuit of revenge.) It is at this moment, when Kohlhaas refuses to abandon his attacks on the decoy (that he recognizes as such), that the difference between his document and the State's abuse of mandates is obliterated:

> Vergebens ließ der Magistrat . . . Deklarationen anheften, mit der bestimmten Versicherung, daß der Junker nicht in der Pleißenburg sei; der Roßkamm, in *ähnlichen Blättern* . . . erklärte, daß, wenn derselbe nicht darin befindlich wäre, er mindestens verfahren würde, als ob er darin wäre. (MK, 41–42, my emphasis)

> In vain did the magistrate post declarations that affirmed definitely that the Junker was not in the Pleißenburg; the horse dealer declared, using similar pages, that if the same was not located there, he [Kohlhaas] at least would proceed as if he were there.

The circulation of legal papers subverts, by multiplying the misunderstandings, any reform that Kohlhaas hopes to establish. Finally, unsigned documents are introduced that only contribute to the confusion. No one in the text can identify the source of the new but deliberately falsifying declarations, nor describe even the chaos in the Dresden Residence that results from the false rumor: "und niemand beschreibt die Verwirrung, die ganz Sachsen und insbesondere die Residenz ergriff" (MK, 42) ["and no one can describe the confusion that overcame all of Saxonia and, in particular, the Residence"].

In "Die Heilige Cäcilie" the destructive force—unleashed by the appeal to subjectivity during the Reformation—could be averted through Music, but, at the same time, the logic of the Reformation (with its stress on "inner" truth) pervaded the narrative account of this "miracle." In "Michael Kohlhaas," the narrative structure also cannot resist the subversion of Authority produced by the Reformation; it too unmasks the loss of a stable center of power. Even though Kohlhaas willingly returns to Dresden and to the social order, neither can the political stability be maintained nor can the exchange of letters be suspended any longer. Luther denounces the corruption of Dresden, thereby defying the authority of the elector; Johann Nagelschmidt counterfeits Kohlhaas's signature in order to augment and profit from the anarchy in the state; and the political relation between Brandenburg and Saxony deteriorates. The juxtaposition of the two legal systems leads to a conflict of interests, highlighting the impossibility of determining what might be the proper legal sentence to be imposed on Kohlhaas.

What remains to be said, then, is how the Law (and, by extension, the written word) is subverted by the narrative structure of "Michael Kohlhaas." The Viennese Emperor's letter may seem to reestablish a just law, which will halt the endless circulation of property. After all, not only can the endless rumors and letters concerning the objects of contention be stopped, the unjustly confiscated horses themselves become "honest." They are saved from their symbolic death by being retrieved from the no-man's realm of the butcher, whose very claim to them undermines the possibility of imposing a citizen's name on the property, be this name Kohlhaas or Tronka. Yet, circulation or endless exchanges are actually not controlled at all, even despite the reintegration of the horses into the social order.

Even if we leave the introduction of the gypsy's note to one side for the moment, we can see that the *Erzählung* does not end with a new, more stable social order, as Propp's and Greimas's narrative models might lead us to expect. The Emperor's Law—his reestablishment of a singular judgment—can only occur through the mediation of another exchange. This new substitution, where Kohlhaas's property is returned to him in exchange for his life, creates the condition for the return to order.[18]

The symmetry of this ending cannot mask, moreover, the continued subversion of a logic of causality, where the sequence of narrative consequences only obfuscates the possibility of deciding who is at fault. For instance: Kohlhaas can be killed only because he accepted the plan of his anarchistic successor [Nagelschmidt] to break the new law of amnesty. Equally unsettling is the insurrectionist motive attributed to Kohlhaas, when he actually means only to withdraw from the legal struggle rather than to return to his policy of destructive revenge. His crime in wishing to flee from Dresden is, in addition, tempered by the fact that his stay in Dresden had begun to resemble an imprisonment; his crime is preceded, in fact, by the official law-givers' transgression. They are themselves ignoring the new code of amnesty.

This deliberate confusion of cause and effect is reinforced by the very end of "Michael Kohlhaas," where the death of the father brings about an even more drastic exchange. Kohlhaas's necessary execution ends up buying the nobility of his sons, so that the scene of death, which is meant to retrace the boundary separating the leaders from the people, becomes the place where such a line is effaced. Kohlhaas's appropriation of power, which marked the crisis of law in the narrative, leads, then, in the course of the story to the symbolic reshuffling of the power structure. The end, which supposedly marks the overthrow of the thrust toward reform, actually brings about the realization that the aristocratic and conservative order—by being constituted in part by the Anarchist's family—is fundamentally an arbitrary one.

CRITICAL RESPONSES TO KLEIST

Certainly it becomes compelling to read Kleist's narratives as self-destructive. Both "Die Heilige Cäcilie" and "Michael Kohlhaas" condemn the revolutionary forces explicitly, only to subvert political or religious conservatism through the narrative structure, through the logic governing the sequence of events. The force of the Revolution is not only implicitly acknowledged, it even seems to be rewarded: the four brothers' claim to a privileged, religious knowledge, validated by their joyous death, and Kohlhaas's personal triumph over his enemy as well as the integration of his family into the ranks of the leaders, are both examples of at least partially successful insurrectionists. Most troubling is the conjunction of explicit and implicit readings; such a juxtaposition seems to lead necessarily to aporia, to the suspension of meaning.

It would be tempting, then, to agree with the analysis Cynthia Chase provides of Kleist's "Unwahrscheinliche Wahrhaftigkeiten" ["Improbable Veracities"], to extend the principle of deconstruction she discovers in that anecdote to all his narratives. In the short anecdote, Chase points out that the cognitive effects achieved by Kleist's text are undone by the force unleashed by the performative aspect of his language. The stories she analyzes are about the disjunction between unbelievable but real experiences and the unbelievable narrative accounts of these, that reenact, on a metatextual level, the breakdown that constitutes the subject matter of the anecdotes.[19]

To argue that the performative and cognitive levels of language are inconsistent with one another, or, to use Chase's vocabulary, to say that the text mutilates or even explodes itself through its own rhetoric certainly might be one way to unmask Kleist's preoccupation with death in his narratives. Still, if the loss of "truth" in narrative or the plurality of contradictory, mutually exclusive meanings created through language can be interpreted as narrative enactments of death, another, more insistent question must be raised. Why does the death of meaning have to be repeated over and over again, and how can the specificity of such repetitions be described? Most significantly: what alternative ideals can a poetics of death offer?

The plurality of different, contradictory, mutually exclusive meanings that undermine the easy identification of Kleist's ideological, epistemological or political ideals can be perceived no better than through the prism of the myriad critical approaches to his oeuvre. Accounts defining Kleist's "alternative ideals" or his literary specificity fall, roughly speaking, into three camps. To introduce a third mediating or synthesizing term as a solution to Kleist's playing one antithetical term against its opposite marks the most traditional response to the crisis of interpretation offered by his narratives. The second group of critics attempts to identify Kleist as a purer mimetic artist, who can even double as a demystifier. And the third category, which will be treated later and includes Helmut Schneider, David Wellbery, and Werner Hamacher, abandons the purely mimetic reading of Kleist's narratives in order to discover a rhetorical trope that could account for the structure of his short prose.

Fritz Lockemann's and Karl Otto Conrady's desire to discover a new third term that could bypass the stalemate resulting from the confrontation of pure chaos and stultified social conventions may appear hopeful, even legitimate from an historical point of view.[20] Yet, this perspective forces a straight, one-dimensional reading of the works. Fritz Lockemann, for instance, attempts to define the order which supposedly represents an alternative to society's conventions, but he is forced to twist and turn before he is able to discover such a new order in each of the stories. Kohlhaas's sense of justice; the power (rather than the violence) of music in "Die Heilige Cäcilie"; the Marquise of O . . . 's sublimity; Elvire's (ineffectual) purity; and the tombstone which ostensibly projects the reconciliation of the two estranged lovers in "Die Verlobung in Santo Domingo" become the symbols of Kleist's new ideal. The appeal to a tombstone as the emblem of a new order seems especially problematic. And Karl Otto Conrady's attempt to recuperate the moral dimension of Kleist's prose,[21] which he interprets as "test cases" of ethical dilemmas and which ostensibly present models of behavior to the reader, still leaves unresolved the problem of determining whose values are to be accepted. In "Michael Kohlhaas," for instance, we have already noted the inadequacy of the Law, be it revolutionary or conservative. And in other texts, clearcut distinctions between good and bad (moral or immoral) behavior are problematized, if not actually effaced.

If a new order, based on *Gefühl* or *Neigung* cannot be supported, and a moral or exemplary dimension is not readily apparent in Kleist's narratives, what function can be attributed to them? How are they to be read? Instead of suppressing the (ethical) contradictions in the texts, a second group of critics, including Walter Müller-Seidel, Klaus Müller-Salget, Wolfgang Kayser, and René Girard affirm that a mimetic impulse is at work in the stories. Such a claim must be analyzed especially carefully, since a poetics of death seems to exclude the possibility of a purely mimetic project. The representation of death—on a theoretical level as well as on the level of Kleist's literary concerns—must be directed at subverting rather than supporting mimesis.

The ambiguities of the world are either joyously celebrated—as Müller-Seidel suggests in his reading of "Die Marquise von O . . ."[22]—or the plurality ("Mehrdeutigkeit") of the world is acknowledged and loyally recorded,[23] simply in order to demonstrate the relativity of truth. Klaus Müller-Salget, for instance, emphasizes the crisis in "Die Verlobung in Santo Domingo," by noting that the distinctions of black and white, or faithful and unfaithful, are suspended by Toni, who paradoxically bears all characteristics at once. Mimesis must then be identified by both Müller-Seidel and Müller-Salget with the refusal to place an ideological grid on the enigmas posed by experience and the world.

An interpretation that equates a commitment to mimesis with the refusal to impose any single belief system on the works may seem more tolerant than one that prefers to suppress contradictions in the text in its search for one stable (and affirmative) reading. But such an analysis still leaves unanswered the question, Why is the simple reproduction of an enigmatic world so important to Kleist? What lies behind the gesture to repeat the frustration of not interpreting the world adequately? Other critics turn to a closer analysis of language itself and, instead of stressing the opacity of the referent, argue how it is the act of writing that makes impossible any totalizing representation of the world. For them, "discourse" makes any adequate cognition, any ordering of experiences in the world, unattainable.[24]

Language in Kleist's texts can also be analyzed as the trace of history. Here it would be the conflicting discourses of society that are responsible for generating the cognitive dilemmas to be found in Kleist's narratives. Christa Bürger, for instance, notes how the aesthetic value of story telling had begun to fluctuate in Kleist's time, so that both "moralism" and "sensationalism" had come to be associated with popular art forms. Even if situating Kleist in a literary context—one that seems to expose him to charges of "banality"—seems crucial and helps to explain his rejection of a narrative frame or of a "coherent" plot, such an analysis easily lapses into a moralizing position. In his choice of isolated, "sensationalist" elements, Kleist may very well be rejecting the French tradition, established in part by Diderot, of coherent, framed plots and moral tales. Still, by equating Kleist's refusal of a "moralizing" art with his desire, judged superficial, to attain the status of a "serious" (elitist) artist, Bürger is forced to suppress Kleist's philosophical concerns. His anxiety with defining the relation between "Wissen" [Knowledge] and proper "Handeln" [Action] is very real, quite clearly articulated in a letter addressed to Wilhelmine v. Zenge, dated August 1801. Here he agonizes over a theoretical possibility: if writers had done half of what they had written in their great works, the world would be far improved. He goes on to formulate his own dilemma:

> Ohne Wissenschaft zittern wir vor jeder Lufterscheinung, unser Leben ist jedem Raubtier ausgesetzt, eine Giftpflanze kann uns töten—und sobald wir in das Reich des Wissens treten, sobald wir unsre Kenntnisse anwenden, uns zu sichern und zu schützen, gleich ist der erste Schritt zu dem Luxus und mit ihm zu allen Lastern der Sinnlichkeit getan. (KB, 682)

> Without knowledge, we tremble before every airy appearance [illusion], our life is exposed to every animal of prey, a poisonous plant can kill us—and no sooner do we step into the realm of knowledge, no sooner do we make use of our knowledge, in order to secure and protect ourselves, then the first step toward extravagance has immediately been taken and with it the sins of sensuality have been committed.

His concern that a correct balance between knowledge and action cannot be achieved leads him to consider the possibility of classifying any action as purely evil. Judging by his letter to Wilhelmine, Kleist's anxiety over the insufficiencies of a political or ideological art detracts from a critical account that would delimit his poetics primarily through the analysis of his literary precursors or aesthetic context.

Here it is more tempting to situate Kleist's prose in the aftermath of the French Revolution, as Friedrich Kittler does. Kittler shows how an idealistic *Bildungsdiskurs* [discourse of education], aiming to achieve an Edenic democracy, necessarily conjures a *Kriegsdiskurs* [discourse of war]. Democracy, according to Kittler's Kleist, must lead to the violent liquidation of differences—for instance, to the confusion between legitimate and illegitimate offspring. Kittler stresses that in "Das Erdbeben in Chili" ["The Earthquake in Chili"], at least, it is not the impossibility of meaning that is staged, but Kleist's radical pragmatism. A deep pessimism seems to govern his interpretation of political structures.

> Und mag jene Novelle noch so inständig versucht haben, Demokratie aufs Phantasma "*einer* Familie" und Familiarität auf Mütterlichkeit

> zu gründen, der Kriegstechniker weiß es besser als alle Bildungsdiskurse. Wahrhaft demokratisch vergehen die Unterschiede zwischen Fürsten und Bettlern, Staatsbeamten und Tagelöhnern in jenem Wahnsinn, den nur "Wahnsinn" nicht wollen könnte—wenn am Novellenende eine bewaffnete Menge alle Standesunterschiede liquidiert.[25]
>
> And no matter how urgently that novella attempts to found democracy on the phantasm of "*one* family" and familiarity on motherliness, the war strategist knows it better than all educational discourses. The differences between rulers and beggars, between state functionaries and day labourers, disappear in a truly democratic manner in that craziness that only "craziness" could not want—when an armed mob liquidates all class differences at the end of the novella.

Kittler shifts the mimetic impulse of the text from the surface of the work (its opacity) to its "deeper" level, that is, to the argument created by the sequence structuring the narrative. Kleist's social analysis, Kittler argues, leads him to affirm the necessity of an armed, violent mob, both in order to define what truly constitutes democracy (*Versöhnung aller Gemüter,* that is, "reconciliation of all minds") and what act can bring such a state about.[26] Similar to René Girard's analysis of the same story (which demonstrates how Kleist's narrative represents the "process of mimesis" itself),[27] Kittler's interpretation uncovers how "Das Erdbeben in Chili" seems to demystify the origins of society or community by describing how an act of violence can become the common ground on which an otherwise splintered community can draw together.

All these mimetic readings help to situate Kleist's texts temporally as well as to shed light on the poetics operating in Kleist's narratives. And yet, by foregrounding the mimetic process, whether on the "surface" or on the "deep" level, these critics fail to recognize how the primacy of death in Kleist's oeuvre suspends or at least undermines the mimetic process. In short, by relying on mimetic readings of Kleist's *Erzählungen,* it becomes impossible to describe how the self-reflexive nature of Kleist's narratives subverts its overtly referential task.

THE DEATH OF MIMESIS

Friedrich Kittler's and René Girard's readings are both compelling in that they uncover a pragmatism and political lucidity in Kleist's writings that others, as we noted, have either hastened to deny or to transform into aestheticized idylls. And yet, despite some of Kleist's explicitly political texts (like the *Katechismus der Deutschen* [*Catechism of the Germans*] or the *Hermannsschlacht* [*Battle of Hermann*]), it is questionable to treat the "deep" level of the work as the "true" locus of Kleist's ironic, even disillusioned political views. Such a reading assumes a little glibly that Kleist's reaction to language is an unproblematic one, that for him his "political unconscious" can be consciously recuperated in the service of social subversion.

If we briefly examine another "politicized" text that Kleist began in 1809, we soon realize that Kleist is not unmasking a myth fundamental to society but that his work actually dramatizes the impossibility of a knowledgeable, powerful, or even demystified view of social progress. *Prinz Friedrich von Homburg*, by being structured dramatically as a series of reversals, unmasks the impossibility of any progress. No constant relation between a self's intentions and his actions can be maintained. The promise of a subject's influence on his environment is repeatedly undermined, so that a mechanical series of reversals becomes the principle governing the logic of the entire text.

What is meant by influence in the context of the play? The prince may win a decisive battle for the Prussians, he may stop the anarchy threatening his uncle's state, he may even win the hand of Natalie; nonetheless, each of these actions is paradoxically ineffectual. The important battle is won, for instance, but the state of Prussia is still threatened by the potential execution of its heir apparent. The same logic applies to the prince's successful quelling of his officers' mutiny. He can only reestablish order by asserting that his death is voluntary. Again, it is this death that will jeopardize the survival of the state. The laws meant to assure the stability and protection against decay are themselves, inexorably, the mark of political suicide.[28]

Each of the Acts—and, in particular, Act II (with its numerous contradictory reports of the *Kurfürst*'s [Elector's] death and his actual survival) is constructed according to the double rhythm of advancement and of back-tracking. It is, however, Act I that is especially interesting to us, since it is here that the progress-obliterating motion becomes primarily a linguistic movement. The prince begins by recognizing Natalie in his dream state—by addressing her as "mein Mädchen" [my girl] and, yet, when he awakens from his trance, this knowledge has been lost. Half of the Act is spent, subsequently, attempting to recover the lost proper name of the mysterious female apparition. Rather than contributing to the forward-driving suspense of the entire play, however, this enigma (which is prolonged by Hohenzollern's subterfuge) is solved at the end of the same, initial Act.

In this play, language almost receives the status of a character, although this character, rather than being identified as "das Wort" [the Word] would be named "die Parole" [password/motto]. For the dramatis personae in *Prinz Friedrich von Homburg* the word *is* power and if this power is called into question (for example, if a command or personal statement of intention is subverted), there can only be one consequence: anarchy.

The passages in *Prinz Friedrich von Homburg*, in which power is subverted by the ambivalence of language, are manifold. At the end of Act I, for instance, the prince quite clearly challenges *Fortuna* with an exaggerated emphasis of his own power:

> Heut, Kind der Götter, such ich, flüchtiges
> Ich hasche dich im Feld der Schlacht und stürze
> Ganz deinen Segen mir zu Füßen um.[29]
>
> But today, elusive offspring of the gods,
> I shall capture you upon the battlefield
> And spill out all your blessings at my feet.[30]

The prince's choice of the verb *umstürzen* confuses the link between his assertion of will and the outcome of this statement. On the one hand, he will win the battle but this victory will not be the mark of his glory. It will be the cause of his death sentence. In effect, this series of reversals makes incomprehensible the concepts of "glory" and "power." We are left with the question, Does the glory lie in the adulation of the officers at the end of Act V or does it actually lie in the prince's renunciation of his life?

The same paradox is created by another one of the prince's "paroles": "Und jetzt ist die Parol', ihr Herrn: ein Schurke/Wer seinem General zur Schlacht nicht folgt!" (P, 11.492–93) ["And now the word is, men: a scoundrel, he/Who disregards his general's battle call!"].[31] As it turns out, the villain is both he who does and he who does not follow the "parole." He who does follow will be accused of mutiny by the elector; he who does not, must watch the defeat and destruction of his state. And another example: the prince says after learning of his uncle's supposed death, "Könnt ich mit Blut, aus diesem treuen Herzen, / Das seinige zurück ins Dasein rufen!—" (P, 11.568–69) ["Oh, would that with the blood of my own heart/I could call his heart's blood back to life."].[32] The prince's grief-stricken expression of desire will both be fulfilled and suspended. His uncle's reappearance is the condition for the prince's death sentence. And yet, we cannot speak of an *ironic* fulfillment of desire either, since, in the final analysis, the prince will not be executed. The same logic governs most of the expressions of power, so that this sequence of reversals leads to the creation of paradoxes, which, in turn, hinder us from drawing any conclusions based on a logic of mimetic causality.

Prinz Friedrich von Homburg is a play obsessed with two parallel concerns. First, the central protagonist attempts desperately to determine the proper relation to his death. Paradoxically, his flight from death is countered by the voluntary (but suspended) assumption of his death penalty. On a metatextual level, the relation between the word and its signified is also inverted. Each attempt to stabilize language—to confer the proper interpretation upon a situation—leads to a reversal of that statement. As a consequence, the relation between language and what language designates is problematized. The logical construction of the text, in effect, does more than subvert the social or political goals. It enacts the subversion of mimesis, in that the speaker's intention is never reflected accurately—is actually contradicted—by the words he speaks.[33]

Significantly, the series of reversals—by separating forcibly word from will—also makes the belief in a linear, causal development an impossible one. Such a metatextual enactment is not limited to the example of *Prinz Friedrich von Homburg* alone. Both "Über das Marionettentheater" (December 1810) ["On the Marionette Theater"] and "Betrachtungen über den Weltlauf" (October 1810) ["Reflections on the Way of the World"] exploit a structure of inversion in order to subvert traditional models of progress. The logical reversals described in both essays emphasize that a subject attempting to accumulate knowledge and power will only place an ever greater gap between itself and its ideal. As the narrator concedes, at the end of "Über das Marionettentheater":

> Mithin, sagte ich ein wenig zerstreut, müßten wir wieder von dem Baum der Erkenntnis essen, um in den Stand der Unschuld zurückzufallen? Allerdings, antwortete er, das ist das letzte Kapitel von der Geschichte der Welt.[34]

> Consequently, I said slightly absent-mindedly, would we have to eat once again from the tree of knowledge, in order to fall back into the state of innocence? Certainly! he answered, that is the last chapter of the story [history] of the world.

Any reading of Kleist's narratives that attempts to link the political subversiveness of his writings with a strong ideological position (with a "plaidoyer" for an anarchic democracy or with the demystification of a *civilized* society) is forced to overlook an even greater subversiveness, one that questions even the *possibility* of demystifying. To argue that demystification is possible implies, after all, that a certain kind of masterful and controllable discourse is still an alternative. And yet, as both the structure of *Prinz Friedrich von Homburg* and the fortunes of the *word* in that play reveal, all strongly affirmed positions are reversed in order to show up the futility of insight and choice.

Following the analysis of *Prinz Friedrich von Homburg* we can argue that the focal point of Kleist's literary project is primarily inward-turned, concerned with dramatizing the play of language. For Kleist, the signifier seems to have priority over the signified; at stake in his texts is the problematized relation between the speaker's will and his speech. In *Prinz Friedrich von Homburg*, as well as in Kleist's narratives, the function of language to distinguish between terms is called into question. We can note, then, that the conflict of sociohistorical discourses is certainly significant in Kleist's work. Nonetheless, it is the crisis of language itself that lends rhetoric priority over mimesis, that generates the dynamic of his works, and that relates, finally, to his preoccupation with literal and figurative forms of death.

To determine now which rhetorical figure dominates in Kleist's literary works is not easily settled, however, since the structure of reversal can be supplanted by Kleist's explicit choice to privilege "metonymy," as in "Über die allmähliche Verfertigung der Gedanken beim Reden" ["On the Gradual Composition of Thoughts While Speaking"]. Language, Kleist argues in 1805 and 1806, is a force that precedes a thought or thesis so that, paradoxically, it is the "vehicle" that creates the "tenor."

> Die Sprache ist alsdann keine Fessel, etwa wie ein Hemmschuh an dem Rade des Geistes, sondern wie ein zweites, mit ihm parallel fortlaufendes, Rad an seiner Achse. Etwas ganz anderes ist es, wenn der Geist schon, vor aller Rede, mit dem Gedanken fertig ist. Denn dann muß er bei seiner bloßen Ausdrückung zurückbleiben, und dies Geschäft, weit entfernt ihn zu erregen, hat vielmehr keine andere Wirkung, als ihn von seiner Erregung abzuspannen. (II, p. 322)

> Language is then no fetter, like a brake shoe on the wheel of the mind, but is rather a second wheel running parallel to its [the mind's] axle. It is something completely different when the mind, before all speech, is already finished with the thought. For then it must remain behind with its simple expression, and this business [activity], far from stimulating it, has rather no effect than to remove the tension from its stimulation.

If the speech act becomes the new object of discourse, so that a theory of "articulation" replaces the theory of "representation, "[35] we should finally be able to equate the (deep) level or logic of a text with its rhetoricity. We should be able to diminish the importance of the referent.

To Hans-Peter Hermann (who begins by redefining "selfhood," so that is no longer identified with terms like "Ganzes" or "Gebilde"),[36] the primacy of language over its referent does not lead him to conclude that mimesis has become obsolete, indeed invalidated by his own new categories. Instead he argues that the Kleistian narrative transforms mimesis into an experience of the world. (And Karlheinz Stierle, by emphasizing that it is the "enigma of the pure now, the abysslike certainty of an emerging present that becomes perceptible through the process of speaking,"[37] seems to agree with Hermann.) Both seem to annihilate the difference between writing and experience.[38]

For both Stierle and Hermann the act of writing enters the order of experience, perhaps conferring durability on the ethereal, passing moments,[39] nonetheless making impossible any general or universal "meaning." Once again, despite the grounding in a "rhetorical" approach, we stand before the enigma of the world. We stand, in fact, before the simple doubling of these enigmas, so that the act of writing ends up increasing the futility of existence. As a result, Hermann's and Stierle's interpretations leave unanswerable the question of why Kleist still engages in his literary projects.

Both Hermann and Stierle identify metonymic continuity with (a "real") temporal linearity in order to deny ultimately the difference between language and experience, and they also note a significant trend in Kleist's poetics. The suppression of teleology (of a belief in God or in absolute knowledge) leads to a structure which privileges mere progression *(Ablauf)* or the empty substitution of one event by another. The uncontrollable, cognitively empty substitution of signifiers (and of narrative sequences) can be identified, then, as the cornerstone both of a Kleistian theory of language and of narrative. At this point we can still only point to two narrative examples. The structure of "Die Heilige Cäcilie" is composed of fluctuating narrative sequences that help to destabilize rather than to fix meaning. The series of substitutions (both of written laws and of individuals: Kohlhaas's death for the nobility of his sons) represents the second example of cognitively empty substitution. The claim of "rhetorical" critics interested in exposing the primacy of the signifier over its referent emphasizes this prevalence of metonymy. Let us remain, therefore, within the perspective carved out by such "rhetorical" critics. Once we analyze the connection between the key figure of metonymy (substitution) and narrative representation, it will be possible to demonstrate how Kleist's 1801 discovery of the mortality of truth becomes the foundation both of his narratives and of his poetics of death.

One final turn of the critics' lens is useful to pinpoint the connections between rhetorical analysis and Kleist's narratives. Helmut Schneider, David Wellbery, and Werner Hamacher all read Kleist's *Erzählungen* as an allegory of narrative representation and each uses "Das Erdbeben in Chili" ["The Earthquake in Chili"] in order to map out the implications of such an interpretation. All three critics isolate the final scene of the tale (with its sequence of innocent and "guilty" murdered victims) as the moment, where the inadequacy of narrative mastery is unmasked. This inadequacy is revealed primarily through the play of mistaken identity, such a confusion highlighting especially the discrepancy between sign and referent.

For one "rhetorical" critic, Helmut Schneider, the narrative project consists in substituting order for arbitrariness. His list of such (metatextual) substitutions includes the suppression of coincidence by interpretation, contingency by coherence, event by speech, and happening *(Geschehen)* by history *(Geschichte)*.[40] The thrust of Kleist's project, and of its simultaneous inadequacy, is symbolized by Don Fernando's double response to the loss of his only child. Don Fernando's attempt to draw a meaning out of the survival of his *Ersatz* child cannot mask his (silent) grief completely. The inadequacy of such a project, Schneider argues, is historically determined; the rejection of a religious mythology for a more enlightened rationality was not sufficient to repress the irrationality implicit in the reality of the French Revolution.[41] For Schneider, then, the meaning of Kleist's narrative allegory can be summed up as the inability of language to (re)arrange ["verfügen"] reality completely.

In Wellbery's analysis, the allegory is a moral one. Here, the inadequacy of narrative order becomes translated into Kleist's self-critical warning that the substitution or repression of coincidence through (falsifying) narratives can only result in violent death.[42] According to Wellbery's analysis, Kleist's narratives must be deadly, because they are always necessarily false.

Wellbery's and Schneider's references oppose "narrative" to the coincidental or arbitrary real. On the one hand, contingency or *Zufall* is perceived as a threat; on the other, narrative must respond to this menace both by explaining it away and by reaffirming its own primacy. ("Coincidence," of course, can never be explained away completely or adequately.) The narrative structure, once it has been perceived as "substitution," will always point to a lack. Since the very real coincidences precede accounts destined to order them, narrative will always be accused of not controlling the arbitrary. Essentially, then, the difference between narrative and contingency can never be clearly articulated. Only the position that one occupies in relation to the other can be identified.

The distinctions between narrative and contingency that are established by the two critics are quite useful, and this despite the overlapping of the two terms. While both emphasize the importance of substitution, they use the term not to describe the process structuring the internal logic of a narrative, but mainly as a metatextual concept, one that provides insight into the crisis facing *any* poetics. The narrative act, they imply, is torn between two poles, between "coincidence" (an opaque "reality") and "order," so that the act of writing will ultimately always be unable to resolve the tension between the two opposites.

Werner Hamacher also exploits the metatextual dimension attributed to the principle of substitution, but radicalizes it through a connection only hesitantly sketched in by Schneider and Wellbery. Hamacher emphasizes, namely, that the repeated substitutions in "Das Erdbeben in Chili" enact the Derridean logic of the supplement. Each replacement (representation) stands in for an original, missing term without being able to mask its own "secondariness" and its excess of difference. The term that is introduced from the "outside" of an originally intact structure may recreate the sought-after completeness, but only at the price of importing an external element. The boundaries meant to distinguish the inside from the outside, or the "improper," are thereby permanently unbalanced.[43]

How does the supplement operate in "Das Erdbeben in Chili?" Hamacher analyzes several key moments for us. A central example of such instability is perceptible, once the Law attempts to reestablish itself, to replace the chaos with order. ("Chaos," defined from the perspective of the Law, would be the [sacrilegious] sexual union between Josephe and Jeronimo.) However, by allowing the legitimate child, Juan, to die in place of the bastard, Philipp, the Law becomes indistinguishable from transgression. Or, if we draw on the vocabulary of the idyll that is evident in the second part of "Das Erdbeben in Chili," the harmony of society ("die Einheit der Familie") is represented by the image of Josephe nourishing Elvire's son. Through this act Josephe displaces *legitimate* maternity. Elvire can only be reintegrated as the mother of her own family, after Pedro the shoemaker (the one who repairs)[44] has murdered Josephe. The newly unified family, however, still points to its lack of wholeness, since the true son has been replaced by Philipp.

By focusing on these central moments of replacement, we can argue that the project to represent "reality" has been redescribed, on an allegorical level, as the logic of the supplement. "Das Erdbeben in Chili" demonstrates that it is impossible to repress the *différance* implicit in signification. To use Hamacher's words: "es ist die Erfahrung der Differenz, die das Vorstellen ermöglicht und seine Form, seine Ausschließlichkeit und seine Wahrheit zerstört"[45] ["it is the experience of differance that makes imagining possible and that destroys its form, its exclusivity, and its truth"].

The "logic of the supplement" accounts for more than the structure of "Das Erdbeben in Chili." The undecidability of the ending—which, in "Das Erdbeben," confuses the distinction between legitimacy and illegitimacy, or law and transgression—is common, as we saw, to "Die Heilige Cäcilie" and to "Michael Kohlhaas." In a sense, we are back to Cynthia Chase's argument that the rhetoricity of the text—here, the primacy of metonymy and substitution—makes knowledge impossible. And since we know that for Kleist uncontrollable, meaning-undermining "substitution" is contaminated as a marker of death, it is not surprising that particularly the death scenes unbalance cognitive distinctions.

In three of Kleist's *Erzählungen* the sensational details distract the reader from drawing either moral or political conclusions. In "Der Findling" ["The Foundling"], Nicolo, the rebellious adopted son, repays an old man's generosity with the attempted rape of his wife. But through his own violent death at the hands of the old man, the impression of Nicolo's brutality is replaced by one in which he himself seems a victim. In "Das Erdbeben in Chili" the murder of the protagonists by a mob undoes the initial opposition between a hierarchical society and a democracy. By the end it is no longer clear whether the evils of democratic anarchy or the rigors of a stratified society are under fire. The violence of the murder scene undoes the radical difference between the two. Even in "Der Zweikampf" ["The Duel"], where the death of the criminal, Jakob der Rotbart, seems to reestablish social justice, the distinction between right and wrong remains shadowy. First of all, the introduction of the final clause "if it is God's will" modifies the clearcut equation of a duel's outcome (a standard signifier) and truth (signified). And secondly, the opening death scene, which destabilizes the social structure, actually *follows* the *legitimate* duke's plot to dispossess his half-brother (Jakob) in order that his own *illegitimate* son be instated as the rightful successor to power.

The difficult triangle between the crisis of knowledge, the narrative representation, and the predominant figure of substitution may be established, but only at the price of *supplementing* Kleist's own poetics. In other words, to read Kleist's narratives simply as enactments of the Derridean supplement is equivalent to alienating Kleist's work from its historical context. The particularity of his literary project is necessarily lost through such an interpretative act.

BEGINNINGS OF A POETICS OF DEATH

Readings centered on discerning the "logic" of a text have provided us with a key: the rhetoric of *substitution* has replaced purely mimetic interpretations. Indeed, Kleist's obsession with substitution—his realization that the relation of one signifier to another is purely arbitrary is quite evident in a playful text written in 1809 and entitled "Brief eines politischen Pescherä über einen Nürnberger Zeitungsartikel" ["Letter of a political Pescherä on a newspaper article of Nuremberg"]. In the Utopia Kleist describes satirically, the following linguistic principle is at work:

> Bekanntlich drücken wir mit dem Wort: Pescherä, alles aus, was wir empfinden oder denken; drücken es mit einer Deutlichkeit aus, die den andern Sprachen der Welt fremd ist. Wenn wir z.B. sagen sollen: es ist Tag, so sagen wir: Pescherä; wollen wir hingegen sagen: es ist Nacht, so sagen wir: Pescherä. Wollen wir ausdrücken: dieser Mann ist redlich, so sagen wir Pescherä; wollen wir hingegen versichern: er ist ein Schelm, so sagen wir: Pescherä. Kurz, Pescherä drückt den Inbegriff aller Erscheinungen aus, und eben darum, weil es alles ausdrückt, auch jedes einzelne. (II, 374)

> It is known that we express everything that we feel or think through the word Pescherä; we express it with a clarity that is foreign to other languages of the world. When we are to say, for instance, that it is day, we say: Pescherä; should we want to say however: it is night, then we say: Pescherä. If we want to express: this man is honest, we say Pescherä; on the other hand, if we want to affirm: he is a rogue, then we say: Pescherä. In short, Pescherä expresses the epitome of all manifestations, and precisely because it expresses everything, it also expresses every single thing.

Still, the inadequacy of a "representational" project has mainly been based on the deconstruction of interpretations supporting the primacy of mimesis and on the analysis of self-reflexivity in *Prinz Friedrich von Homburg*. It is time now, as a final step, to reexamine Kleist's own metatextual remarks about representation. His explicit criticism of a poetics of the *Bild* [the image] will allow us to orientate our search, so that we may discover how a writer is able to salvage a poetics of death from the abyss of silence.

In a series of letters and anecdotes spanning at least seven years (1800–1807), Kleist considers how the inadequacy of mimesis (of *das Bild*) parallels the shortcomings of Bildung and true knowledge. The image—and this implicates the figure of mirroring—leads simply to a reduplication of the subject who perceives the world. Kleist's critique of a metaphor based solely on the "mirror" is evident in a letter he writes to Wilhelmine von Zenge in November 1800. Here he describes the aesthetic viewer as a "dead" eye, whose perceptive abilities are indistinguishable from the surface of the sea.

Kleist considers mistaken the view that supposes the structure of reflection (or mirroring) to be binary. In fact, either the subject is passive (as in the example of the dead eye) and merely reduplicates the object, or (as in the case of an actively critical viewer) such criticism reveals more about the spectator himself and is, therefore, not sensitive to the specificity of the described world. A genuine interplay between two terms can never be maintained. As a result, with the inevitable obliteration of the subjective or the objective term, mimesis yields no new knowledge.

Beyond the "physical" instability of a figure based on the mirror lies the inadequacy of any model meant to organize and guide the development of the mind. In his ironic text, "Allerneuester Erziehungsplan" ["Very Latest Educational Plan"], Kleist advocates the usefulness of contradiction for education. Through paradox, children can learn to be better than their parents. After all, the narrator argues, a simple doubling of the imperfections of the parents will hardly lead to improvement or progress. Put in artistic terms, as Kleist's "Brief eines jungen Dichters an einen jungen Maler" ["Letter of a young Poet to a young Painter"] shows that the mere imitation of great masters would only efface the creativity of a young artist. The reliance on Bild (as image or as model) cannot help but repeat the inadequacy of Bildung. The process of mirroring, besides being potentially deadly (as in "Über das Marionettentheater"), cannot contribute to the accumulation of knowledge or to any sort of progress.[46]

What might replace a spatial model for art is hinted at, paradoxically, in Kleist's praise of a particularly excellent painting. The image of a dying soul that he describes in 1807 is a masterpiece, but not because its lines are drawn accurately. "In einer der hiesigen Kirchen ist ein Gemälde, *schlecht gezeichnet zwar*, doch von der schönsten *Erfindung*" (KB, 783, my emphasis) ["In one of the local churches there is a painting, which, *while badly drawn*, still (is characterized) by the most beautiful *invention*"]. In fact, it is the invention itself that he praises in place of the painterly object, a replacement that in this example becomes possible because the "object" is itself ethereal—is *now* losing its quality of being-in-the-world. And how is this "absent" quality portrayed?

> Sie [die *Seele*] liegt, mit Blässe des Todes übergossen, auf den Knieen, der *Leib* sterbend in die Arme der Engel zurückgesunken. Wie zart sie das Zarte berühren; mit den äußersten Spitzen ihrer rosenroten Finger . . . das liebliche Wesen, das der Hand des Schicksals jetzt entflohen ist. Und einen Blick aus sterbenden Augen wirft sie [die Seele] auf sie [die Engel]. (KB, 783, my emphasis)

> [The *soul*] lies, bathed in the pallor of death, on its knees, the dying *body* [lying] sunken back in the arms of the angels. How tenderly they touch the tender one, with the extreme tips of their rosy pink fingers . . . [they touch] the lovely creature that has now fled [escaped] the hand of destiny. And out of dying eyes the soul casts a glance upon them.

Kleist describes this depiction of a death by emphasizing its transitions, by noting how delicately and briefly the angelic fingers brush the human hand. The effect of movement is achieved even more strikingly in Kleist's decision to *split* the object of representation. Both a soul (with its excess of almost liquid paleness) *and* a body are painted, and through this doubling it becomes impossible to reconstruct a centered object. Also the juxtaposition of the phrases "already fled" and "dying glance" suggests that the object of representation has disappeared into a space above and beyond the canvas; yet, this "object" is also present in its momentary glance which still lingers in the world. Through Kleist's act of interpretation, the glance of the eyes becomes the fleeting center of the painting.

It is not a static realism, not the accuracy of the perceived or reflected object that Kleist posits as the goal of an aesthetic project. That goal is movement, represented both as the passage from life to death within the painting and as a "stimulation of emotions" *(Gemütserregung)* outside of it. This is what exalts an otherwise mediocre portrait. Below the surface of the verbal icon of his letter—organizing the disparate, seemingly random remarks of Kleist's enthusiasm—lies a conception of art that draws its inspiration from music. Here the search for transitions, for a correct succession of spatial moments, orientates creative expression.

The image of the dying soul helps Kleist to break away from the sterility associated with mimesis but also leads him back to his preoccupation with death. And yet, while the abstract, dynamic qualities of the painting do not free him from his crisis with progress and (cognitive) art, it does mark a turning point in Kleist's literary venture.

Up to now we have only marked his frustration with tradition (with the conventions of representation and of Bildung). His flight from its deathly sterility could only precipitate him into more encounters with death. On an empirical level, the wild travels of 1801 exposed him to actual brushes with death. But even on a metatextual level, the structure of endless substitutions only repeats his realization that knowledge has died, become mortal. In his narratives, the death scenes continue the work of the substitutions structuring the narratives by allowing traditionally opposed terms to be equated, so that their differences are blurred, becoming almost identical.

With his appeal to an alternative ideal—one explicitly bound up with the figuration of death—Kleist experiences a radical turnabout. He counters his flight from death with a flight toward it, willing to explore and define the subversive strategies made possible through a poetics of death. His turn to a musical model marks but the first step of his active attempt to counter the traditions of Bild and of Bildung. His later narratives, "Das Bettelweib von Locarno" ["The Beggarwoman of Locarno"], "Der Zweikampf" ["The Duel"], and "Die Verlobung in Santo Domingo" ["The Engagement in Santo Domingo"] all constitute much clearer examples of his subversive, "reverse" Bildung. In the next chapter we will begin, then, with a more detailed analysis of the tradition of Bildung, so that the more affirmative, as well as innovative, aspects of Kleist's poetics of death can come to light.

Chapter Two

Bildung and Mortality

Kleist's Search for a Poetics of Death

BILDUNG AND ITS SUBVERSION BY A POETICS OF MUSIC

Traditional readings of the death scene in literature tend to give it supreme value on account of its uniqueness. Garrett Stewart, in his analysis of death scenes in British fiction, isolates that quality in his analysis of literary death:

> If all death is a kind of closure, then any death, at any point in a novel, coinciding with or anticipating "The End," may summon the sense, and suspended apprehension, of such a formal limit. The prose of the fictional death sentence may thus, at the circumscribed level of the stylistic microcosm, compact and so dramatize the very premises of representation that permit and condition it.[1]

Stewart recognizes that the radicality of the death scene grants it a special, metatextual status in any literary project. But the metatextual function he bestows on death scenes relies on the self-evident link between death and closure; better: it relies on the unique (that is, never recurring) quality of death. Such a connection cannot hold, of course, for a writer like Kleist, who is obsessed with showing the pervasiveness of death, its unavoidable presence in every mode of existence. Consequently, once death is no longer singular, its link with truth—not even necessarily an "immortal" truth—can no longer be sustained.

Once again, we stand before the fundamental dilemma. Even if the work of art contains certain repeated enactments of death, it still is a conscious act and, as such, does not simply happen to the writer. In other words, by being willed, the experience of writing differs extremely from the experience of death. One can't help wondering: if the substitutions that seem to constitute the structure of Kleist's narratives act as contaminated signifiers of death, why, then, does Kleist keep these substitutions in play? What does he achieve through the act of writing?

Our method of addressing this question so far has been to consider that death, for Kleist, is not so much of an obsession but, rather, more of a trap.[2] Once we consider how Kleist articulates his poetic project, how, in effect, his repeated representations of death impact on such a project, we can note a certain ambivalence. Even his preliminary sketch of a "musical" progression in time, that would replace the inadequate Bildungs-model, tends to foreground the scene of death while, at the same time, transforming it into a symbol of something else: here, imaginative perfection. The death scene is celebrated only incidently. In this example, then, the poetics of movement and music still attempts to subordinate, even repress, death.

The strategy to displace the primacy of death through the privileging of a musical model can to some extent be explained by Kleist's historical context. He is writing partially against Goethe, searching for a concept that can counter the dominance of a poetics concerned with visual effects or color (*die Farbenlehre*). An example of Kleist's "anxiety of influence" can be perceived in a letter dated the summer of 1811, in which Kleist presents his own alternative to the massive literary project defined by Goethe. Kleist's tone may seem flippant, but, as the suppression of Goethe's name reveals, it does not quite mask Kleist's anxiety:

> Denn ich betrachte diese Kunst [die Musik] als die Wurzel, oder vielmehr, um mich schulgerecht auszudrücken, als die algebraische Formel aller übrigen, und so wie wir schon einen Dichter haben—mit dem ich mich übrigens auf keine Weise zu vergleichen wage—der alle seine Gedanken über die Kunst, die er übt, auf Farben bezogen hat, so habe ich, von meiner frühesten Jugend an, alles Allgemeine, was ich über die Dichtkunst gedacht habe, auf Töne bezogen. Ich glaube, daß im Generalbaß die wichtigsten Aufschlüsse über die Dichtkunst enthalten sind. (KB, 875)

> For I consider this art [music] as the root, or—to express myself properly—as the algebraic formula of all else, and since we already have a poet—with whom, moreover, I do not dare compare myself in any way—[a poet] who has applied all his thoughts on the art that he practices to colors, so have I, from my earliest youth, applied all general thoughts that I have had on poetry—to sounds. I believe that the most important explanations of the art of poetry are contained in the continuo.

The familiar opposition of a musical to a painterly model has far-reaching consequences for Kleist's theory of representation, since his emphasis on "tones" reveals that "succession" (and thus, a tendency toward "abstraction") replaces the importance of the image, both as "painting" and as "mirror"—in his artistic project.[3] Music, by emphasizing the positive, more dynamic aspect of succession, offers a liberation from a poetics that foregrounds the intersection of Bild and Bildung[4] too strongly—a tendency that is represented rather visibly, by contrast, in Goethe's *Wilhelm Meisters Lehrjahre.*

Before considering how a poetics of music might manifest itself in Kleist's narratives, it is necessary to examine a little more closely *what* Kleist is rejecting when he resists the primacy of an aesthetic (visually oriented) Bildung. In order to understand why he rejects the literary account of a gradual, unfolding self, we must first consider—this time through an analysis of Bildung—how Bild and Bildung implicate one another.[5]

Wilhelm Meisters Lehrjahre [1795–96] is perhaps the most famous of all *Bildungsromane*[6] and, as such, can function as the *exemplum* of its type. It contains, moreover, one of the most striking scenes, during which a connection between Bild and Bildung is enacted in the narrative. The plot follows the formation of a main character, Wilhelm, who develops gradually into an artist by acting as an apprentice in the theatrical world. His gradual development is paradigmatic, leading him to grasp the great paradox inherent in all education.

His crisis comes about when he realizes that his development cannot simply be understood as an arbitrary encounter between his unformed self and "experience" or the "world." There has been an unknown third term at work, guiding and forcing him into various situations. His individuality is not simply spontaneous; he has been led to assume a certain form.[7]

The enigma facing Wilhelm is never solved. The narrative leads him to discover a mysterious *Turmgesellschaft* [Tower Society], presumably responsible for his adventures. But when he presses the society's members for explanations, they disclaim any direct responsibility for his experiences. Already here this mystical third force—one that Kleist could not accept, even in March 1801—is bound to an authority, even if this authority is not to be equated with a traditional straight-laced establishment.

> Nicht vor Irrtum zu bewahren ist die Pflicht des Menschenerziehers, sondern den Irrenden zu leiten, ja ihn seinen Irrtum aus vollen Bechern ausschlürfen zu lassen, das ist Weisheit der Lehrer. (WML, 518)

> It is not the task of the educator of humans to protect [them] from error, but rather to guide the erring individual, to allow him/her to drink the last drops of his/her error out of full cups; that is the wisdom of teachers.

This confrontation with a secretly manipulated formation does lead Wilhelm to an unresolved crisis—one that is carried over to the end of the novel.

Wilhelm is explicitly liberated from the influence of the society but never quite succeeds in freeing himself of its involvement in his life or even its company. Even more significant is the fact that the formation the society submits him to also provides him with a written portrait, an image that is not *identical* with his self but acts, nevertheless, as a stabilizing force. Writing and formation join hands, as do Bildung and Bild: Wilhelm is allowed access to his *Lehrbrief* and even analyzes the documentation of his life. [Incidentally, *Lehrbrief* is a term with literary and legal overtones. The *Lehrbrief* can be read as Wilhelm's biographical portrait, but its primary meaning is the apprentice's indenture, that is, the text that legitimates his apprenticeship.]

> Er sah zum erstenmal sein Bild außer sich, zwar nicht wie im Spiegel ein zweites Selbst, sondern wie im Porträt ein anderes Selbst: man *bekennt* sich zwar nicht zu allen Zügen, aber man freut sich, daß ein denkender Geist uns so hat fassen, ein großes Talent uns so hat darstellen wollen, daß ein Bild von dem, was wir waren, noch besteht und daß es länger als wir selbst dauern kann. (WML, 529–30, my emphasis)

> For the first time he saw his image outside of himself, although not (as) a second self as in the mirror, rather, (as) another self as in the portrait: one does not perhaps *acknowledge* all the traits, but one is happy that a thinking mind has grasped us in such a manner, that a great talent has wanted to represent us so, that an image of what we were still remains and that it will last longer than we ourselves can.

Even if this image is not the one he chooses to accept as a completely authentic or truthful copy of himself, Wilhelm is able to recognize himself. His formation has literally created a substantial self. Moreover, with the emphasis on *bekennen*, the question of considering the *Lehrbrief* as an impartial, objective evaluation cedes to whether it is judged as truthful, whether it can be accepted. Wilhelm hesitates to *acknowledge* or even to *admit* to the self-image, but this hesitancy seems to reflect more the (slight) immaturity of the beholder rather than, simply, the inadequacy of the portrait.

This moment in the *Lehrjahre* allows us to note how Goethe skillfully blends the Bildung of Wilhelm with his Bild. In addition, the juncture of Bildung and Bild accounts, at least partially, for the very existence of the *Lehrjahre*. This *mise en abyme* explicitly places the author at the source of all three projects—of Wilhelm's formation and of his two portraits (one metatextual, the other the novel itself). The project of writing—which remains a mysterious one, cloaked by the enigmatic *Turmgesellschaft*—allows Goethe to harness the unfolding of time to both a moral and an aesthetic purpose. Kleist is, however, not able to privilege such mastery in his own works. No *Turmgesellschaft* or other mystical frame exists for him, and so his poetics leads him to hope that "music" will be able to bestow a more durable quality on the succession of sounds and sequences in his narratives.

Kleist's shortest tale, "Das Bettelweib von Locarno" ["The Beggarwoman of Locarno"], is perhaps the best example of a tale that abandons an aesthetic of the image. The story is almost musical in its construction, since its entire plot consists in repeating an (acoustic) scene of death. The structure of the story is simple: a Marchese, returning to his castle from a hunt, finds a beggarwoman in one of his rooms and orders her to place herself behind a stove. As she is following his command she slips, barely manages to drag herself to the stove, and dies there, invisible to the Marchese—and to the narrator. The scene is repeated four times (the invisible ghost returns again and again to haunt the room), and the story ends with the Marchese's despair and suicide by fire.

In this story it is an anonymous narrator who records the events as a witness with no privileged information:

> Die Frau, da sie sich erhob, glitschte mit der Krücke auf dem glatten Boden aus, und beschädigte sich, auf eine gefährliche Weise, das Kreuz; dergestalt, daß sie zwar doch noch mit unsäglicher Mühe aufstand und quer, wie es vorgeschrieben war, über das Zimmer ging, hinter den Ofen aber, unter Stöhnen und Ächzen, niedersank und verschied.[8]

> The woman, as she raised herself, slipped with her crutch on the smooth floor and hurt the small of her back dangerously; to such an extent that she was, it is true, able to stand up and cross the room with unspeakable effort, as had been ordered. However, [once] behind the stove, she sank down amidst moans and groans and passed away.

The central episode—namely, her death—remains curiously hidden, as invisible as the old woman behind the stove. The scene is very much an auditory experience; the groans and sighs are the only (recurring) signs of her disappearance.

Once death is no longer associated with the lifeless body but is equated with the sounds that accompany the woman's dying, the finality of this moment is put into question. This is the meaning of the story's structure, since what begins as a groan echoes as a ghostly sound ["ein gespensterhaftes Geräusch"] which, in turn, disperses itself in rumors ["Gerücht"] that circulate both in and outside the Marchese's castle.

The circulation of sound is not harmless: it displaces the exchange of money in devaluing the Marchese's Castle, which he was desperate to sell because of financial difficulties. An even more serious consequence: the echoing dispersion of sounds alienates the Marchese not only from society but even from himself. He is finally driven mad by his inability to answer his own question, Wer da? [Who's there?]. And why? Because the disembodied groans of the invisible old woman are themselves displaced echoes of the Marchese's original indignant ["unwillig"] command. Following this narrative structure, he is both speaker and addressee, since the succession of sound can end only after he has taken the place of the old woman. His whitened bones are put in the corner of the room where the woman had once lain. And so, figuratively at least, her crutches that had been displaced by his initial command are returned to their proper resting place.

The implications of such "moral retribution" are extremely grim; he who speaks condemns an "other" to death, and thereby also condemns himself. Indeed, the death scene, especially its uncontrollable repetitions, undoes the reassuring difference between a self and an other, a rather important precondition for knowledge, not to mention the exercise of power. As in "The Purloined Letter"—particularly in Lacan's reading of Poe's story—the position of power remains radically empty; neither the beggar woman nor the Marchese occupies it.

Music is meant to replace the dominance of the mirror and the model, whose drawbacks, outlined by Kleist, help hollow out the ideal of progress in the Bildung ideology. And clearly, music, with its emphasis on the dynamic succession of sounds, structures a narrative like "Das Bettelweib von Locarno" ["The Beggarwoman of Locarno"], where visual details are almost completely omitted in order to make room for the proliferation of sounds. But where Kleist's thematic analysis of the "dying soul" allows him to circumvent the pervasiveness of death, his narrative only ends up accenting its omnipresence. A poetics of music can hardly resist becoming a poetics of death for Kleist: after all, sequences cannot be distinguished from the aimless series of substitutions that constituted his early voyages, whether these be the uncontrollable repetitions (of the death scene) that structure "Das Bettelweib" or even the dizzying proliferation of phenomena that begin to dominate his experience of day-to-day living.[9] And once the possibility of differentiating between sounds or experiences is obliterated, the problem of fixing meaning reemerges. Once again, Kleist is haunted by the loss (or death) of meaning:

> Aber zu schnell wechseln die Erscheinungen im Leben und zu eng ist das Herz, sie alle zu umfassen, und immer die vergangnen schwinden, Platz zu machen den neuen—Zuletzt ekelt dem Herzen vor den neuen, und matt gibt es sich Eindrücken hin, deren Vergänglichkeit es vorempfindet. Ach, es muß öde und leer und traurig sein, später zu sterben, als das Herz. (KB, 661)

> But the manifestations in life alternate too quickly and the heart is too narrow to be able to contain them all, and always the past [manifestations] disappear in order to make room for the new ones—Finally,

the heart is disgusted by the new ones, and wearily it submits to impressions whose transitoriness it senses in advance. Oh, it must be barren and empty and sad to die later than one's [own] heart.

This particular instance of Kleist's sense of crisis in experiencing life is not limited to July 1801. Later, in the summer of 1811, months before he commits suicide, Kleist writes to Marie von Kleist:

> Ich kann, von zu viel Formen verwirrt, zu keiner Klarheit der innerlichen Anschauung kommen; der Gegenstand, fühle ich unaufhörlich, ist kein Gegenstand der Einbildung: mit meinen Sinnen in der wahrhaftigen lebendigen Gegenwart möchte ich ihn durchdringen und begreifen.... Das Leben, mit seinen zudringlichen, immer wiederkehrenden Ansprüchen reißt zwei Gemüter schon in dem Augenblick der Berührung so vielfach aus einander, um wie viel mehr, wenn sie getrennt sind. An ein Näherrücken ist gar nicht zu denken; und alles, was man gewinnen kann, ist, daß man auf dem Punkt bleibt, wo man ist. (KB, 873)

> Confused by too many forms, I cannot come to any clarity concerning my inner contemplation; objects, I feel continuously, are no objects of imagination: with my senses in the true, living present, I would like to penetrate and to grasp them. Life with its intensive, always recurring demands tears two minds—already in the instant of contact—so frequently apart, how much more, then, when they are separated? One cannot even think of a *rapprochement*; and all that one can attain is that one remain at the point where one is.

This crisis of life has its corollary in writing. Since all experience is really an experience of one's own instability, it becomes increasingly difficult to write anything down. The crisis that had been created by the act of writing (or by the futility of the mimetic project) now seems to turn back on that act, making it impossible.

> So geschäftig dem weißen Papier gegenüber meine Einbildung ist, und so bestimmt in Umriß und Farbe die Gestalten sind, die sie alsdann hervorbringt, so schwer, ja ordentlich schmerzhaft ist es mir, mir das, was wirklich ist, vorzustellen. Es ist, als ob diese in allen Bedingungen angeordnete Bestimmtheit meiner Phantasie, im Augenblick der Tätigkeit selbst, Fesseln anlegte. (KB,873)

> No matter how industrious my imagination is when facing the white paper, and no matter how distinct the figures, brought forth [by my imagination], are in outline and color, yet how difficult, how truly

> painful it is to me, to imagine what is real. It is as though, in the instant of activity, the latter [imagination] placed fetters on my fantasy with a certainty appropriate to all conditions.

If we return to Kleist's description of his living death (cf. KB, 661), we can note that the negativity of endless substitutions is not only perceptible through the frightening lack of traces left by daily occurrences. Even more disconcerting is that in Kleist's description the two terms *life* and *death* have become interchangeable. What used to signify life has become the sign of death. And in a very late text, familiarly known as "Die Todeslitanei" ["The Liturgy of Death"],[10] the substitutions become so radical that no difference of meaning distinguishes one signifier from another. Each word in the prose poem, which is structured almost completely as a simple sequence of nouns, always signifies "Henriette," the woman with whom Kleist commits suicide. The anxiety that Kleist seems to associate with a loss of difference leads to his false hope that within the chain of endless equations he has found in the name Henriette his Master-Signified.

The succession of sounds meant to supplant the more oppressive, inadequate Bildung leads in this instance, then, to the willful gesture of chaotically equating disparate referents while paradoxically obliterating the possibility of establishing differences. In this late text, we can note the impact of a Kleistian poetics of music: here, at least, simple juxtaposition replaces progression.

DEATH SCENES: WITHIN AND WITHOUT THE BILDUNGSROMAN

Kleist's representation of death still seems almost involuntary; it is as if each search for more narrative sequences, more signifiers, only leads him to rediscover one ultimate signified: death. His predicament is not shared, however, by his contemporaries. To return to the earlier example of *Wilhelm Meisters Lehrjahre*, we find a more "masterful" manipulation of the death scenes. Goethe, quite simply, controls the intervention of death by subsuming it under the category of life. He places it in the service of Bildung, so that death falls within boundaries that are easily fixed.

There are several unrelated examples in the *Lehrjahre* that allow us to perceive this transformation of death quite clearly. Wilhelm's father dies and, although this generates a crisis of identity in Wilhelm, it also forces him to assume responsibility for his own existence. But there is more. The father reappears both in the guise of his mentor and during a theatrical representation of *Hamlet*. Although the figure of the father remains shadowy—impossible to recognize clearly—his mysterious resurrections in the novel tend to underplay the menacing quality (finality) usually associated with death.

Equally significant is the example that appears in "Bekenntnisse einer schönen Seele" ["Confessions of a Beautiful Soul"], a text that plays a paradigmatic role within the narrative. The character is exemplary; she achieves a spiritual purity rarely to be found among individuals. Through her confrontation with her own mortality we learn that death has no power over her. It is represented as a kind of rending, acting as a tear between the body and the soul. But this tear also lacks finality; the soul remains intact and immortal, especially through the mediation of the memory. The action of the mind is able to compress and control time, so that in this account it can even survive the experience of death.

> Es war, als wenn meine Seele ohne Gesellschaft des Körpers dächte; sie sah den Körper als ein ihr fremdes Wesen an, wie man etwa ein Kleid ansieht. Sie stellte sich mit einer außerordentlichen Lebhaftigkeit die vergangenen Zeiten und Begebenheiten vor und fühlte daraus, was folgen werde. Alle diese Zeiten sind dahin; was folgt, wird auch dahingehen: der Körper wird wie ein Kleid zerreißen, aber *ich*, das wohlbekannte ich, *ich* bin. (WML, 434–35)

> It was as if the soul were thinking without the company of the body; she [the soul] regarded the body as a creature foreign to her, as one might consider a dress. She pictured with extraordinary liveliness past times and occurrences and sensed through these what would follow. All these times were over; what follows will also pass away: the body will tear to shreds like a dress, but *I*, the well-known I, *I* am.

This moment of writing grants the "schöne Seele" a kind of immortality. She almost seems able to write retrospectively, as if speaking to us from the place of the dead.

The conscious mastery of death is not only documented in the written confessions of a "beautiful soul." The death scenes are not all relegated to narratives meant to enhance Wilhelm's education theoretically. When his "adoptive daughter," Mignon, dies (of a broken heart), death becomes a reality for Wilhelm. Mignon dies irrevocably; her soul cannot be called back to join the body. Still, despite that failure, Art is used in several ways to reconstruct the corpse, to draw death back into life, to give life, as it were, the last word.

To put it most simply, her body is preserved almost fetishistically, so that it becomes possible to represent, at least verbally, the state of "being dead" as sleep, as a rest that awaits all others. Indeed, through the work of language, death enters into the *cycle* of a day, by becoming the evening; it is described as a nocturnal sleep that refreshes [*erquickt*].[11]

It is the artistic ceremony accompanying Wilhelm's loss of Mignon, however, that primarily reworks the status of death in the Bildungsroman. The ritual attempts to close the gap between reality and thought, so that thought can actually replace or at least reintegrate the lost being. The ceremonial ritual includes the following words:

> Wohl verwahrt ist nun der Schatz, das schöne Gebild der Vergangenheit! hier im Marmor ruht er unverzehrt; auch in euren Herzen lebt es, wirkt es fort. Schreitet, schreitet ins Leben zurück! Nehmet den heiligen Ernst mit hinaus, denn der Ernst, der heilige, macht allein das Leben zur Ewigkeit. (WML, 619)

> Safely kept is the treasure now, the beautiful creature of the past! Here in marble it rests undevoured; in your hearts also it lives, it continues to have an effect. Stride, stride back into life! Take with you the holy solemnity, for solemnity, the holy one, alone transforms life into eternity.

In the narrative, Mignon's death is not portrayed as a moment of rupture. The loss itself cedes quickly to the work of mourning necessary to the surviving individuals. Death again must be reintegrated into the process of Bildung; it helps to strengthen the survivor, much like in Goethe's "Selige Sehnsucht" [Holy Nostalgia]. Through the line "Stirb und werde" [die and become], death is transformed metaphorically into an example of "becoming." The narrative function of death shifts, losing its (menacing) specificity in order to demonstrate how "art" (here: the funeral songs) is able to elide the finality of death.

The clearest example of death being appropriated into the service of social assimilation occurs in the case of Mignon's father, the mysterious, mad harp player. His fear of death, which had initially alienated him from society, can only be banished by his possessing a phial of poison. By carrying with him the means for potential suicide, the harp player succeeds in suppressing an essential quality of death. Death is for him no longer an imposed or fateful event. By taking physical possession of its threat, he has been able to become the master of his own fate.

> Das Gefühl, daß es wünschenswert sei, die Leiden dieser Erde durch den Tod geendigt zu sehen, brachte mich zuerst auf den Weg der Genesung; bald darauf entstand der Gedanke, sie durch einen freiwilligen Tod zu endigen, und ich nahm in dieser Absicht das Glas hinweg; die Möglichkeit gab mir Kraft, sogleich die großen Schmerzen zu ertragen, und so habe ich, seitdem ich den Talisman besitze, mich durch die Nähe des Todes wieder in das Leben zurückgedrängt. (WML, 626)

> The feeling that it might be desirable to see the suffering of this earth ended through death, brought me initially onto the path of recovery;

> soon thereafter the thought emerged, to end them through a voluntary death, and with this purpose in mind I took the vial; the possibility gave me strength immediately to endure great pain and so, ever since I own the talisman, through the proximity of death, I have pressed myself back into life.

Here the work to subsume death under the dominant term *life* is at its strongest. The physical mastery over death allows the mad harp player to become a social being. Indeed, the proximity of death acts as the condition actually permitting him to live. But, as the harp player makes clear, preceding this physical possession of a death-giving instrument is the work of the mind that prepares his ready renunciation of life.

In contrast to Kleist, where the proximity of death overshadows all life, where life is experienced, even translated, as a form of loss or death (KB, 661), the process of representing death for Goethe works in the opposite direction. For Goethe death begins to be the support of life, and through the appeal to a naturalizing (cyclical) language, it actually almost becomes a metaphor for life.

As mentioned earlier: *Wilhelm Meisters Lehrjahre*, written in 1795, may be the clearest and most paradigmatic example of a Bildungsroman. And yet, it is not the only novel that stresses how, within the Bildungsroman, death can be reworked into a positive life-enhancing term. We can easily take another example, which is less canonical, less of a conventional Bildungsroman, but which still displays the same tendency to transform the term *death* into a productive, even necessary stage during the process of formation. This second example is a fragment, Schlegel's *Lucinde*, written in 1799.

Most striking in the following example is the conscious aestheticization of death. Such a "revisioning" functions especially well, of course, when death is considered abstractly, without reference to any particular character:

> Und dann weiß ich's nun, daß der Tod sich auch schön und süß fühlen läßt. Ich begreife, wie das freie Gebildete sich in der Blüte aller Kräfte nach seiner Auflösung und Freiheit mit stiller Liebe sehnen und den Gedanken der Rückkehr freudig anschauen kann wie eine Morgensonne der Hoffnung.[12]

> And then I know now that death also allows itself to be perceived as beautiful and sweet. I understand how the freely created, while in the bloom of all its forces, can yearn with quiet love for dissolution and freedom and [how it can] regard the thought of return like the morning sun of hope.

Aside from the linguistically sweet rendering of an actually traumatic experience (that, as an aestheticizing depiction, helps to make the otherness of death familiar to reader and writer alike), the reworking of the model of progression helps to transform death into a comforting and comfortable concept. Death enters into the cycle of formation, and the cycle is presented here in organic terms, as the culmination of blooming. Once it is organic, death can then be described as a *return*, no longer frightening as a leap into the unknown void.

In Kleist's works, death is not represented as organic or as part of a natural life cycle. Indeed, his transformation of death into the Master-Signified of all manifestations of life potentially makes for a rather barren art. Differences in experience are constantly being reduced to sameness in his narratives—especially in "Das Bettelweib von Locarno," where the ultimate disjunction between the "you" and the "I" is undone by the repeated sequence of dying and deathly sounds. For Kleist, even the more hopeful strategy to construct a poetics of music forces him to recognize that sequence, as the horizontal substitution of one sound for the next, becomes ultimately the enactment of death—here, primarily the death of meaning.

And yet, despite the contamination of a poetics of music by one of death, Kleist does not relinquish narrative. Instead of abandoning his obsession with sequences, especially with the successions carefully ordered by a Bildungsmodel, he continues to strain against that convention, twisting and inverting it, undermining the mastery over experience that Bildung seems to promise. If "Das Bettelweib," or even "Die Heilige Cäcilie" and "Michael Kohlhaas," used sequence in order to demonstrate the emptiness, even fatal threat, of sheer linearity, "Der Zweikampf" ["The Duel"], which was to end the collection of Kleist's short prose, most skillfully ties together his subversion of Bildung with an active poetics of death.

To consider "Der Zweikampf" as a subversive text may seem enigmatic, since, traditionally, it has been classed with "Die Marquise von O . . . ," as one of the few optimistic narratives that Kleist ever wrote.[13] Still, already the form of "Der Zweikampf" reveals how Kleist makes use of succession in order to subvert the traditional progression of plot. No central character dominates in the narrative, no one intrigue can be identified as the master intrigue.

The story begins with the murder of the *Herzog* [the Duke], but the perspective of the bereaved family is quickly abandoned in order to adopt that of his suspected (and actual) murderer, his half-brother Jakob. At this point, a technique obliquely—even if rather anachronistically—related to stream of consciousness, is used. Jakob, the accused murderer, cites as his alibi his supposed lover Littegarde von Auerbach, and the narrative follows this cue in order to focus on the new character and her past. Only after the narrative has described her exile, resulting from Jakob's accusation, do we reach the famous duel, which, on the surface, seems to judge in favor of the adulterer and murderer. But even at this culminating point, the narrative perspective shifts again, this time to concentrate on an intrigue that had previously occurred between Jakob and Littegarde's chambermaid, an intrigue that now manages to clear Littegarde's name and to reveal how Jakob himself has been deceived into believing that he had had an affair with Littegarde. Once this misunderstanding is clarified, and once Jakob also admits to having murdered his half-brother (the *Herzog*), Littegarde and her supporter can be liberated, whereas Jakob finally dies. Even the ending of the tale brings about another shift of narrative perspective, since we suddenly share the Kaiser's [the Emperor's] vision, when he undertakes to modify the laws governing duels and the interpretation of their outcome.

These shifts in perspective are reminiscent of "Die Heilige Cäcilie," except that the gap between the various displacements seems to be greater in the later story. No one character's questioning can act any longer as the organizing principle of the narrative. The only other alternative to deciphering the shape of "Der Zweikampf" is to note the succession of deaths that help to structure it. One death, the *Herzog's*, sets the narrative in motion and thus acts as the catalyst responsible for the succeeding deaths. In the small universe of "Der Zweikampf," death—especially the violent kind—functions as a contagious disease, connecting otherwise unrelated characters. Littegarde's father and Jakob both succumb, and Littegarde as well as Friedrich, her supporter and the Duke's chamberlain, are nearly annihilated.

The abundance of deaths in "Der Zweikampf" allows us to recognize at least three different representations of death. Death through contagion (aside from its narrative function) accounts for at least two deaths in the story: Littegarde's previous husband (already dead by the beginning of the intrigue) has died of a contagious fever, and Jakob, of course, is gradually consumed by a spreading, cancerlike growth resulting from his duel-inflicted wound.

In "Der Zweikampf," however, the representation of death is most closely linked to acts of writing and of reading; the experience of death seems to find its most adequate expression through the trope of writing. In the case of Littegarde's father, for instance, the physical document becomes the bearer of death. The written text begins to assume dangerous overtones, at least for the old man already weakened by age, having fixed his sights on the goal of all living things ("das Ziel schon ins Auge fassend, das allem was Leben atmet gesteckt ist") [already fixed on the goal that is set for all that breathes life].[14] Indeed, even his fatal fall ends up following the fall of the document.

The act of writing is used—no longer simply to translate the experience of death adequately, but to describe, at least metaphorically, the act of killing. This is true in the case of the *Herzog*, as he is pierced by an arrow. The arrow is described both as a text that can be deciphered (that is, read) and traced back to its source.[15] Loving detail is expended on its description:

> Starke, krause und glänzende Federn steckten in einem Stiel, der, schlank und kräftig, von dunkelm Nußbaumholz, gedrechselt war; die Bekleidung des vorderen Endes war von glänzendem Messing,

> und nur die äußerste Spitze selbst, scharf wie die Gräte eines Fisches, war von Stahl. (Z, 231)

> Large, stiff, shiny feathers were set in a strong and slender shaft of finely turned walnut; the forepart was sheathed in shining brass and only the very tip, sharp as a fishbone, was made of steel.[16]

The reference to the feathers and to the sharp point of the arrow ("Pfeil") reinforce the parallels between the weapon and the writing tool.

During the duel, the interplay of writing and death is no longer limited to the tool; it is represented through the actual act of inflicting death. This is less clearly perceptible, perhaps, in the case of Friedrich, whose side is pierced [*gestoßen*] three times by Jakob's sword. Jakob's wound, which proves to be fatal, is, however, all the more explicitly described as an inscription, as a mark that only breaks the skin superficially. Jakob is, moreover, wounded fatally at the wrist, at the point that joins the arm with the hand, at the point, in fact, which governs, at least physically, the act of writing.

> Herr Friedrich verwundete gleich auf den ersten Hieb den Grafen; er verletzte ihn mit der Spitze seines, nicht eben langen Schwertes da, wo zwischen Arm und Hand die Gelenke der Rüstung in einander griffen . . . [Jakob] . . . fand, daß, obschon das Blut heftig floß, doch nur die Haut obenhin geritzt war. (Z, 245)

> Sir Friedrich wounded the Count with his very first blow, slashing him with the tip of his sword, which was not especially long, just at the point between arm and hand where his armor was linked together; the Count . . . found that, though the blood flowed freely, it was only a scratch.[17]

Jakob's grazed wrist may, at this point, seem to have little to do with the act of writing; nonetheless, by the end of the narrative it is Jakob himself who points both to the significance of the wound and to the strict correlation between the superficial inscription and its effect on the inner core or the essence of his being.

> Denn er [Friedrich], von drei Wunden, jede tödlich, getroffen, blüht, wie ihr seht, in Kraft und Lebensfülle; indessen ein Hieb von seiner Hand, der kaum die äußerste Hülle meines Lebens zu berühren schien, in langsam fürchterlicher Fortwirkung den Kern desselben selbst getroffen, und meine Kraft, wie der Sturmwind eine Eiche, gefällt hat. (Z, 259)

> For the one of us who got three wounds in the duel, each of them a mortal injury, now flourishes, as you can see, in all the fullness of strength and vigor; while a blow from his hand that scarcely seemed to scratch the husk and surface of my life has eaten its way with terrible patience into the kernel of my being and toppled my strength like the tempest does the oak.[18]

The metaphor of writing that is used to describe Jakob's death undoes the distinction between inner and outer self. At least, it seems to reverse the laws of causality, so that "outside"—the skin (or parchment) separating inner from outer self—is transformed into the vulnerable inner core of the individual. We noted earlier that the act of writing, when analyzed metatextually, leads to the unbalancing of differences. This particular narrative enactment of an effaced opposition now is portrayed explicitly as fatal. Inscription has become the bearer of death.

The metaphorical crossing of writing and death, where the infliction of death can be represented as an inscription, leads to a rather compelling question. Are we simply to conclude that all writing is fatal or are we to assume that the process of naming—where substitutions make all signifiers equal—has sucked even the act of writing into the endless chain of equations?

Both possibilities seem to fall short of the mark, especially since there has been a significant reversal. No longer do the numerous representations of life cede to the pull of death as the hidden Master-signified. Now it is the moment of death that seeks its own adequate representation. In the third category of deaths to be found in "Der Zweikampf" (deaths that are neither caused by contagion nor by "inscription") such a reversal is most clearly perceptible. This third category contains deaths that remain suspended. The annihilation of the characters is no longer directed solely at the body but becomes a spiritual one. By transforming death into an abstraction, Kleist attempts to rid death of its frightening quality as "tenor" of the metaphor. He gives it instead the status of "vehicle," of a signifier easily replaced by other signifiers.

"Der Zweikampf"—as the last story of Kleist's collection and written in the summer of 1811—can be read, then, as a series of variations on "death abstracted." The deaths are symbolic, social or even moral, and they are inflicted primarily on Littegarde, who is led to the very limits of her identity, by experiencing a radical self-alienation. "Der Zweikampf" can, in effect, be interpreted as the inverted Bildung of Littegarde, where all the experiences that are to form her, actually mark various kinds of deaths that she barely survives. In this way, then, Kleist can invert the Bildungs-model most radically, by transforming stages of the process of formation into more and more complete forms of loss.

Littegarde's experiences begin under the sign of renunciation. She is urged by her brothers to give up all claims on a worldly existence by becoming a nun. This act—already a symbolic death to all the pleasures in the world—is to have as its greatest consequence her lack of any progeny. In order that she lay no claim to her father's heritage, her brothers decree that no traces of her existence are to survive.

Jakob's claim that his adulterous affair with Littegarde provides him with an alibi concerning his half-brother's murder removes her from the threat of the nunnery. However, since her purity is called into question, her brothers use this pretext in order to submit her to an even worse exile—banishment from the family home. Initially, her reaction is simply to lose all consciousness. Her powerlessness is evident both in her struggle with her brother within the castle and outside of it, after she has been physically threatened by her brother and banished from the family.

Once this physical exile and isolation from society does not represent a sufficient means for the brothers to guarantee the ostracism, more importantly to them the sterility, of their sister, they turn to a more symbolic structure.

> Dabei trugen sie zur Ehrenrettung der durch sie beleidigten Familie, darauf an, ihren Namen aus der Geschlechtstafel des Bredaschen Hauses auszustreichen, und begehrten, unter weitläufigen Rechtsdeduktionen, sie, zur Strafe wegen so unerhörter Vergehungen, aller Ansprüche auf die Verlassenschaft des edlen Vaters, den ihre Schande ins Grab gestürzt, für verlustig zu erklären. (Z, 241)

> To redeem the honor of their family, they proposed that her name be blotted from the family tree of the house of Breda, and offered far-fetched legal arguments to support their wish to have all her claims on their noble father's estate, whom her disgrace had driven to his grave, declared null and void as punishment for her shocking transgression.[19]

In addition to striking Littegarde's name from the future, now even her past is to be annihilated. Her social (abstract) identity is placed squarely under attack; it is threatened with complete effacement.[20]

The final attack on her from the outside occurs after Friedrich loses the duel against Jakob, a failure that leads to the death sentence both of Friedrich and Littegarde. And yet, worse than the threatened death by fire that awaits Littegarde is her self-alienation, resulting from her inability to interpret the outcome of the duel. Friedrich's defeat leads her to question her own memory, her own coherent and consistent identity. She discloses her own madness,[21] once she feels unable to reconcile God's judgment with her experience, with her own subjective perceptions of truth.

> Wie kannst du [Friedrich] dem, was dir mein Mund sagt, Glauben schenken? . . . "Wahnsinniger! Rasender!" rief Littegarde; "hat das

geheiligte Urteil Gottes nicht gegen mich entschieden? Hast du dem Grafen nicht in jenem verhängnisvollen Zweikampf unterlegen, und er nicht die Wahrhaftigkeit dessen, was er vor Gericht gegen mich angebracht, ausgekämpft?" (Z, 253)

How can you believe a single word that comes from my mouth? . . . "Madman! Maniac!" cried Littegarde. "Hasn't God's sacred judgment gone against me? Weren't you beaten by the Count in that fatal duel? Hasn't he vindicated with his arms the truth of what he accused me of before the court?"[22]

This moment marks the greatest crisis of Littegarde's experience. She is even split within herself, unable to discern her own core of identity. In not being able to decide between two contradictory voices, she willingly renounces her own position in order to assume God's—in this case, society's—verdict of her guilt. The moment could be described as a symbolic or moral suicide; it marks the total loss of integrity and of selfhood.

In a staggered series of experiences the plot of "Der Zweikampf" uncovers an increased loss of confidence, loss of will, and loss of self-knowledge. This process of emptying out the self reverses the formation of a Wilhelm Meister or even of a Julius (in Schlegel's *Lucinde*). In contrasting the two trajectories of a conventional Bildung and its inverted double, it becomes a puzzle to decide how Littegarde's constantly intensified annihilation is actually stopped, finally even brought around to reintegrate her with honor into the society that had effectively cast her out.

Without any reference to the corpus of Kleist's texts, the sudden reversal at the end of "Der Zweikampf" is quite enigmatic. Isolated, this narrative *peripeteia* is only explicable as divine intervention, as an example of *deus ex machina.* The Rosalie intrigue, the sudden discovery of Jakob's own illusion and of Littegarde's purity occurs without being planned, so that the human strategies or projects are incidental to the text's conclusion. All that can be ascertained is that Littegarde is completely helpless. If the boundaries of the Kleistian corpus are expanded, however, it soon becomes clear that Littegarde belongs to a group of characters who are saved from their almost complete annihilation because of their willing renunciation of life. Littegarde resembles Amphitryon (in the comedy of the same name), for instance, and like Prinz Friedrich (in Kleist's *Homburg*) humbly accepts the death penalty imposed by a rigorous, even unjust society.

In effect, all three characters willingly sacrifice their own causes (and lives) in a supreme gesture of confidence in those they love or admire. And all three, by renouncing their own claims, end up gaining more than they have lost. Amphitryon, for instance, publicly recognizes the faithfulness of his wife despite overwhelming evidence to the contrary and thereby renounces the enforcement of his marital rights, even offering his life.[23] His gesture seems to motivate Jupiter to confess his guilt to having seduced Alkmene, Amphitryon's wife, thus clearing her name of any crime.

Prinz Friedrich, by accepting his uncle's verdict (which would bring about his own death, because of his martial and filial disobedience), can—because of this acceptance—be crowned as a hero in his uncle's state. And Littegarde, by accepting God's "verdict" in place of her knowledge that she is innocent, by accusing herself readily, can thereby redeem herself, at least in Friedrich's eyes. And Friedrich's acceptance of her innocence is doubled symbolically at the end of the narrative, through the intervention of the Rosalie intrigue, which leads, finally, to the reintegration of both Littegarde and Friedrich into society.

What are the implications generated by reading Littegarde's development as an example of a reverse Bildung (which is shared by other central characters of Kleist's literary work) and where such a formation strips her of everything, even threatening the very core of her identity? Such a reading points to the precept that it is only through annihilation that a character can be redeemed; moreover, this principle works the other way, too. Jakob's perfect control over his features, indeed his circumstances, leads him to perdition rather than to a position of power. Indeed, if we turn to the literary essays written in 1810 and 1811, we can begin to notice how Kleist's fascination with a "redeeming principle of annihilation" leads him to try to develop a tenable alternative to the more conventional Bildungs-model—grounded on mastery—advocated by Goethe and Schlegel.

In his "Betrachtungen über den Weltlauf" ["Reflections on the Way of the World"], Kleist describes the impossibility of progress, by stressing the disjunction between a never-to-be-attained origin and a far from perfect present. His desire for a return in time, even a chronological reversal, equates the advancement in time with historical (and aesthetic) decline. The conventional structure assuming the correspondence of temporal and cognitive development is turned on its head and this point-by-point inversion of the conventional model undermines even the theoretical possibility of progress. Reality, he seems to suggest, bears out the priority of decline over progress.[24]

In "Über das Marionettentheater" ["On the Marionette Theater"], the desire for return is more pronounced, since Kleist no longer only comments on the order of the world, but rather begins to sketch out a trajectory that could counter a model of mere temporality. One such alternative is described by "Herrn C.":

> Solche Mißgriffe, setzte er abbrechend hinzu, sind unvermeidlich, seitdem wir von dem Baum der Erkenntnis gegessen haben. Doch das Paradies ist verriegelt und der Cherub *hinter* uns; wir müssen die Reise um die Welt machen, und sehen, ob es vielleicht von *hinten* irgendwo wieder offen ist. (II, 342)

> Such mistakes [loss of grace], he added, breaking off [the conversation], are unavoidable, ever since we ate from the tree of knowledge. Paradise is bolted shut and the cherub is *behind* us; we must make the trip around the world and see if perhaps it is open somewhere from *behind*.

"Herrn C.'s" alternative model attempts to weld two opposites together. The movement forward is to be simultaneously a return to a lost past. This theoretical dilemma is given its practical counterpart, albeit confusedly, by "Herrn C.'s" interlocutor, who advocates that the original sin be repeated in order to permit the individual to fall back into grace. By sinning again, the acting individual would suspend, indeed willingly renounce, his mortal sin, indeed knowledge. This renunciation of knowledge would then have the status of a sacrifice; it would mark the voluntary surrender of power. The relinquishment of knowledge would act as the precondition for the individual's return to a state preceding the creation of time and reminiscent both of birth and death. The return to paradise becomes, through its dependence on an imagery of loss, a return to nothingness.

"Über das Marionettentheater" and "Der Zweikampf" seem on the surface to emphasize Kleist's triumph over a poetics of death. Here he is finally able to harness the "principle of annihilation" to an ideal, so that self-abnegation can become the path leading to redemption. And yet, the ending of "Der Zweikampf," during which Littegarde is saved somewhat arbitrarily, also acts as the marker signifying the ambivalence inherent in death. The symbolic deaths suffered by Littegarde may prepare the victory of her victimization, but the coexistence of the violent death sentence imposed upon Jakob points to the still uncontrolled shadow side of mortality. Death still carries the weight of a threat; it still is the most intense punishment possible.

Kleist's appropriation and reworking of death differs from conventional ones in essentially one respect. Whereas Goethe and Schlegel transformed death into a life-affirming principle, supporting the gradual formation of their fictional characters, Kleist pursues a reverse Bildung, one structured around symbolical deaths, in order to demonstrate the impossibility of mastery and power. We can conclude, then, that his poetics of death has a two-fold orientation. Death is the tool used to unmask the myth of mastery and it, in turn, becomes the foundation of a new myth of redemption.

Kleist's subversion of the illusion of power can be seen if we turn again to the wider corpus of his work. The realization that even strong figures are vulnerable, that, indeed, they are threatened *because* of their strength, is a repeated message. Familiar examples in Kleist's canon—besides "Jakob der Rotbart"—are Adam in *Der Zerbrochene Krug* ["The Broken Jug"] and Homburg's uncle, leader of the Prussian state. Both seem to wield immeasurable power and both are unable to wield that power unambiguously. In Adam's case it is his own speech that constantly threatens to unmask him. And Homburg's uncle, by not swerving from the logic of military justice, ends up threatening both the stability and the survival of his state.

It is in *Penthesilea*, however, where the equation between ostensible power and actual vulnerability is expressed most clearly. After the death of the tragic (eponymous) hero we hear two moralizing voices attempting to seize on a meaning that could explain the catastrophe. The play closes with the interpretation:

> Sie sank, weil sie zu stolz und kräftig blühte!
> Die abgestorbne Eiche steht im Sturm,
> Doch die gesunde stürzt er schmetternd nieder,
> Weil er in ihre Krone greifen kann.[25]
>
> Her blooming was too proud and glorious!
> Vainly the gale will shake the withered oak,
> But with a crash he flings the living down,
> Grasping with ruffian hands her copious locks.[26]

It is *because* of Penthesilea's vitality that she is singled out, thereby becoming more susceptible. The state of death, in absolute terms, may be a weaker position, but it does manage to be a constant one. The dead oak survives, where the healthy and powerful tree must fall.

The rhetorical sleight of hand in Kleist's metaphor of the oak becomes more explicit in his final writings—his farewell letters to Marie von Kleist. We should recall: the quotation from *Penthesilea* does not exalt the survival of the oak yet. By simply emphasizing the contrast between vitality and death it reverses the usual relation of the two terms to one another. More interesting than the transformation of powerlessness into strength is the hint that death permits survival. Death imperceptibly loses its finality and begins to assume the characteristics of a stage in a sequence (although Kleist, in contrast to Goethe, does not harness death as a means to validate the primacy of life). Still: once the oak has died, it can resist a storm more successfully than it could have while alive.

Kleist's suicide letters—in opposition to the letters written at the time of his Kant crisis—tend to concentrate on the relation between earthly existence and an afterlife. Almost facetiously Kleist writes of his vision of celestial life (shared by Henriette von Vogel, the woman accompanying him into suicide): "Wir, unsererseits, wollen nichts von den Freuden dieser Welt wissen und träumen lauter himmlische Fluren und Sonnen, in deren Schimmer wir, mit langen Flügeln an den Schultern, umherwandeln werden" (KB, 886) ["We, for our part, want to know nothing about the joys of this world and dream of nothing but heavenly meadows and suns, in whose gleam we, with long wings at our shoulders, will wander about"]. This preoccupation serves, on the one hand, simply to prepare the suicide. Death is made familiar, less final through the mediation of traditional images.

Still, this preparatory work follows the trajectory tentatively mapped out by "Der Zweikampf." The act of dying is metamorphosed into the passage that can lead Kleist beyond the restrictions of his earthly existence. Life on earth is perceived—apparently through the mediating influence of Henriette Vogel—as inadequate to his needs.

> Nur so viel wisse, daß meine Seele durch die Berührung mit der ihrigen, zum Tode ganz reif geworden ist; daß ich die ganze Herrlichkeit des menschlichen Gemüts an dem ihrigen ermessen habe, und daß ich sterbe, weil mir auf Erden nichts zu lernen und zu erwerben übrig bleibt. (KB, 884–85)

> Now know this much, that my soul—through contact with hers—has become ripe for death; that I have gauged the whole splendor of her human mind, and that I die, because nothing on earth is left to me to learn and to acquire.

The store of earth's treasures can be depleted, so that with his renunciation Kleist seems to indicate that he seeks some other domain, more adequate to his search for knowledge.

An even clearer example that shows how renunciation (here, suicide) can become for Kleist the necessary preliminary to a richer, more perfect existence, can be found in another letter addressed to Marie von Kleist. Here death is no longer simply represented as renunciation. It begins to resemble an intense sexual experience.

> Ein Strudel von nie empfundner Seligkeit hat mich ergriffen, und ich kann Dir nicht leugnen, daß mir ihr Grab lieber ist als die Betten aller Kaiserinnen der Welt. Ach, meine teure Freundin, möchte Dich Gott bald abrufen in jene bessere Welt, wo wir uns alle, mit der Liebe der Engel einander werden ans Herz drücken können. (KB, 888)

> A whirl of never experienced bliss has overcome me, and I cannot deny to you that her [Henriette's] grave is dearer to me than the bed of all the empresses of the world. Oh, my dear friend, may God call you away soon to that better world, where we all—with the love of angels—will be able to press each other to our hearts.

The tension within Kleist's obsession with death between its subversive and its redeeming functions allows the writer to defer the detailed description of

Eden (or, *das Nichts*) that he seems to be striving for in "Über das Marionettentheater." Instead, by constructing parallels between the sensuality of love and that of death, he can transform the experience of death into one of birth. Death has become rebirth; self-sacrifice has reaped greater, purer (albeit mystical) pleasures.

If in "The Duel" voluntary self-abnegation brings about the return to an enhanced, richer life for the protagonists, the suicide letters show how Kleist has relinquished the hope for a better earthly existence in favor of a heavenly, unknown one. He is able to repress the finality of death, by representing it instead as the necessary condition for happiness. In one of his anecdotes, Kleist writes for instance: ". . . der Weise freut sich der *Vernichtung* . . . weil er weiß, daß in ihr der Keim zu neuen und schöneren Bildungen liegt" (II, 310) ["the sage feels joy for *annihilation* . . . because he knows that in it lies the seed of new and more beautiful formations"]. An even more dramatic example is the one in Würzburg, at a low moment in Kleist's life. He is oppressed by the fear of death, by the necessity of one day removing his presence from all things. The image that redeems that depression is also based on a reversal. Rather than turning to a life-affirming example, Kleist chooses to transform an image of falling into a redemptive image:

> Warum dachte ich, sinkt wohl das Gewölbe nicht ein, da es noch *keine* Stütze hat? Es steht, antwortete ich, *weil alle Steine auf einmal einstürzen wollen*—und ich zog aus diesem Gedanken einen unbeschreiblich erquickenden Trost, der mir bis zu dem entscheidenden Augenblick immer mit der Hoffnung zur Seite stand, daß auch ich mich halten würde, wenn alles mich sinken läßt. (II, 573)

> Why, I thought, does the arch not cave in, since it has *no* support? It stands, I answered, *because all stones want to collapse at once*—and from this thought I drew an indescribably refreshing comfort, that—until the decisive moment—always stayed with hope at my side, that I also would conserve myself, when everything lets me fall.

KLEIST AND MODERNITY: THE IMPACT OF A BILDUNG OF DEATH ON MODERN ACCOUNTS OF IDENTITY FORMATION

Kleist's suicide letters mark the most radical example of his need to rework death as a stage in an ongoing sequence.[27] His attempt to transform death into a threshold experience and, especially, his construction of a reverse Bildung, meant to unmask the hollow illusions inherent in a power-oriented Bildung, make him an important precursor of contemporary accounts of "identity formation." Perhaps the most radical Bildungs-model that concerns itself with the centrality of the death phenomenon can be found in Lacanian psychoanalysis. Just as Kleist rejects Goethe's recuperation of death through his encomium to the mastery of Art and Language, so, too, is Lacan interested in unmasking the (blind) vulnerability of power. Kleist may prepare the way for these modern accounts of identity, but these, because of their pragmatic bent, can also help to illuminate how Kleist can sustain his (precarious) poetics of death.

The models of individual development presented by psychoanalysis do seem more concerned with sexual development than with death.[28] Still, the unbalancing of oppositions which haunts Kleist's narratives can be rediscovered in the Freudian text concerned with defining the status of death in the psyche. In *Jenseits des Lustprinzips [Beyond the Pleasure Principle]* Freud's difficulty to distinguish between desire and the death drive (or the more conservative *Ichtrieb*) shows that the unobtrusive drive toward death is more central to the development of an individual than first admitted. Freud is not only uneasy about the antithesis of the *Ich-* and *Sexualtrieb*.[29] Toward the end of the text he suddenly reveals that the pleasure drive—usually described as the life-affirming impulse—in reality chooses as its goal the elimination of all stimuli. This, in fact, can be equated with the desire to return to an "anorganic calm," or death.[30] The antithesis between desire and the death drive is radically undermined by such an equation, although this act of unsettling the difference between life and death drives is quite in keeping with Freud's earlier assertions that "The goal of all life is death," that "The anorganic ["das Leblose"] preceded the living," and that the deferment of death is due to circumstances and stimuli imposed by the external world.[31] If the death drive is so pervasive, it becomes rather difficult to explain how life can be sustained.[32] Nonetheless, these radical assertions all mark the beginning of an attempt to define the role, even the primacy, of death during the formation of an individual.[33]

Jenseits des Lustprinzips simply designates death as the final stage of the living organism without elaborating too much on the details of that last moment. How the existence of a deferred (but inner)[34] death can bestow meaning or, at least, a shape on life is an enigma that Freud does not explain but that several theorists, following his lead, have attempted to solve. One tendency is to shift the emphasis away from an empirical to an artistic level in order to show how the creative act is determined by the threat of death.

For Michel de M'Uzan, for instance, unmediated existence is indistinguishable from a traumatic experience of discontinuity and death. So, the act of creative representation must establish a liveable reality for the writer, although it is never able to shake off completely his subjection to the threat of being submerged, either by inner or outer destructive impulses.[35] M'Uzan writes: "[La représentation créatrice] . . . cherche sans cesse à saisir un présent, dont l'émergence se produit à tous les instants, et par là même constitue une micro-expérience traumatique" ["(Creative representation) . . . seeks unceasingly to seize a present whose emergence is taking place at every moment, and precisely because of that, [it] constitutes a traumatic 'micro-experience'"].[36] Through the creative act "chaos" can be dispelled according to M'Uzan, but never entirely, since every mastery of death cannot help but bear the mark of the initial threat. Most disturbingly, creative representation cannot sustain a stable order ("un nouveau silence fonctionnel");[37] it cannot forestall the new onslaught of destructive impulses.

M'Uzan's recuperation of death as the motivation and the subject matter of writing implicitly restricts the significance of death in a self's Bildung to the artist or to the artistically inclined individual. In contrast, Lacan, as well as Lacanian critics like Shoshana Felman, Helga Gallas, and Stuart Schneiderman, make an even more radical claim. Where M'Uzan describes the preoccupation with death as a conscious experience that needs to be actively (and aesthetically) mastered, Lacanian psychoanalysis tends to designate the unconscious as the place where death structures *every* individual's relation to reality. Lacan writes:

> Il faudrait que vous lisiez d'ici la prochaine conférence *Oedipe à Colone.* Vous y verrez que le dernier mot du rapport de l'homme à ce discours qu'il ne connaît pas, c'est la mort. Il faut aller en effet jusqu'à l'expression poétique pour découvrir jusqu'à quelle intensité peut être réalisée l'identification entre cette prétérité voilée et la mort en tant que telle, dans son aspect le plus horrible. Dévoilement qui ne comporte pas d'instant au-delà et éteint toute parole.[38]

> By the next lecture it is important that you will have read *Oedipus at Colonus.* You will see there that the last word [denoting] the relationship of man to this discourse that he does not know, is death. One must turn to poetic expression in order to discover what intensity can be achieved through the identification of this veiled preteriteness and death as such, in its most horrible form. An unveiling which does not include an instant Beyond and which extinguishes all speech.

Representable reality for Lacan is never an undefined entity. It is a symbolic, therefore social, structure, and assumes the integration of each individual into a system grounded on the order of discourse.

Helga Gallas explains most lucidly how the individual must experience a kind of death—she calls it "symbolic castration"—in order to be introduced into the world of language and to survive in the social order. Freud, in his *Drei Abhandlungen zur Sexualtheorie* [*Three Treatises on the Theory of Sexuality*] had already been able to establish the primacy of sexual development in a theory of psychoanalysis common to all, by isolating and analyzing the stages of childhood. Lacan and, following him, Helga Gallas repeat Freud's gesture by concentrating on the child's development. They are then in the position to insist on the centrality of the initial "deathly" moment for every human being.

The Lacanian narrative retold by Gallas is quite compelling. The child begins by identifying itself with the mother. It acts as her appendage, so that, by being nurtured by her, its status becomes that of the Mother's phallus.[39] More significantly, since the child must be desired by the mother in order to be nurtured, it begins to desire the mother's love for itself. Whether the child perceives that it fills a "lack" in the mother is a corollary of the more convincing point, that the play of desire between mother and child is of a specular, inwardly locked kind.

Logically, separation must occur, so that the child is not trapped in a closed situation; and it occurs, necessarily, because of the father's intervention.[40] His very presence bars the child from continuing the mirroring play of desire between itself and the mother. By accepting the law of the father, the child must renounce its original object of desire and pursue other, substitute, objects. This is the moment of renunciation and separation crucial to the child's development. This marks its symbolic castration or its death.

Why the experience of death becomes the child's introduction to language can only be understood, Gallas argues, within the context of Saussure's linguistics. Quite simply, the child has just experienced the essential structure of language. Language, in this case, can no longer be interpreted as a tool devoted to the representation of the world. It must be analyzed as a closed system, where difference (or the pertinent trait) governs the (meaningful) classification of sounds. The "pertinent trait," in effect, becomes the key, permitting the production of meaning.[41] This "radicalization of difference, "[42] which organizes the play of the signifiers, can then be carried over to the order of the signified (of the thought). Once it can be established that the structural relation of signifiers to one another is arbitrary, and that it is the same as the principle distinguishing one thought from another, a radical theory of the signifier becomes possible. Language does not reflect—rather, it *precedes*—thought. The signifier is the *condition* for the signified.[43]

The logic generally associated with the metaphor makes it possible to demonstrate the primacy of the signifier over the signified more clearly. The figure of the metaphor essentially places two signifiers in a relation of identity, usually subordinating a familiar signifier to an unfamiliar one in order to produce a meaning for the unknown term. In short: through the work of the metaphor the familiar (suppressed) signifier is transformed into a signified. In the words of Helga Gallas:

> Im Unterschied zur Metonymie, die immer auf einen fehlenden Signifikanten verweist, auf eine Leerstelle (Seinsmangel)—daher nur "ein Weniges an Sinn" produziert—erzeugt die Metapher einen Sinneffekt: indem ein Signifikant einen anderen verdrängt, rutscht dieser in die Position des Signifikats.[44]

> In contrast to metonymy, which always refers to the missing signifier, to a lacuna (lack of being)—and therefore produces only a "little meaning"—metaphor generates an effect of meaning: in that one signifier represses another, the latter slips into the position of the signified.

The parallel between the structure of language and the child's introduction to the social order of discourse should be evident. By transforming the manifest desire for the mother into a latent and forbidden desire, the child is finally in possession of its first signified and can then continue to search for other signifiers to replace its initial, suppressed desire. (Needless to say, such a replacement is necessarily always inadequate and thus explains the endless *glissement* of the signifier and desire.) Most significantly, renunciation, as a kind of voluntary death, can be interpreted as the foundation of each individual's access to speech.[45]

This is precisely the logic at play in Lacan's psychoanalytic school—in the emphasis on the "pass." This stage prepares the transformation of the analysand into an analyst. The candidate must narrate the course of his/her personal analysis to an anonymous committee of Lacanian psychotherapists; his/her own analysis must be told, so that s/he can learn to fall silent—to occupy, as it were, the place of the silent dead.[46] In effect, rather than helping to affirm the analysand's control and mastery, both the analysis and the telling of it are to be experienced in order to prepare the analysand/analyst for a kind of death:

> What interested Lacan ultimately was not the subject's assimilation of love objects but rather the subject's gaining of ex-sistance. And this must imply an ability to occupy the place of the Other, not in the sense of identifying with someone who is taken to be one's counterpart or little other, but rather in this sense: having appropriated something that does not properly belong to the living, the analysand finds himself detached from humanity and the life cycle. But he is also away from the place of the dead from which he has stolen speech.[47]

Not surprisingly, a model of development that stresses how death is a necessary threshold experience easily constructs a goal for itself that validates deathly silence over speech. Kleist faces a similar dilemma. His project to articulate a reverse Bildung—a poetics of nonmastery and death—is a constantly threatened one, and his theoretical shifts are repeated, two centuries later, by Lacanian psychoanalysis. Once a death experience, or a symbolic gesture of self-abnegation, is analyzed as the condition for speech or the necessary precursor of a successful life, it becomes virtually impossible to move beyond that threshold. How can one posit a goal in a strategy devoted to self-sacrifice? How can any values even be affirmed?

Within the context of psychoanalysis all motivation is described in terms of the patient and his or her desire. Psychoanalytic sessions find their purpose in helping the patient to conjure up an unnamed desire, to make that desire become present to the patient. Lacan writes: "En le nommant [le désir], le sujet crée, fait surgir, une nouvelle présence comme telle, et du même coup, creuse l'absence comme telle"[48] ["By naming [desire], the subject creates, makes a new presence as such spring up, and as a result, hollows out absence as such"]. The work of psychoanalysis combines the pursuit of mastery and nonmastery. The patient may control the desire by naming it, but s/he is unable to conjure it up completely, following the law of the signifier. As in "Le stade du miroir" ["The Mirror-Stage"] the patient's insight is always accompanied by the recognition of his or her own powerlessness. In the earlier essay the child discovered its control over the image in the mirror, but this discovery was accompanied by the threat of its own potential enthrallment.[49] According to the same logic, the naming of desire must always point back to the (necessary) suppression of an original and unnameable desire.

The absence that Lacan refers to is not simply limited to the law of the signifier. This absence essentially becomes the quality that can define the otherness of Desire. In Lacan's account, no doubt influenced by *Jenseits des Lustprinzips*, Desire is no longer simply life sustaining. Its singularity, or difference from particular desires, can only be explained, if Desire is defined as a lack, as fundamentally unnameable, in short, as Desire for nothing.[50]

> Le désir, fonction centrale à toute l'expérience, est désir de rien de nommable. Et c'est ce désir qui est en même temps à la source de toute espèce d'animation. Si l'être n'était que ce qu'il est, il n'y aurait même pas la place pour qu'on en parle. L'être vient à exister en fonction même de ce manque. C'est en fonction de ce manque, dans l'expérience de désir, que l'être arrive à un sentiment de soi par rapport à l'être.[51]

> Desire, the mortal function of all experience, is desire for nothing nameable. And it is this desire that is, at the same time, at the source of all types of life. If the being is only what he is, there would not even be space to speak of it. The being comes to exist according to what is lacking, it is as a function of this lack, in the experience of desire, that the being attains a feeling of self in relation to being.

This account of desire defines existence, then, as a Heideggerian *Sein-zum-Tode*. The individual can confer meaning on her own life only by confronting nothingness, by facing her own desire for death. In the Lacanian account, then, death stands both as the threshold experience, as the condition for meaning, and as the goal of life. As one of Lacan's students remarks:

> Nous arrivons à ceci—la démystification accomplie, on se trouve en présence de la mort. Il n'y a plus qu'à attendre et contempler la mort.[52]

> We arrive at this: once demystification has been accomplished, one finds oneself in the presence of death. One can only wait and contemplate death.

The act of naming becomes incidental, once psychoanalysis defines as its task the necessity of facing one's own death.

A DEATHLY SELF-REFLECTION

For a writer—in particular, Kleist, who is obsessed by his failure to produce—to adhere to a reverse Bildung, where self-abnegation is the goal of his characters' development, means to be threatened constantly by his own self-destructiveness. Besides the obvious temptation of stifling his own voice, such a writer is faced with an ideological dilemma: if he rejects strong, powerful assertions, how can he articulate, much less even choose, a set of values? What can motivate and sustain his writing?

Kleist's "Die Verlobung in Santo Domingo" ["The Engagement in Santo Domingo"] constitutes one complex response to the writer's ideological dilemma. He uses the *Erzählung*—by drawing on its developed metatextual level—in order to articulate his poetic concerns. The story is quite self-reflexive, since it is structured as a series of many different narratives. We hear Babekan's story of exploitation, Gustav's first tragic love story, accounts of the revolt on the island, as well as purely fictional tales meant to seduce and deceive the listener.

On the one hand, "Die Verlobung" may appear to be an anomaly. The death motif is as prevalent as ever, but here it seems to lose its redemptive quality. Although written a few months earlier than "Der Zweikampf," "Die Verlobung" seems to be constructed with rather more rigor. Whereas Littegarde is redeemed (a little arbitrarily) through her suffering, Toni dies, because Gustav is seduced into believing the false narrative of her betrayal. The bleak ending—one that associates the listener's belief in a narrative with death for the teller of the tale—sheds the most light, however, on the ideological stalemate of a writer devoted to the two dimensions of a poetics of death. The obsession with death highlights in Kleist the seductive, indeed inevitable pull of the death of meaning while also emphasizing the accompanying skepticism, subversive of any value systems and one generated by the sense of an impending limit or even of limitations.

"Die Verlobung in Santo Domingo" opens with the beginning revolt of the slaves on the island. Here, the antithesis that is immediately created divides the revolutionary blacks from the conservative whites. The one group believes in the necessity of change, while the other group insists on the truth of the old order. And yet, the unbreachable split between those fighting for active social transformations and those defending the old, conservative order is a false one. As is usual for Kleist, neither position is presented as a tenable one.

The "terrible" Congo Hoango, leader of the revolutionaries, is introduced first. By selecting a well-rewarded, favorite slave as the representative of the oppressed, Kleist already calls into question any absolute justification due to the rebels. The slaves' motivation is, moreover, presented under the sign of madness. The natural laws of gratitude, of proper exchange, are suspended by Hoango's rising up against his master. The list of plentiful rewards bestowed upon Hoango precedes and therefore alienates the description of his revenge:

> Und doch konnten alle diese Beweise von Dankbarkeit Herrn Villeneuve vor der Wut dieses grimmigen Menschen nicht schützen. Congo Hoango war, bei dem allgemeinen Taumel der Rache, der auf die unbesonnenen Schritte des National-Konvents in diesen Pflanzungen aufloderte, einer der ersten, der die Büchse ergriff, und, eingedenk der Tyrannei, die ihn seinem Vaterlande entrissen hatte, seinem Herrn die Kugel durch den Kopf jagte.[53]

> And yet, all these proofs of gratitude could not protect Mr. Villeneuve from the wrath of this ferocious man. In the general frenzy of revenge that flared up in the plantations following the National Convention's ill-considered steps, Congo Hoango was one of the first to reach for a rifle and, remembering the tyranny that had torn him from his native land, blow his master's brains out.[54]

If the revolutionary position seems to diverge from the logic of cause and effect, in that Hoango first saves his master's life, only to murder him later, the conservative ideology is presented as no less questionable. When Toni asks Gustav for an explanation of the uprising, Gustav speaks of the madness of freedom, emphasizing the *general* strengths of his system over its *particular* weaknesses. But he ends with a narrative that demonstrates the quite particular violence of one slave toward her former master. Gustav concludes his "theoretical" discussion, having reversed his original assertion:

> Der Fremde versetzte . . . daß, nach dem Gefühl seiner Seele, keine Tyrannei, die die Weißen je verübt, einen Verrat, so niederträchtig und abscheulich, rechtfertigen könnte. . . . die Engel selbst, dadurch empört, stellten sich auf Seiten derer, die Unrecht hätten, und näh-

> men, zur Aufrechthaltung menschlicher und göttlicher Ordnung, ihre Sache! (V, 171)

> The stranger . . . said that the feeling of his own soul was that no amount of tyranny ever practiced by the whites could justify a treachery so base and dreadful. . . . the angels themselves in their outrage would side with the unrighteous and, to uphold the human and the divine order, plead their cause.[55]

Both Gustav's line of argumentation as well as his vehemence point to a fundamental irrationality.

Kleist seems to make very little distinction between the irrationality of the revolutionary and that of the master aristocrat. Both Hoango and Gustav believe in their own self-righteousness, and both are blinded by this belief. No other scene is quite as explicit about this shared blindness as the moment when Toni has bound Gustav to the bed. Both interpret Toni's gesture at face value, unable to recognize her betrayal of the rebel cause or her loyalty to her lover. Even Babekan's duplicity does not allow her to recognize that same *Verstellung* [disguise] in her daughter. Nor do the two narratives that seem to constitute the sum total of Gustav's relation to women help to orientate him.

Gustav's interpretative quandary is essential, since it unmasks the instability inherent in the knowledge offered by narratives. In his story of the plague-ridden slave girl, language had been used to seduce the listener [a former, cruel owner] into proximity, so that he could be contaminated with the yellow fever. In the story of Gustav's first love, Mariane, however, the lie was used to *protect* him from the guillotine. By having to draw on polarily opposed narratives, Gustav is unable to interpret Toni's gesture. Instead of reading her actions in the light of Mariane's self-sacrifice, he chooses to interpret Toni's behavior as a repetition of the slave girl's seductions and, as a result, he murders his fiancée.

Kleist does not only equate the blindness of Hoango and of Gustav. He emphasizes how both self-righteous characters easily use violence and murder in the service of their beliefs. Gustav feels he is justified to punish Toni and, similarly, Babekan (following Hoango's lead) does not question her right to transgress the law of hospitality.[56]

Kleist's skepticism vis-à-vis both positions is a familiar phenomenon to us. As early as August 1801 he had questioned the opposition of knowledge and action, critical of an empty, apathetic knowledge but equally frightened of the extremes permitted by uninformed but devout conviction. Both the pursuit of knowledge and the desire to cling to ignorance are tainted positions for him.

> Auch ist immer Licht, wo Schatten ist, und umgekehrt. Wenn die Unwissenheit unsre Einfalt, unsre Unschuld und alle Genüsse der friedlichen Natur sichert, so öffnet sie dagegen allen Greueln des

> Aberglaubens die Tore—Wenn dagegen die Wissenschaften uns in das Labyrinth des Luxus führen, so schützen sie uns vor allen Greueln des Aberglaubens. (KB, 682)

> There is also always light where there is shadow, and vice versa. If ignorance secures our simplicity, our innocence, and all pleasures of peaceful nature, in contrast, it opens the gates to all horrors of superstition. If knowledge leads into the labyrinth of luxury, it still protects us from all the horrors of superstition.

By rejecting both knowledge and the grace of ignorance, Kleist in effect banishes himself to a no-man's land, to the vacuum of an existence lacking orientation. And in an earlier letter Kleist reveals that he is aware of his self-imposed exile to "no-place." In July 1801 he writes:

> Wer die Welt in seinem Innern kennen lernen will, der darf nur flüchtig die Dinge außer ihm mustern. Ach, es ist meine angeborne Unart, nie den Augenblick ergreifen zu können, und immer an einem Orte zu leben, an welchem ich nicht bin, und in einer Zeit, die vorbei, oder noch nicht da ist. (KB, 677)

> Whoever wants to know the world from the inside, may only scrutinize the things outside of him in passing. Oh, it is my innate bad habit, never to be able to be in the moment, and to live always in a place, where I am not, and in a time that is either over or not yet there.

This lament is a corollary of another Kleistian preoccupation, of his inability to control the wild abundance of experiences. His painstaking, lucid analysis of events forces him into a state of limbo, which excludes him necessarily from experiencing life completely. And this analysis forces him to demonstrate the impossibility of any one ideological position. After all, the movement of his narratives effaces the boundaries between opposites, thus blocking him from assuming any one course.[57] This expropriating analysis acts as the focus of his narratives, so that, finally, it is the texts Kleist is writing, which make up the exile and timelessness of his existence. How seriously Kleist takes his predicament is articulated no more clearly than in one of his suicide notes. He describes how he has been displaced both from the future and the past after his sisters' remark that he is a useless member of society ["nichtsnutziges Glied"], worthy of no more help ["Teilnahme"].[58]

In "Die Verlobung" it is Toni who most clearly shares the author's own dilemma. Besides functioning as the master tactitian, Toni, like Kleist, belongs nowhere. She is neither black nor white, since her mother is a mulatto and her father—who has dispossessed her, by perjuring himself in a court of law—is white. And by the end of the narrative, even her mother disowns and curses her. Most importantly, Toni belongs to neither ideological camp. At best, she is a revolutionary who rebels against the new order. But she reverses the direction of the revolution out of apolitical motives. She acts primarily for personal, rather than social, reasons. And by choosing this middle ground, Toni shows herself to be the most vulnerable of all characters. She is attacked on both fronts and, despite her resourcefulness, is unable to survive.

It is important to note, however, that Toni is the one character in "Die Verlobung in Santo Domingo" who comes closest to experiencing a reverse Bildung. On one level, at least, she distances herself from the lessons taught to her by Congo Hoango and Babekan, lessons which have as their goal the entrapment and murder of white refugees.

Leaving aside the paradox that Toni's reverse Bildung results in her death, it is essential to try to understand what motivates her transformation and development. But it is at this point that the story points to its own inadequacy; language breaks down. The turning point of the text, where Toni abandons her family's cause, is narrated as unnarratable. After hearing Gustav's account of Mariane's (displaced) death, Toni begins to identify with his grief.

> So übernahm sie, von manchen Seiten geweckt, ein menschliches Gefühl; sie folgte ihm mit einer plötzlichen Bewegung, fiel ihm um den Hals, und mischte ihre Tränen mit den seinigen.
>
> Was weiter erfolgte, brauchen wir nicht zu melden, weil es jeder, der an diese Stelle kommt, von selbst liest. (V, 175)

> A feeling of compassion, awakened by many things, came over her; with an abrupt movement she followed him to the window, threw her arms around his neck, and mingled her tears with his.
>
> There is no need to report what happened next, as any reader who has reached this point in our narrative can supply his own words.[59]

Toni is, in effect, seduced through language, although the effect of that seduction is left undescribed.

Once again, the story advertises both its inadequacy and its seductive power, a power that can, moreover, seduce the listener to desire death. It is easy to demonstrate the inadequacy of the sign in "Die Verlobung in Santo Domingo" because of the text's developed self-referentiality. Either a truthful account is perceived as insignificant or as a lie: Babekan's overt bitterness regarding her betrayal by a white man is ignored by Gustav; Toni's denunciation of Babekan's plan is not taken seriously; and Gustav is unable to recognize that Toni is lying to Babekan and Hoango in order to protect him. Or a deceitful story is interpreted as a truthful one: the story of the plague-ridden girl deceives her owner; Babekan entraps Gustav with her (false) denunciation of Hoango; and Toni betrays Babekan and Hoango successfully. Even the decision to remain silent is a dangerous one. Toni's silence becomes, in effect, her own death sentence, since Gustav never hears from her the confession that could motivate him to believe in her continued loyalty to him.

The story of Mariane's self-sacrificing lie has a double narrative function. It reveals, on the one hand, how a lie can carry more positive value than truth. By pretending not to recognize Gustav, Mariane is able to save him, even if she must die in exchange for saving her lover's life. But the deadliness of the Straßburg tale is only deferred. The story seduces Toni into transgressing her mother's law; after hearing it she submits to Gustav. Toni's sexual initiation thereby brings about her voluntary subjection to the curse of death:

> Sie [Babekan] ermunterte dieselbe (Toni), den Fremden keine Liebkosung zu versagen, bis auf die letzte, die ihr bei Todesstrafe verboten war. (V, 161)
>
> She encouraged her to refuse none of the strangers' caresses except the ultimate one, which was forbidden her on pain of death.[60]

The threatened death penalty may not be carried out by Babekan; still, the curse is effective, since Toni is murdered, in a sense, because of her relation with Gustav. The end of "Die Verlobung" thus brings about the realization of the curse, and it also brings about the ending to the displaced story of Gustav's first love. Through the detour of his experiences on the island, Gustav finally commits suicide, which he had initiated with his overt denunciation of the French Revolution.[61]

The link between language and its deferred truth (its *différance*) is repeated in most of the key scenes. Gustav's note to his waiting family is intercepted twice (besides being misplaced), and is used both in Babekan's plan—to trick the Strömli group—and by Toni—in order to sabotage her mother's strategy. The signifier (Gustav's note) in effect possesses two antithetical signifieds.

The most self-conscious demonstration of the link between language and its necessary displacement occurs during Gustav's dream. Toni confesses first to the "redeemer" in order to muster up the strength to speak truthfully with her lover. Here already the addressee is displaced. But even her confession is suspended by Gustav's unexplained, strange dream:

> Sie . . . rief ihn, seinen süßen Atem einsaugend, beim Namen; aber ein tiefer Traum, von dem sie der Gegenstand zu sein schien, beschäftigte ihn: wenigstens hörte sie zu wiederholten Malen, von seinen glühenden Lippen das geflüsterte Wort: Toni! Wehmut, die nicht zu beschreiben ist, ergriff sie; sie konnte sich nicht entschließen, ihn aus

> den Himmeln lieblicher Einbildung in die Tiefe einer gemeinen und elenden Wirklichkeit herabzureißen. (V, 183–84)

> Gently . . . inhaling his sweet breath, [Toni] spoke his name; but he was lost in a dream that seemed to be about herself, at least she heard his ardent, trembling lips whisper the word "Toni!" several times. An indescribable sadness came over her; she could not gather the resolution to pull him down from the blissful heavens of his imagination into the middle of a common and wretched reality.[62]

Toni believes that he will awaken sooner or later and so watches Gustav in his relation with her imaginary self. He addresses a displaced dream figure, and this imaginary union defers, indeed makes impossible, a true meeting of the two. (Hoango's unexpected arrival cuts short their meeting.) Gustav's calling of Toni's name is echoed by her calling his name. In both cases the speaker is never heard by the addressee.

Even the final articulation of the truth must be mediated, since death robs Toni of her speech: "Was sollen wir ihm sagen? fragte Herr Strömli, da der Tod ihr die Sprache raubte" (V, 192) ["'What shall we tell him?' cried Mr. Strömli—but the approach of death robbed her of the power of speech"].[63] And once the truth is spoken—in retrospect, since it can be of no more practical use—it, like Mariane's story for Toni, becomes Gustav's death sentence.

Language in "Die Verlobung in Santo Domingo" seems, at best, able to articulate the truth only in a deferred manner. Its status is almost like that of Toni's (displaced) social standing. And yet, if Toni shares the qualities and the fate of a writer, why can she not be saved, as Littegarde is in "Der Zweikampf"? We could surmise that, to a certain extent, her death is presented not as a negative state, but as one of a liberating displacement: "aber alle Bemühung, wie gesagt, war vergebens, sie war von dem Blei ganz durchbohrt, und ihre Seele schon zu bessern Sternen entflohn" (V, 194) ["but all efforts, as we have said, were in vain, the lead had gone clean through her and her soul had alreay fled to a better star"].[64] This most radical of displacements is presented in the terminology of an escape; here displacement is equated with liberation. And Toni's escape from the restrictions of an earthly life is soon followed by another explosion of limits—figured this time as Gustav's quite horrible suicide.

Whereas both Toni and Gustav experience a form of transgression, annihilating physical, even bodily restrictions, the description that separates Toni's death from Gustav's helps to reinforce the duality to be associated with death. Again, the ambivalence of mortality cannot be suppressed. Both Toni's murder and Gustav's suicide clearly stand under the heading of extreme punishment. Even the reference to better stars cannot mask the negativity of the event. Still, death is also desired by both. Gustav, it is clear, has been haunted by images of death since his Straßburg experience. Even in Toni's case, the desire for death is quite as strong, especially following her interaction with Gustav.

By allowing herself to be seduced by Gustav, Toni, we have seen, effectively places herself under her mother's curse. For Toni, sexual desire—or submitting to that desire—cannot be divorced from submitting to death. The turn toward autonomous life must bring about her own death. This is what she realizes soon after the (unnarrated) union with Gustav. The affiliation with Gustav, in effect, ties her both to a conservative cause (that of the doomed white man) and to her personal death. And this voluntary subjugation to death (a transformation which has even been motivated by a narrative of death) finds its expression in her apathy following the sexual act:

> Doch da sie auf alles, was er vorbrachte, nicht antwortete, und, ihr Haupt stilljammernd, ohne sich zu rühren, in ihre Arme gedrückt, auf den verwirrten Kissen des Bettes dalag: so blieb ihm zuletzt nichts übrig, als sie, ohne weitere Rücksprache, aufzuheben; er trug sie, die wie eine Leblose von seiner Schulter niederhing, die Treppe hinauf. (V, 176)

> But she said nothing in reply to all his urgings, only huddling motionless amid the tumbled pillows of the bed . . . and at last he had no choice . . . but to lift her up without further ado; she hung lifelessly over his shoulder as he bore her upstairs to her room.[65]

The symbolic death that Toni experiences here has far-reaching consequences on her relation to the world. From this point on, she lives with a goal, a goal that entails risking her life. She begins by appealing to her own extreme engagement in her debate with Babekan (cf. V, 177), and soon acts in accordance with this verbalized position, willing to die in order to save Gustav:

> Sie nahm aus dem Schrank der Mutter den Brief . . . und auf gut Glück hin, ob die Mutter ihn vermissen würde, entschlossen, im schlimmsten Falle den Tod mit ihm zu leiden, flog sie damit dem schon auf der Landstraße wandernden Knaben nach. (V, 181)

> Trusting to luck that her mother would not miss it, she took from the cupboard the letter . . . and, resolved, if worst came to worst, to die together with him, she raced down the road after the boy.[66]

Already at this point there is an interesting shift in Toni's project. Previously, her death was a risk she was willing to take. Now the failed project becomes the pretext for the desire to share her lover's possible death. Imperceptibly, Toni starts to devote herself more and more to the fate of death.

By the time Gustav has lost faith in her loyalty, Toni has begun to exult in her impending death:

> Es mischte sich ein Gefühl heißer Bitterkeit in ihre Liebe zu ihm, und sie frohlockte bei dem Gedanken, in dieser zu seiner Rettung angeordneten Unternehmung zu sterben. (V, 187)

> A feeling of burning bitterness began to mingle with her love for him, and she exulted at the thought of dying in this attempt to rescue him.[67]

Toni's sacrifice of her honor and her family has occurred under the sign of death, but rather than being imposed solely from the outside, the drive toward death is fueled from the inside as well. Toni's development is presented as a steadily increasing desire for death, so that Gustav's murder of her becomes the logical culmination of that development.

"Die Verlobung in Santo Domingo" ends with a troubling image, one that resists the displaced, retrospective union of lovers joined in one grave. This grave is first described as the "dwellings of eternal peace" (V, 194–95), but the potential idyll is undermined by the final lines of the narrative:

> Herr Strömli kaufte sich daselbst mit dem Rest seines kleinen Vermögens, in der Gegend des Rigi, an; und noch im Jahr 1807 war unter den Büschen seines Gartens das Denkmal zu sehen, das er Gustav, seinem Vetter, und der Verlobten desselben, der treuen Toni, hatte setzen lassen. (V, 195)

> There Mr. Strömli, with the remainder of his small fortune, bought a piece of property near the Rigi; and even in the year 1807 one could still see, amid the shrubbery of his garden, the monument he had erected to the memory of his nephew, Gustav, and the latter's bride, the faithful Toni.

This image of the monument belongs to an altogether other, metatextual order. The monument acts as the place of safe-keeping; it guarantees that the experiences of Toni and of Gustav are remembered. Here, at least, the many different forms of life ["Ich kann, von zu viel Formen verwirrt, zu keiner Klarheit der innerlichen Anschauung kommen" (KB, 873) ("Confused by too many forms, I cannot come to any clarity concerning my inner contemplation")] do not simply cancel one another without leaving a trace. The act of writing desperately attempts to stabilize the experiences of the world, even if these experiences are ones of missed encounters, of displacements, and of deaths.

But this is only the one side of the image. Much like the murder and suicide scenes, the monument bears two, antithetical faces. Although the stone has survived until 1807, it is also half-buried in the bushes. The trace of Gustav's and Toni's story is on the verge of being masked, of being lost from sight for ever. More significantly, the monument replaces the (missing) tombstone that could not mark the lovers' grave on the island. The tombstone in Switzerland points to a story of displaced truth, but through its act of designating the lovers' grave, it is, in turn, displaced. As a result, the tomb is empty, and the bodies lost. Even the act of documenting and stabilizing the story enters necessarily into the trajectory of displacement that governs the entire narrative, so that the marker of the empty grave becomes, in turn, a poignant image of Kleist's own (inherited) dilemma. To repeat the passage:

> Wer die Welt in seinem Innern kennen lernen will, der darf nur flüchtig die Dinge außer ihm mustern. Ach, es ist meine angeborne Unart, nie den Augenblick ergreifen zu können, und immer an einem Orte zu leben, an welchem ich nicht bin, und in einer Zeit, die vorbei, oder noch nicht da ist.(KB, 677)

> Whoever wants to know the world from the inside may only scrutinize the things outside of him in passing. Oh, it is my innate bad habit, never to be able to be in the moment, and to live always in a place, where I am not, and in a time that is either over or not yet there.

The ideological dilemma in the context of the narrative—pitting revolutionary against conservative—ends with an unpeopled scene that does not defend either strategy. But if this stalemate leads us to Kleist's own ideological dilemma, which urges, paradoxically, the necessity of a Bildung devoted to powerlessness and silence, we can see that he has found a way to articulate a poetics of death, by banishing himself from ever living in his own time. The work of his narrative has been directed primarily at designating its own self-annihilating movement, pointing out the emptiness of two opposite positions and the even more lonely but necessary emptiness of the demystifier. A reverse Bildung can be described and even almost mastered, but only at the price of an exile imposed on the writer who attempts to advocate the necessity of subverting all power.

KLEIST'S POETICS OF DEATH: WRITING AS DYSTOPIA

Kleist's obsession with death pervades the plots of all his *"Erzählungen."* Even his most optimistic one—"Die Marquise von O . . ."—bears the imprint of his preoccupation.[68] The violent death scenes in Kleist's narratives mark, however, only one facet of his confrontation with his own mortality. His discovery in

March 1801 that knowledge is mortal means that his obsession with death cannot simply be shrugged off as sensationalist or thematic. Kleist's confrontation with death unsettles more than his belief in Bildung; it suspends even the possibility of a poetics founded on mimesis.

To consider Kleist's Bildung centered on death—devoted, as it is, to the subversive critique of all power—as a mimetic, socially enlightened one—would be misguided. Kleist cannot be reappropriated into the ranks of mimetic writers, since he is quick to demonstrate the inadequacy of any ideological position. Indeed, this is the common denominator of all his *Erzählungen.* They each, unfailingly, efface the primacy, even the difference of any one ideology.

A dramatic example highlights the complex contradictoriness implicit in a stance determined by ideology. Penthesilea finds herself caught between two positions: her loyalty to her people and her passion for Achilles, which has cost the life of several of her Amazons. She accepts the need to destroy her lover, and her hatred and love are confused by her obsession to consume or literally devour her lover. But precisely this extreme, expiatory act results in her becoming "nameless," "unclassifiable" to her own people ["Sie, die fortan kein Name nennt"[69] ("She, who henceforth can be named by no name")]. The final death scene dramatizes how Penthesilea's ideological predicament finally destroys her:

Denn jetzt steig ich in meinen Busen nieder,
Gleich einem Schacht, und grabe, kalt wie Erz,
Mir ein vernichtendes Gefühl hervor.
Dies Erz, dies läutr' ich in der Glut des Jammers
Hart mir zu Stahl; tränk es mit Gift sodann,
Heißätzendem, der Reue, durch und durch;
Trag es der Hoffnung ewgem Amboß zu,
Und schärf und spitz es mir zu einem Dolch;
Und diesem Dolch jetzt reich ich meine Brust:
So! So! So! So! Und wieder! Nun ists gut.
[Sie fällt und stirbt.] (PE, II. 3025–34)

For now I will step down into my breast
As into a mine and there will dig a lump
Of cold ore, an emotion that will kill.
This ore I temper in the fires of woe
To hardest steel; then steep it through and through
In the hot, biting venom of remorse;
Carry it then to Hope's eternal anvil
And sharpen it and point it to a dagger;
Now to this dagger do I give my breast:
So! So! So! So! Once more! Now it is good.
[She falls and dies.][70]

Kleist's poetics of death seems to sustain itself in only one form: by becoming self-referential. But this specularity serves mainly to unmask the illusions of a referential, meaningful language. His works can, in fact, all be read in light of their metatextuality. "Die Heilige Cäcilie," "Michael Kohlhaas," and "Das Bettelweib von Locarno" disclose how the substitutions of narrative sequences gradually invade and undermine the difference between religious or political oppositions, finally even annihilating such differences. All three narratives thereby stage the play of language.

Later narratives only reinforce the self-referentiality of Kleist's prose. In "Der Zweikampf," for instance, the trope of writing becomes the most adequate metaphor used to describe death. Within the universe of his prose we see that it is his fictional characters who succumb most often to the murderous captivation of narratives. "Das Erdbeben in Chili," "Die Verlobung in Santo Domingo," and "Der Zweikampf" offer up enough repetitions of such deadliness.

Kleist himself, however, is caught in the most deadly scene of all: in the timeless self-referentiality of his narratives. His path prepares, in a sense, the trajectory of analysis mapped out by a Lacanian psychoanalysis intent on defining the relation between death and language. Preempting Lacan's radical theory, Kleist's stories disclose how narrative can only posit as its goal the confrontation of the storyteller with his own death. For Kleist, the confrontation with death takes the form of a repetition, one that must point over and over to the disjunction between the word and its referent. This repetition forces him to dwell in a poetic limbo. Mortality has two faces, then, even for the writer. The obsession with death sustains the endless substitutions propelling his stories forward, but it also places his literary venture under the mark of sterility, dedicating him, as it were, to a poetics constantly threatened with silence.

Kleist recognizes that his art places him in a no-man's land, where the lucidity of his gaze can only always be self-destructive, telling him that no true lucidity can ever be possible. He himself describes his own exile of paradox in August 1800, when he welcomes his friend Rühle to the world of Art:

> Ich dichte bloß, weil ich es nicht lassen kann. . . . Es gibt nichts Göttlicheres, als [die Kunst]! Und nichts Leichteres zugleich; und doch, warum ist es so schwer? Jede erste Bewegung, alles Unwillkürliche, ist schön; und schief und verschroben alles, sobald es sich selbst begreift. O der Verstand! Der unglückselige Verstand! (KB, 769)

> I only write poetry, because I can't stop it. . . . There is nothing more divine than [art] and simultaneously nothing easier; and yet, why is it so difficult? Each first movement, everything spontaneous is beautiful; and crooked and odd, as soon as it comprehends itself. O reason! Unfortunate reason!

Kleist's intuition in 1801—that through the death of truth he has been alienated both from the past and the future—reaches its climax when even his present is displaced, trapped by the dystopia of his narratives. His is a self-imposed exile and its most haunting symbol can be no more eloquently expressed than at the end of "Die Verlobung in Santo Domingo" as the tombstone marking the empty grave.

Chapter Three

In Pursuit of Power

From "Honorine" to César Birotteau

> Que les ignorants le sachent! Si l'artiste ne se précipite pas dans son oeuvre, comme Curtius dans le gouffre, comme le soldat dans la redoute, sans réfléchir; et si, dans ce cratère, il ne travaille pas comme le mineur enfoui sous un éboulement: s'il contemple enfin les difficultés au lieu de les vaincre une à une, à l'exemple de ces amoureux des féeries, qui, pour obtenir leurs princesses, combattaient des enchantements renaissants, l'oeuvre reste inachevée, elle périt au fond de l'atelier où la production devient impossible, et l'artiste assiste au suicide de son talent. (*La Cousine Bette*, V, 82)
>
> Be it known to all who are ignorant! If the artist does not throw himself into his work as Curtius sprang into the gulf, as a soldier (within the trenches) leads a forlorn hope without a moment's thought, and if when he is in the crater he does not dig on as a miner does when the earth has fallen in on him; if he contemplates the difficulties before him instead of conquering them one by one, like the lovers in fairy tales, who to win their princesses overcome ever new enchantments, the work remains incomplete; it perishes in the studio where creativeness becomes impossible, and the artist looks on at the suicide of his own talent.[1]

DEATH AS EXILE

The anxiety (which so tormented Kleist) of finding himself without a place in the world does not seem to threaten the author of *La Comédie Humaine*. Balzac's immense creation, firmly situated in nineteenth-century France, is almost overrun with images of himself. Through the disparate figures of Z. Marcas, Balthasar Claës, Albert Savarus, Louis Lambert, or Séraphîtüs/

Séraphîta, Balzac can explore his own hidden capacities as politician, scientist, lawyer, madly exalted philosopher, and even that of an angel. The roles of dandy, sculptor, musician, painter, or simply that of the stand-up comedian are enacted, respectively, by the more familiar Rastignac (as well as Lucien de Rubempré and Raphaël), Sarrasine, Gambara, Frenhofer, and, finally, Bixiou of *Les Employés*. Each of these characters resembles Balzac in some way, but each shares a common fate—that of an (often mad) genius destroyed by society or consumed by his own desires.

An account of Honoré de Balzac as a writer filled with energy and vision, easily and masterfully projecting himself, Vautrin-like, upon his new world, forging it, as it were, in his own image, conveniently ignores the sheer labor of the artist struggling to define his subject. Moreover, to assume that Balzacian narratives represent or even enact "desire" implies a readily perceptible relation of continuity between Balzac and his doubles. And yet, in *Les Proscrits [The Exiles]* (1831), the only text in which the author of *La Comédie Divine* appears, we have a clear example of how disruptively complex the relation is between the "double" and the "writing self." The fictional Dante's creativity can be interpreted as an exalted copy of Balzac's own, in that he draws words from silence and ideas from the night.[2] But here the concept of Oedipal rivalry helps to illuminate the ironic reversal that apparently reduces Dante to a figment of Balzac's imagination.

There is another double in this text, even if he is less recognizable and less central. This is Honorino, the sole male character in the entire *Comédie humaine* to bear a variant of Balzac's own name. Honorino does not even belong to the fictional world of *Les Proscrits*; he is a character in Dante's vision, used to warn against the perils of suicide. The hierarchy of paternal creativity, which transformed Dante into a latecomer and imitator, is here once again inverted; now it is Honoré/Honorino who becomes, in effect, an image created by the poetic text.

Honorino does resemble Honoré; both are able to "lose" themselves in other characters. Honorino's self-sacrifice is extreme—he commits suicide in order to share the destiny of his love—whereas Honoré as narrator loses himself only figuratively. In *Facino Cane* (1836), for instance, we learn that a storyteller must obliterate himself in order to enter fully into the lives of others ["devenir un autre que soi" (IV, 257–58)], in order to find stories to narrate.[3] The cost of narrating, which presupposes becoming another, is, then, personal annihilation.

The state which follows Honorino's suicide intensifies the parallels between double and writer. While his experience in Hell does not allow him to share the fate of the woman he loves, it still resonates with figures and images often identified with Balzac's own poetic fantasy.

> Puis tout à coup l'ombre prit son vol à travers la *cité dolente* et descendit de sa place jusqu'au fond même de l'Enfer; elle remonta subite-

ment, revint, se replongea dans les cercles infinis, les parcourut dans tous les sens, semblable à un vautour qui, mis pour la première fois dans une volière, s'épuise en efforts superflus. (VII, 283)

Then the shadow suddenly flew off across the mournful city and descended to its place, to the bottom of Hell itself; it climbed up again suddenly, returned, dove again into the infinite circles, traveled the length of them in all directions, resembling a vulture, who—placed for the first time in an aviary, exhausts itself with superfluous efforts.

Honorino's exile is characterized by solipsistic, bleak isolation and by the free, multi-directional movement of the banished soul, and this ambivalent image affects our evaluation of his suicide. If the swooping movements of the damned soul can be associated metaphorically with poetic imagination, then it follows that the necessary precondition of writing is an (at least symbolic) self-obliteration.[4] The playful undermining of Balzac's authorial mastery in *Les Proscrits* masks the more serious threat of (self-)annihilation implicated in the process of poetic creation, even if the terms *annihilation* and *creation* remain undefined and their relation to one another as yet unclear.

In *Les Proscrits*—through the analogy produced by the names—we have two contradictory statements: on the one hand, a voluntary suspension of the writer's identity leads to the frame of mind necessary to literary creation. On the other hand, once achieved, this state of metaphorical death is equated with exile, with extremely negative values producing an impression of deep-seated ambivalence toward the (represented) experience of literary production.

Whether death is simply to be interpreted as the limit of what can be written or whether it can be appropriated as a trope for the act of writing as such remains an enigma that extends throughout the relation of Honorino to Balzac's Dante. Even for Dante death is dominant as the source of the poet's inspiration; it ends by hollowing out the writer himself. In effect, the fact that Balzac has chosen to depict Dante's exile in Paris is hardly insignificant. Exile acts as a metaphor for the writer's more fundamental alienation from the world of sensation and experience.[5] Dante exclaims:

Oh! fouiller dans les tombes pour leur demander d'horribles secrets; . . . apprendre des mots que les hommes vivants n'entendent pas sans mourir; toujours évoquer les morts, pour toujours les traduire et les juger, est-ce une vie? (VII, 282)

Oh, to comb through tombs, to ask horrible secrets of them; . . . to learn words that living men don't hear without dying; to evoke always the dead, to translate and to judge always, is this a life?

After recording the deaths of others, transforming them into works of art, the writer finds his own life depleted. He is able to write about death, it seems, only at the cost of his own life.

Les Proscrits is only one vivid example of the conjunction of writing and death—a conjunction which takes place, we should note, not within Balzac's confessional writings but within the framework of a fictional account. (We shall look at Balzac's letters later.) Our preliminary question remains: to what extent does the scrutiny of the representation of death better illuminate an oeuvre more often interpreted in the light of structures of desire?

We could begin by considering how desire is used to explain the scope of Balzac's text, the "insatiable" quality of his literary genius.[6] Gaëtan Picon, for instance, uses literary and personal documents in order to identify a dynamics of desire both in Balzac's fictional characters and in the writer himself. From letters written to Zulma Carraud and Mme de Hanska between the years 1834 and 1850, Picon concludes:

> Espoir ou souci, la vie n'existe qu'en projet, qu'en perspective. Jamais nous ne voyons l'existence balzacienne bloquée dans son présent. Jamais nous ne la voyons trouvant sa mesure dans une possession quelconque. L'objet du désir balzacien est la Totalité.[7]
>
> Hope or worry, life only exists as a project, as a prospect. We never see the Balzacian existence blocked in its present. We never see it taking its measure by some possession or other. The object of Balzacian desire is Totality.

A simple method of problematizing the primacy of desire is to use Picon's own reading against him. Picon continues:

> La limite à laquelle se heurte le héros balzacien, et dont la mort n'est qu'un symbole, ce n'est pas la totalité inaccessible: *c'est la totalité déjà faite.* La vie humaine n'a pas de sens en dehors de la création. Et nous ne sommes pas le créateur.[8]
>
> The limit against which the Balzacian hero comes up, and of which death is only a symbol, is not inaccessible totality: *it is totality already achieved.* Human life has no meaning outside of creation. And we are not the creator.

If the desire (for Totality) motivates the Balzacian project, and if the realization of that desire implies collision with a limit, symbolized as a form of death, the drive at the root of Balzac's *Comédie humaine* inescapably becomes a death drive. The never-to-be-realized thrust toward totality borders here on a drive toward death. And so, in Picon, the firm distinction between desire and death begins to disappear. The confusion in determining the meaning of desire is mirrored, moreover, by the critic's inability to maintain the essential difference and undefinability expressed by the word *death.* Death is made familiar by being translated into a symbol, and this metaphorical transformation is represented as an effect of a masterful project of achieving totality. In such formulations nothing radically different survives; the reading succeeds only by suppressing complete powerlessness rightly associated with death.

Of greater importance to our argument than the instability of the term *death* is the following claim—that Balzac writes in order to achieve immortality. Picon cites Balzac's letter of 1822 to his mistress, Mme de Berny, as indicative of that desire: "Inaperçu sur la terre, et c'est un de mes plus grands chagrins, j'aurai vécu comme des millions d'ignorés qui sont passés comme s'ils n'avaient jamais été" ["Unnoticed on earth—and this is one of my greatest sorrows—I would have lived like millions of unknown people who have passed as if they had never been"].[9] One would expect a great emotional investment in texts that are meant to secure the immortality of their author. But Picon's story of Balzac's masterful projection of the self is marked by a strange phenomenon.

> Cette oeuvre à laquelle il a voué sa vie, comme il l'a peu aimée, peu relue! Mais s'il lui préfère l'amour et la gloire, n'est-ce point parce que l'oeuvre est une réalité moins indéfinissable, s'incarnant en des objets tangibles, vers lesquels on peut se retourner, alors que l'amour et la gloire sont des limites vers lesquelles on avance toujours sans pouvoir les saisir.[10]

> This work to which he dedicated his life, how little he loved it, reread it! But if he prefers love and glory to it, isn't this because the work is a less undefinable reality, embodied in tangible objects, toward which one can always turn back, whereas love and glory are limits toward which one advances continuously without being able to seize them.

This passage makes it clear that the text cannot simply be interpreted as a projection of the self; it is even rather separate from the writer. Or, if we prefer the family metaphor: Balzac's texts are cast-off, disowned children rather than the guarantors of his godlike creation, necessary to validate his paternal Creator's role.

Finally, Picon's depiction of Balzac's relation to his doubles is equally ambivalent. Although it is meant to serve as another example of the continuity between the writer and his text, his description could easily be perceived as an expression of Balzac's violent attempt to disengage himself from those doubles.

> Les victimes sur lesquelles le destin s'acharne . . . sont autant de victimes sacrificatoires offertes par Balzac à son propre destin.

> Mais les vaincus qui lui ressemblent? Ceux qui, justement, mènent son combat? En eux, il ne contemple pas, apitoyé et serein, des défaites étrangères; il exorcise la hantise de sa propre défaite, il interroge passionément, assumé par d'autres lui-mêmes, un échec qu'il évitera peut-être puisqu'il le crée, le prévoit, et surtout le délègue à ces représentants fraternels.[11]

> The victims which destiny dogs unrelentingly . . . are as much sacrificial victims offered by Balzac to his own destiny.
>
> But the defeated ones who resemble him? Those who, precisely, lead his battle? In them he does not contemplate, moved to pity and serene, foreign defeats; he exorcises the obsession with his own defeat; he questions passionately a failure assumed by other "himselves," a failure that he will avoid perhaps, since he creates it, anticipates it and, especially, delegates it to these fraternal representatives.

Reading Picon against the grain, we could argue that the violence directed by Balzac against his doubles proves that his writing is not meant to extend the self infinitely but rather to shatter its productions, tending to mask and even perhaps to destroy the self at the source. Here Balzac's disassociation from his doubles is reminiscent of Rousseau's confessed account of the effect of writing upon him:

> C'est une de mes singularités de ma mémoire qui méritent d'être dites. Quand elle me sert, ce n'est qu'autant que je me suis reposé sur elle: sitôt que j'en confie le dépôt au papier, elle m'abandonne; et dès qu'une fois j'ai écrit une chose, je ne m'en souviens plus du tout.[12]

> This is one the peculiarities of my memory that merits being told. When [my memory] serves me, it is only in so far as I rely on it: as soon as I entrust it to paper, it abandons me; and as soon as I have written a thing down, I don't remember it any longer at all.

In this account writing does not affirm the self but supplants it rather; it leads to a loss—the death of memory—within the writing self. Rousseau's case may appear more extreme than Balzac's but it allows us to reflect on how central the consciousness of loss is to the project of writing. This consciousness informs *La Comédie humaine.*

If the preoccupation with death or the exorcism of doubles allows us to supplement analyses of Balzac's narrative based on desire, several questions present themselves. We must consider first in what ways Balzac attempts to represent the "nonrepresentable" and how these constructs affect a simpler theory of straightforward (self-)reflection.[13] Next we must question what narrative functions and values are attributed to death (to its representation) and if these functions help determine the structure of his fiction, especially of his short fiction. Only then can we hope to situate Balzac in a larger cultural context to see what values he affirms or subverts through his fascination with the topic of death.

One of the most troubling representations of death occurs not in Balzac's fictions but in his letters. By studying the trajectory of Balzac's letters preceding the day of his death, May 21, 1850, we can follow Balzac struggling—in the face of his impending death—to articulate his anxiety. In 1847 Balzac writes to Mme Hanska:

> Je suis sans âme ni coeur; tout est mort. . . . Je mourrai épuisé de travail et d'anxiété, je le sens. . . . Ecoute: non seulement le coeur et l'âme sont attaqués; mais je te le dis bien bas, je perds la mémoire des substantifs, et je suis prodigieusement alarmé.
>
> J'éprouve un vide, un ennui, un dégoût de tout, qui agit sur mon cerveau.
> Mon ennui est incurable.
> La tête se brouille.[14]
>
> I am without soul nor heart; all is dead. . . . I will die, exhausted by work and anxiety, I feel it. . . . Listen: not only are my heart and soul attacked; but I tell you very softly, I'm losing my memory of nouns, and I am tremendously alarmed.
>
> I feel an emptiness, a boredom, a disgust with everything, which acts on my brain.
> My boredom is incurable.
> My head is becoming blurred.

It is crucial to be aware of the way in which Balzac's own representations attempt to master the threat of death. Unlike Montaigne, for whom death chiefly threatens the integrity of the body, Balzac's account profiles the "mind" (or "head") as the controlling center, as the place where he suffers "loss" and aphasia. In Balzac's personal experience death is signaled by the "emptiness of self" and the "loss of a center." The passage also reminds us, finally, that none among the abundant accounts of death in Balzac's fictions contains any suggestion of a playful attitude. The drive to finding narrative solutions that might overcome the primacy of death is a very serious anxiety, one that implies especially that the narrating self is at risk.

Nevertheless, Balzac's personal anxiety is not reflected in his narrative accounts with a comparable intensity. Those characters portraying artists are not themselves stricken with death. They find their art and their productivity threatened, but this is not depicted, strangely enough, by a rhetoric of loss.

Here it is precisely the artist's controlled, theoretical analysis that leads to his failure or madness. The pattern extends from 1831 until 1846, spanning, in effect, Balzac's most creative years. Whether the artist is figured as a primary or secondary character, he seems to fall into one of two categories. Either he literally defaces his own work because of his hyper-lucid reflections upon art, or the careful, preparatory analysis leads him to defer his "execution" endlessly, so that he ultimately condemns himself to speechlessness or sterility.

Claude Vignon in *Béatrix* (1839) is a fairly straightforward example of this. Clearly, he possesses an almost divine ability to penetrate and understand the world around him. But this power turns against him, since it also forces him to see all those obstacles that might hamper his creation. The result is a loss of artistic power; he is finally reduced to fleeing his mastery: "Indifférent aux plus petites comme aux plus grandes choses, il est obligé, par le poids même de sa tête, de tomber dans la débauche pour abdiquer pendant quelques instants le fatal pouvoir de son omnipotente analyse" (II, 41) ["Indifferent to the smallest as to the greatest things, he is obliged, by the weight of his head [mind] itself, to fall into debauchery in order to abdicate for a few instants the fatal power of his omnipotent analysis"].[15]

Vignon's metaphorical self-dissolution is a weak version of the rather flamboyant self-destruction of Frenhofer in *Le Chef-d'oeuvre inconnu* (1831). Frenhofer's destiny is also marked by a curious antithesis, in that his artwork is destroyed by his intense redefinition of the medium. Initially obsessed with evading the deathly immobility of the painterly copy, he calls up the need to redefine the object of mimesis. According to him, nuances of color (as opposed to the sketch or line) must attempt to reproduce the *invisible* world. His artistic vision rejects as secondary the opaque, material world: "Nous avons à saisir l'esprit, l'âme, la physionomie des choses et des êtres" (VI, 579) ["We must seize the mind, the soul, the physiognomy of things and beings"]. The light liveliness of the artwork is guaranteed by stressing the *causality* rather than the effects of phenomena in the world (and these terms are disturbingly close to Balzac's own when he writes to Mme Hanska in October 1834 that he hopes to "paint the causes of sentiments and ideas" in his *Etudes philosophiques*).[16] The culmination of Frenhofer's painterly vision is an opaque wall ["muraille de peinture" (VI, 586)], one that calls attention primarily to the mimetic "instruments," to the *syntax* or self-reflexivity of painting, rather than to the mimetic object itself. This artistic narcissism ends with the painter's suicide. It also ends with the willful burning of all paintings, for Frenhofer can no longer separate self-referential, chaotic paintings from his earlier masterpieces that continued to follow the discipline of (a more material) mimesis.

Frenhofer's complete self-destruction has already been hinted at earlier in the narrative. Porbus, a more traditional fellow painter, explains to Poussin, the young initiate:

> Il a profondément médité sur les couleurs, sur la vérité absolue de la ligne; mais, à force de recherches, *il est arrivé à douter de l'objet même de ses recherches.* Dans ses moments de désespoir, il prétend que le dessin n'existe pas et qu'on ne peut rendre avec des traits que des figures géométriques; . . . le dessin donne un squelette, la couleur est la vie, mais la vie sans le squelette est une chose plus incomplète que le squelette sans la vie. (VI, 583, my emphasis)

> He has meditated profoundly on colors, on the absolute truth of the line, but by dint of his research, *he has reached the point of doubting [the reality of] his research's object itself.* In his moments of despair, he claims that drawing does not exist, and that one can only render geometrical figures with strokes . . . drawing creates a skeleton, color is life, but life without the skeleton is a more incomplete thing than the skeleton without life.

In the fictional world of the *Comédie humaine* it is the masterful gaze attempting to define art theoretically—Porbus speaks of the quarrel between "le raisonnement" and "les brosses" ["reason" and "brushes"]—that ends up destroying the creation, creativity, and even the creator.

If Vignon and Frenhofer represent artists who destroy their works and creativity through excessive (cerebral) analysis, the characters of Wenceslas in *La Cousine Bette* (1846) and of the eponymous hero in *Gambara* (1837) represent examples of artists, who are faulted for being unable to suspend their control. They thereby become incapable of producing great or intelligible masterpieces; indeed, they are unable to produce anything at all. Wenceslas—a Polish émigré sculptor—is a character not struck down by physical annihilation, although he is afflicted with figurative death, with sterility. He is described as a "charming eunuch" (V, 83), able only to "conceive" and dream about sculptural projects, but unable to summon up the energy necessary to "execute" his visions. His lucid insights paralyze rather than consume him.[17]

It is at this juncture that Balzac defines the terms of what is to be the antidote to creative paralysis. The artist must be willing to bracket out his consciousness; he must submit voluntarily to the (temporary) death of his intellect and will power:

> Que les ignorants le sachent! Si l'artiste ne se précipite pas dans son oeuvre, comme Curtius dans le gouffre, comme le soldat dans la redoute, sans réfléchir; et si, dans ce cratère, il ne travaille pas comme le mineur enfoui sous un éboulement: s'il contemple enfin les difficultés au lieu de les vaincre une à une, à l'exemple de ces amoureux des féeries, qui, pour obtenir leurs princesses, combattaient des enchantements renaissants, l'oeuvre reste inachevée, elle périt au fond de l'ate-

> lier où la production devient impossible, et l'artiste assiste au suicide de son talent. (V, 82)

> Be it known to all who are ignorant! If the artist does not throw himself into his work as Curtius sprang into the gulf, as a soldier [within the trenches] without a moment's thought, and if when he is in the crater he does not dig on as a miner does when the earth has fallen in on him; if he contemplates the difficulties before him instead of conquering them one by one, like the lovers in fairy tales, who to win their princesses overcome ever new enchantments, the work remains incomplete; it perishes in the studio where creativeness becomes impossible, and the artist looks on at the suicide of his own talent.[18]

If the artist fails to suspend his control, he will find his self displaced. He can only be present at the suicide of his talent; he finds himself shifted to the marginal role of spectator, much as Wenceslas is relegated to a secondary narrative position.

Although the emotional response to the experience of death diverges widely depending on context—Balzac's letters or his fictions—the associations that present themselves in conjunction with the word *death* seem to turn on the issue of control and mastery. What is the effect of a strategy that seeks to undermine itself, that turns on the need to suspend narrative mastery over (fictional) artists and their projects?[19]

In *La Cousine Bette* the artist's readiness to endure the threat of being destroyed becomes the very precondition for creating a work of art. It might seem more logical to posit death simply as the limit of what can be represented in short fiction. And yet, for the narrator of *La Cousine Bette*, death comes to mean the artist's refusal to employ a sovereign, masterful strategy for producing a text. He must hurl himself into a void in order to create. The anxiety of death has thus been redirected; the narrator has transformed the limit of mortality into a threshold, thereby marking the writer's ultimate triumph over his own "self-displacement." Through the narrator's description, the risk of death has become, in effect, an essential stage in the process of artistic creation.

THE CRISIS OF DOUBLING: A STUDY OF *HONORINE*

The joyous relinquishing of control that seems to be demanded of the beginning artist clearly relies on his understanding death figuratively. Whereas for Balzac *literal* depictions are accompanied by an anxiety difficult to suppress, the more metaphorical depictions of death, in the final analysis, actually permit greater control or, at least, creativity.

We can pause here to realize that our comparison of Kleist's and Balzac's poetics shows that both writers reflect on how to embrace and justify powerlessness but that they still concern themselves with how to assume a differently defined power. Kleist's preoccupation with death seems overshadowed by the inescapability of the death of meaning; Balzac, on the other hand, attempts a more hopeful appropriation of that limit.[20]

The focus of our study must be: what form of creative power is bestowed upon an artist when he submits figuratively to an experience of death? But first we must determine what might constitute a more traditional and masterful authorship in Balzac's short prose—in other words, what is being replaced by the more radical poetics of death.

A brief return to *Les Proscrits* allows us to perceive that for Balzac the question of originality—represented by the fluctuating position of the double vis-à-vis its creator—determines whether a written text can be considered a projection and affirmation of the writing self. In *Les Proscrits* the doubling of the double introduces a crisis into the assumption that each narrative simply mirrors and extends the powerful author named "Balzac." What, however, is at stake in this crisis of doubling?

The text that continues most radically the questioning of the controllability and adequacy of doubling, raised by *Les Proscrits*, is Balzac's short *récit Honorine* (1842).[21] The title alone signals that the relation between the writing self and its double will be explored. This text contains, namely, the only two other characters of *La Comédie humaine* bearing variations of Balzac's first name: Honoré. Here, however, the assumption of an author's self-mirroring is problematized by the fact that both of these doubles are female: Honorine and Onorina Pedrotti.

In pursuit of the logic associated with "doubling" or "representation," we might first question why the characters in *Honorine*, unlike Honorino in *Les Proscrits*, are masked as female doubles. The pretext motivating the second narrator's story about Honorine provides us with a clue:

> En parlant littérature, on parla de l'éternel fonds de boutique de la république des lettres: la faute de la femme! Et l'on se trouva bientôt en présence des deux opinions: qui, de la femme ou de l'homme, avait tort dans la faute de la femme? (I, 562)

> In discussing literature, they spoke of the perennial stock-in-trade of the republic of letters—woman's sin. And they presently found themselves confronted by two opinions: When a woman sins, is the man or the woman to blame?[22]

Implicit in this question is the very real problem of whether Woman is a controlled, controllable image of Man. Is even her *faute* [erring] to be understood as the attempt to narrate her own story of acquiring autonomy, or can she only be subsumed into Man's fantasy as something forever reacting to his initial mistreatment of her? Is Woman to be understood as Man's double, even when she tries to break free of his masterful gaze? Honorine's resistance to the projection (and loving protection) of her husband Octave, her attempt to seal herself off from the "story" (or "role") that both he and Society are eager to project on her, problematizes within a feminist framework the relation between "author" and text (here: Woman, or Honorine).[23] Honorine's refusal to accept a traditional role allows us to examine the form of her creative struggle to "write" her own story independently.

The structure of *Honorine* can be understood as the conflict between two "writer's" plots—that of Honorine and that of Octave, her estranged, cuckolded, but still loving husband. The figure of the secondary narrator, Maurice, is caught between the two plots, first in his attempt to coordinate the two narratives, and, second, in his apparent imprisonment by his obsession to explain the enigmatic, resisting Honorine. He refuses to accept that his own "totalizing" narrative must remain inadequate to his subject matter.

Octave's plot seems, for the most part, to be a powerful, controlling one. He employs Maurice as his secretary, only to treat the orphan as his "son." The privileges of filial status include the knowledge of how to write exactly as Octave does (I, 567), the story of Octave's troubled relation to his wife, the involvement in the plot to reintegrate Honorine (against her wishes) into the family; the gift of a fiancée; and, not surprisingly, the rivalry (although repressed) for Honorine's love.

Maurice's own answer to the question of Woman's relation to Man is inconclusive. He ostensibly uses the story of Honorine to call into question the traditional definition of a woman's role and of her virtue. And yet, his account of Octave's plot (although undermined subtly by references to a potential madness in Octave) begins by using the image of his employer's self-sacrifice and loving protection as a means to denigrate Honorine's stubborn refusal to return to her husband—especially after Octave is still eager to welcome her back after her adultery and subsequent abandonment by her lover.

Initially, Honorine's plot is more difficult to follow, and it only gradually helps to undermine the self-abnegating, idealistic vision of Octave as paternal and supportive husband. Her plot is based on withdrawal, on the refusal to participate in the community and on the attempt to banish Society from her enclosed, self-sustaining "citadel." Honorine's greenhouse, which is ultimately shattered by the invading gaze of Octave through his various proxies, among them Maurice, seems to figure her attempt to resist the plots of faithful wife and obedient mother that Society would have her enact. The "citadel" marks her resistance to being appropriated as a double into a masculine plot.

The pastime Honorine selects to occupy and support herself within her "separate" world is one that attempts to break free from narcissistic self-representation. In other words, her own "creations" are not presented as necessarily mirroring or extending her producing self. Neither does she wish her signature to be stamped on her art (especially since she hopes to elude her husband's control).

> La fabrication des fleurs et celle des modes nécessitent une multitude de mouvements, de gestes, des idées même qui laissent une jolie femme dans sa sphère; elle est encore elle-même, elle peut causer, rire, chanter ou penser. (I, 577)
>
> The making of flowers and light articles of wear necessitates a variety of movements, gestures, ideas even, which do not take a pretty woman out of her sphere; she is still herself; she may chat, laugh, sing, or think.[24]

Leaving the condescending tone aside, we can still note that her manufacture of flowers extends the hope that such "nonreferential" creativity will not contribute to "fixing" or "enthralling" the creating self.[25] Yet, the pull of perceiving a continuity between the self and its artistic creations is one to which even Honorine succumbs. To Maurice, who has acquired her trust by playing the role of madman (a role assigned to him by Octave), she explains her interest in the reproduction of flowers:

> Cet art, me disait-elle, est dans l'enfance. Si les Parisiennes avaient un peu de génie que l'esclavage du harem exige chez les femmes de l'Orient, elle donneraient tout un langage aux fleurs posées sur leur tête. J'ai fait pour ma satisfaction d'artiste, des fleurs fanées avec des feuilles couleur bronze florentin comme il s'en trouve après ou avant l'hiver. . . . Cette couronne, sur une tête de jeune femme dont la vie est manquée, ou qu'un chagrin secret dévore, manquerait-elle de poésie? (I, 578)
>
> This art, she would say, is in its infancy. If the women of Paris had a little of the genius which the slavery of the harem brings out in Oriental women, they would lend a complete language of flowers to the wreaths they wear on their heads. To please my own taste as an artist, I have made drooping flowers with leaves of the hue of Florentine bronze, such as are found before or after the winter. Would not such a crown on the head of a young woman whose life is a failure have a certain poetical fitness?[26]

This passage is doubly significant, since it hints, first of all, that the act of sealing oneself off from others and their stories begins to resemble a new slavery, the potential imprisonment of the self in its own declining narcissism. There is an even more serious implication, however. The production of flowers as the projection of the self is especially enslaving, since that reproduction soon becomes the trope used to explain the enigmatic nature of Honorine, their creator. In Honorine's case, the flower—which was her creation, meant to remain separate—is fixed upon by Octave and Maurice as defining her being. Here the text (as flower) seems to displace the (absent/veiled) core of the individual.[27] Her creation becomes the means to define and fix the elusive self that Honorine might be.[28]

If the attempt to remain detached from the textual product does not protect Honorine from being determined by it, it seems that the plot of *Honorine* is signalling to us the ultimate impossibility of a strategy of creative disjunction. The producing self will be made vulnerable through its creations, just as the individual can never escape completely from the mastery of another's plot. And, indeed, Honorine will not be able to resist being appropriated by Society. She finally capitulates to Octave's desires. She immolates herself for the sake of Society, bears a son and soon after dies. The violence inflicted upon Honorine does not even stop with her death, since Maurice will attempt to redefine her, by giving her a narrative contour through his account of her "illogical" behavior.

The text clearly associates violence with the act of narrating. When offering Honorine's tale as the means of exploring the threat to masculine authority implicit in Woman's adulterous "erring," Maurice speaks of the necessity of dissecting a "real" corpse rather than simply exploring "un mort imaginaire" (I, 562). His act of narration also constitutes a transgression of his promise to Honorine to bury her secrets. She had written to him, after all: "Gardez mes secrets comme la tombe me gardera" (I, 589) ["Keep my secrets as the tomb will keep me"]. We should note, however, that not only does Maurice in effect invade Honorine's tomb as he invaded her glass house: he also transgresses the law of Octave—the law of discretion that distinguishes a political man (as well as a secretary) (I, 564).

The violence which Maurice directs against Octave can be readily explained, if we consider that he, too, has been used by Octave as the means to reappropriate Honorine into the destructive plot of Society. The violence of rivalry is especially strong, since Octave counts on Maurice's love for Honorine to mask his role of representative spy (for the adoptive father). In other words, this explains the violence of Maurice (as Octave's double) upon the "master-narrator." Octave has, after all, displaced Maurice's desire—appropriating his rival's desire in order to propel his own plot further. Why, however, Maurice should feel the need to appropriate Honorine's image through his narration of her story as a way of "dissecting her cadaver" (I, 562) is a question more difficult to resolve.

By turning to the complex narrative frame of the text we can begin to glimpse an answer. The structure of *Honorine* is itself marked by a radical fragmentation. Here, at least seven different voices interconnect, each potentially displacing the other six: an anonymous narrator, who conjures up a cluster of Balzacian characters abroad, is supplanted by Maurice who orientates their aimless conversation regarding the status of an adulterous woman. Next, in Maurice's account of his childhood, we hear the voice of his first adoptive father (his uncle, a priest) who, in turn, will provide him with a second "father," Octave. Octave's own story sends Maurice into Honorine's world, where the account is now invaded by Honorine's voice, as Maurice communicates the content of their conversations. Maurice then draws on Octave's letters to Honorine (of which he has been the bearer) and on Honorine's letters to himself, after she has been reunited with Octave. The récit ends with conflicting interpretations provided by the narrative audience that had initially motivated the question determining the relation of Man to his (Biblical) double. At this point it has become impossible to distinguish storyteller from narrated subject. In other words, the direction of doubling (or of mimetic representation) can no longer be determined.

Through this list we immediately see that the "Byronesque" Maurice, who seemed poetically enigmatic, apparently has difficulty controlling his own text. His voice is constantly invaded by his "subject" or his story. Indeed, one way to understand this complex narrative structure is to consider that Maurice's project of "organizing" the subject is obsessive because it is at the same time an ordering of his own life through the story. The attempt to uncover and to articulate or master the invisible, enigmatic core—the attempt to break into the tomb—determines the trajectory of the storyteller's life. This imprisonment of the narrator by his story finds its most extreme figuring in the character of Maurice's wife, Onorina Pedrotti—obviously a double of Honorine—and who represents the displaced object of Maurice's desire to possess Honorine herself.

Paradoxically, then, Honorine may seem to have the last word. Through Maurice's obsession and despite Honorine's own appropriation by Octave and her death, she appears as a successful writer. It is she, after all, who shapes Maurice's destiny. Maurice's violence toward her, paralleling his violence toward Octave, can also be read, then, as the double's violence toward one of its would-be creators. Through Maurice's troubled relation to Octave and to Honorine, we note that both the place of the storyteller as well as that of the double implies a determination by an Other. Here, then, is the narrative dilemma: if, on the one hand, there is no mastery to be found in being manipulated by a narrator, the movement to forge another's history can only mean (for Maurice) to find his own narrative trajectory mapped out by the subject matter.

Despite her desire for self-determination, even Honorine, the eponymous protagonist, does not occupy the "masterful" position in the text. This becomes clear in the incapacity of Honorine to escape from a (literal) death or even to name the cause of her death (I, 588). Is it her inability to forget her own enslaving dream of self-determination that consumes her, so that she, unlike Maurice, finds herself displaced by her drive to determine herself? Or is she killed by Octave's consuming need to possess her? Let us turn to her own description, after she has returned to Octave and given up control over her own future:

> A ce jeu terrible [de l'hypocrisie] je prodigue mes forces, la comédienne est applaudie, fêtée, accablée de fleurs; mais le rival invisible vient chercher tous les jours sa proie, un lambeau de ma vie. Déchirée, je souris! Je souris à deux enfants, mais l'aîné, le mort triomphe. Je vous l'ai déjà dit: l'enfant mort m'appellera, et je vais à lui. (I, 588)[29]

> I throw all my powers into this terrible masquerade; the actress is applauded, feasted, smothered in flowers; but the invisible rival comes every day to seek its prey—a fragment of my life. I am rent and I smile. I smile on two children, but it is the elder, the dead one, that will triumph! I told you so before. The dead child calls me, and I am going to him.[30]

To understand Honorine's inward-locked creativity in terms of her maternity seems especially apt, since the figure of nurturing a growing other within oneself also suggests that the growth of this other will deform the self, displacing it by new demands. Maternity, as the interplay of nurturing and displacement, repeats rather than stabilizes the interplay of the narrator's quest for the true, original subject to be narrated, a quest which—in Honorine's case—will deform and finally destroy the self. Both modes of creativity—a maternal as well as a paternal one—seem to lead to the creator's annihilation by his or her "product."

In *Honorine* the violence unleashed by the act of narration is particularly clear—whether it is experienced as conversation (as in the frame involving the figure of Maurice) or as plotting (the Honorine-Octave intrigue). The narrative fragmentation of *Honorine* helps to illuminate the unstable process of doubling. In this récit the desire to control leaves no one in control; there is no nearly masterful or controlling narrator in this text. Neither Octave nor Honorine is able to survive. Both of their attempts—either to determine another's role or one's own—are unsuccessful. Even the surviving narrator, Maurice, does not represent a controlling narrator, since he remains captivated by Honorine's and Octave's story. He is himself a double of both deposed narrators; and this seems to be the connotation underlying the description of him as "poetic" rather than as a "poet." (I, 561)

THE DENIAL OF DEATH: BALZAC'S NOVELS

In *Honorine* we have found an example of a text in which the narrator renounces his dream of control and thereby manages to survive, even if this survival resembles a death-in-life. In fact, the pattern of failure asserts itself on two levels. Success eludes the characters in their experience of the world, and—on the level of narrativity—adequate descriptions or explanations are withheld, inaccessible. Although Honorine's death is ostensibly made legible by Maurice's situating it in a causal sequence and by his introducing "authentic" (autobiographical) commentaries, it remains an enigma to all characters within and without the narrative frame. Indeed, through one listener's opaque conclusion, we can note that even the character of Honorine remains unintelligible, unnarrated and unnarratable. Camille Maupin, a fictional author in the *Comédie humaine*, says:

> Cette femme est une des plus rares exceptions et peut-être la plus monstrueuse de l'intelligence, une perle! (I, 589)
>
> This woman is one of the most rare examples and perhaps the most monstrous in intellect, a pearl.

The self-contradictory terms *monstrous* and *pearl* make Camille's conclusion incomprehensible and, moreover, leave the initial question—who is most at fault when a married woman errs—unanswered. The récit, in short, enacts a form of narrative death by pointing to its own inadequacy either to control the fictional perspective or to order and explain the (narrative) world.

By now it is clear that the anxiety over death dominates Balzac's writing both as theme and as narrative form—with special implications for the narrative voice. But Balzac hardly limits his depictions of death to a few repeated scenes, nor does he assign the same narrative function to all moments of fictional death. This is especially clear in his longer narratives, where we usually find less radical subversions of authorial control. Let us end this third chapter by analyzing how Balzac depicts death in a few novels where the loss of life figures especially prominently; there we can study Balzac's creativity in transforming death into a poetic construct. By analyzing briefly *Le Lys dans la vallée* (1835), *Histoire de la grandeur et décadence de César Birotteau* (1837), *Pierrette* (1840), and *La Rabouilleuse* (1841), we can hope to distinguish between representations of death found in the shorter and the longer narratives. For instance: in the lengthy narratives the texts seem in their drawn-out nature rather impervious to any threat that death—understood as narrative closure or rupture—might pose to their all-encompassing structures. Since a rhetoric of powerlessness is pursued less deliberately in the four novels, we can note how Balzac explores alternatives to such a strategy of "failure." We might then be in a position to determine in the fourth chapter the different ways in which the representation of death functions in Balzac's short prose. This should also allow us to note how Balzac's fascination with death and with the inadequacy of power permits new insights into the culture of his time.

Upon a first glance, Balzac's novels point to a more authoritative ideology; scenes of death do not seem to undermine the narrator's ability to control his text. In the novels under consideration two basic methods are used to counter the threat of death to the integrity of the represented self. In *Pierrette* and *Ursule Mirouët*, for instance, the narratives attempt simply to question and problematize the finality of the dying moment. The novelistic structure helps to depict the resistance of the *body* to its annihilation by exploring situations in which the "cadaver" might continue to survive. Pierrette's corpse disappears but lives on through the political discussions that circle around the mystery of her death, whereas le docteur Minoret in *Ursule Mirouët* discovers the more scientific power of telepathy, which culminates in his reappearing several times after his death in the novel.[31]

In *Le Lys dans la vallée*, in *La Rabouilleuse*, and in *César Birotteau*, the narrator will attempt to confer a more "redemptive" function on the moment of death, where the "redemption" resides in emphasizing a more spiritual self, which might survive beyond its body. This "conquering of the flesh" tends to coincide with the dying character's discovery of the plenitude of its identity.

Let us begin with the novel written in 1835, *Le Lys dans la vallée* [*The Lily in the Valley*] in which the moment of death is constantly glorified (and elided) by the idealizing vision of the surviving "spiritual" self. Henriette de Mortsauf, the "adoptive mother" and unattainable lover of the narrator (Felix), is in the process of dying. She has been "murdered," as it were, by Felix's betrayal (his turn to sensuality, embodied by his affair with Lady Dudley), and Felix recognizes his status as "spiritual murderer," as the (unpunished/unpunishable) criminal, "qui verse goutte à goutte le fiel dans l'âme et mine le corps pour le détruire" (VI, 380) ["who drop by drop pours venom into the soul and undermines the body in order to destroy it"]. By stressing the primacy of *soul* over body, the novel seems to situate the drama of death in the realm of "immateriality." And, in fact, the representation of Henriette's death dwells lovingly on the slowed respiration of the dying woman, as well as on the continuous song of two nightingales at the precise moment of her death (". . . le chant alternatif de deux rossignols qui répétèrent plusieurs fois leur note unique . . ." [VI, 385] [". . . the alternating song of two nightingales who repeated their single note several times . . ."]). Most significant, of course, is the narrator's reference to the perfume that seems to surround him as a continuing consolation of Henriette's incorporeal presence:

> Une âme est en mon âme. Quand quelque bien est fait par moi, quand une belle parole est dite, cette âme parle, elle agit; tout ce que je puis avoir de bon émane de cette tombe, comme d'un lys ses parfums qui embaument l'atmosphère. (VI, 390)

> A soul is in my soul. When some good deed is done by me, when a beautiful word is spoken, this soul speaks, it acts; all the good that I

> can do emanates from this tomb, as a lily's perfumes do make the atmosphere fragrant.

This aesthetic depiction of Henriette's death (and of its effect) seems to promise that the survival of the self as disembodied soul can be effortless. But the graceful elegance of the ending willfully masks the crisis that Henriette has experienced in the effort of dying. The text seems to prefer to displace this process, by calling it meaningless or trivial next to the "true" portrait of Mme de Mortsauf.[32]

> Ses tempes creusées, ses joues rentrées montraient les formes intérieures du visage, et le sourire que formaient ses lèvres blanches ressemblait vaguement au ricanement de la mort. . . . L'expression de sa tête disait assez qu'elle se savait changée et qu'elle en était au désespoir. Ce n'était plus ma délicieuse Henriette, ni la sublime et sainte madame de Mortsauf; mais le quelque chose sans nom de Bossuet qui se débattait contre le néant, et que la faim, les désirs trompés poussaient au combat égoïste de la vie contre la mort. (VI, 383)

> Her hollowed out temples, her sunken in cheeks showed the interior forms of her face, and the smile that her white lips formed vaguely resembled the snigger of death. The expression of her face indicated enough that she knew herself to be changed and that she was in despair because of it. This was no longer my delicious Henriette nor the sublime and saintly Mme de Mortsauf, but that something without a name of Bossuet, which was struggling against nothingness and which hunger and deceived desires incited to the egotistical battle of life against death.

Even Henriette's formerly familiar smile cannot—in its fixity—be deciphered; it signals the possibility of all states of the soul: "the irony of vengeance, the waiting for pleasure; the intoxication of the soul; and the rage of having been deceived or of wanting to deceive" ("la rage d'une déception") (VI, 383).

This indecipherability of death seems to mark the moment of the textual struggle to articulate how a character's identity might disintegrate. In Henriette de Mortsauf's case, this dissolution lies in the disjunction between what the body rejects (food and drink)—in short, refusing to nurture life—and what the soul desperately clings to (materiality, passion, and, especially, sensuality). And it is this disjunction between *corps* and *âme* that marks the moment in which Henriette potentially no longer has a center, a fact that is necessarily accompanied by the chaos in the system of recognition and even of signification (consider her smile, for instance). In the space of dying, there is no longer a stable relation between a *signifier* and its *signified.*

Ultimately, however, Henriette's death does become "successful." The soul is led back to accept its self-abnegation "voluntarily," so that body and soul fuse again, mutually reflecting and reinforcing one another. Felix returns to visit Henriette and describes her moribund peacefulness:

> En ce moment le corps était pour ainsi dire annulé; l'âme seule régnait sur ce visage, serein comme un beau ciel après la tempête. Blanche et Henriette, ces deux sublimes faces de la même femme, reparaissaient d'autant plus belles que mon souvenir, ma pensée, mon imagination, aidant la nature, réparaient les altérations de chaque trait où l'âme triomphante envoyait ses lueurs par des vagues confondues avec celles de la respiration. (VI, 385)

> At this moment the body was, so to speak, cancelled out; only the soul reigned on this face, serene like a beautiful sky after the tempest. Blanche and Henriette, the two sublime aspects of the same woman, seemed again to be more beautiful, since my memory, my thought, my imagination, helping nature, was repairing the deterioration of each feature, where the triumphant soul was sending its lights in waves merged with those of her breathing.

It is not by chance that the body is described as being "almost annihilated" or that it is Felix's memory (his thoughts and his imagination) that helps him to reconstruct Henriette's coherent identity. After all, in order to find again the lost integrity of her soul, Henriette has been drugged by opium. Ironically, it is only through the individual's intoxication that her idealized core can be rediscovered or reimposed on her.

This novelistic attempt to represent death, to harness the threat posed by the disjunction in the self (and to counter the temporary dissolution of meaningful language accompanying such a disjunction) seems to allow the fantasy of the self's endless survival to be triumphant. And yet, even if the horror of the self's death can be overcome, there is still always "a price to pay"; a new anxiety will always surface. In *Le Lys dans la vallée* the survival of the incorporeal self is accompanied by the invasion of the narrator's body by such a soul. The coercive violence imposed on Henriette (her being drugged) turns back on Felix de Vandenesse, so that he is both abandoned by Mme de Mortsauf and by the fiancée to whom he is narrating the story. More significantly, his own identity is displaced by the stronger presence of Henriette's "spirit" (or "memory"); she is his "better" part.[33] In *Le Lys dans la vallée* death loses its finality; its power over the individual is reduced. But in such a fantasy the dead come back to haunt the living, destroying—in the case of Felix—the particularity (and life) of the bereaved self.

Balzac uses the representation of death in the novel in order to plot out a fantasy of survival, but these fantasies, while hardly ever resembling one another, are each flawed in some way. The diversity exists, it seems, in order to discover ways in which the Balzacian characters (and narrators) might evade being fettered by their dreams of immortality. In *La Rabouilleuse* (1841), for instance, Balzac explores a different relation between death and individuality, where death is no longer portrayed as the destructive enemy of the individual but becomes instead an excessive outgrowth of the self, thus remaining, potentially, within the self's control. The redefinition of death as an excessive manifestation of the self is exemplified by one of the major victims/manipulators of the novel *La Rabouilleuse*—herself. She has succeeded in destroying herself by pursuing her own obsession. Her narcissistic vanity and ambitious pretentiousness eventually can no longer be sustained without an accompanying degradation of the self, notably, prostitution: "Quand Philippe a vu sa Rabouilleuse habituée à la toilette et aux plaisirs coûteux, il ne lui a plus donné d'argent, et l'a laissée s'en procurer . . . vous comprenez comment?" (III, 187) ["When Philippe saw his 'Rabouilleuse' used to clothes and costly pleasures, he no longer gave her money and let her procure it herself . . . you know how?"]. Philippe, as "le fléau de Dieu" ["the scourge of God"], has simply turned Flore Brazier's (alias the "Rabouilleuse") mastery over her own victim onto herself. Whereas her earlier tyranny over "le père Rouget" relied on her victim's need for her love, now it is her own need for grandeur that becomes the mechanism that undoes her power.[34]

In effect, the entire novel can be read as a sequence of such "self-continuous deaths," where the overdevelopment of an individual's distinguishing feature becomes the form of his or her own death. The text itself offers the terms that reveal how the mechanism used to redefine death can also be imposed as a grid to explain the otherwise rambling structure of *La Rabouilleuse:*

> "Hélas! mes amis!" dit Bixiou d'un ton qui laissait ses trois compagnons dans le doute s'il plaisantait ou s'il parlait sérieusement. . . . "Voilà! Ma grand-mère aimait la loterie et Philippe l'a tuée par la loterie! Le père Rouget aimait la gaudriole et Lolotte l'a tué! Madame Bridau, pauvre femme, aimait Philippe, elle a péri par lui! . . . Le Vice! le Vice! mes amis! . . . Savez-vous ce qu'est le Vice? C'est le Bonneau de la mort!" (III, 187–88)

> "Alas, my friends," said Bixiou in a tone which left his three companions in doubt as to whether he was joking or speaking seriously. . . . "There it is! My grand-mother loved the lottery and Philippe killed her by the lottery. Old Rouget loved womanizing and Lolotte killed him. Mme Bridau, poor woman, loved Philippe, she perished by

> him. . . . Vice, Vice, my friends! Do you know what Vice is? It's the Bonneau [go-between] of death."

What in *Le Lys dans la vallée* was the fantasy of the self's survival has been redefined in *La Rabouilleuse* as a fantasy where death is subsumed as part of the individual's identity. Such a redefinition necessarily provides new anxieties. First: if death can be defined as the "natural" extension (and therefore cancerous overdevelopment) of the self and its distinguishing feature, then the individual becomes rather vulnerable to the gaze of a masterful decipherer. Anyone clever enough to perceive another individual's dominant tendency (and specificity) will be able to stimulate its overdevelopment and thereby precipitate that character's destruction. This, at least, is what the various character developments in *La Rabouilleuse* seem to suggest.

There is another, equally anxiety-ridden, dimension to the naive fantasy of the self's continuous control (signalled here as the appropriation of death as a "symptom" of the self), and this is: what might be the fate of the masterful decipherer? Can he, at least, sustain his masterful appropriation?[35] He almost does, until the other characters have deciphered his spiderlike activity. Then it is his plots that are undone; his social standing and wealth are wrested from him. Here is the representation of his death:

> En s'apercevant que leur colonel [Philippe Bridau] était cerné, ceux qui se trouvèrent à distance ne jugèrent pas à propos de périr inutilement en essayant de le dégager. Ils entendirent les mots: *Votre colonel! à moi! un colonel de l'Empire!* suivis de hurlements affreux, mais ils rejoignirent le régiment. Philippe eut une mort horrible, car on lui coupa la tête quand il tomba presque haché par des yatagans. (III, 189)

> Upon noticing that their colonel was surrounded, those who found themselves at a distance did not judge it opportune to perish in vain while trying to free him. They heard the words: *Your Colonel! To me! A Colonel of the Empire!* followed by horrible screams, but they rejoined the regiment. Philippe had a horrible death, for they [the enemy] cut his head off while he fell, almost hacked to pieces by yataghans.

Philippe Bridau, the master decipherer, can function as a symbol of the desire for wholeness that characterizes the treatment of death in *La Rabouilleuse.* He wishes to maintain control over the characters surrounding him and in this pursuit finds his own wholeness dismembered. His fate of being fragmented seems to be shared by the structure of *La Rabouilleuse*, a text which—by depicting the individual's quest for completeness and mastery—shifts almost aimlessly from one personal destiny to another. Although the novel overtly seems to suggest the possibility of mastering death by interpreting it as a characteristic natural to the self, that wholeness must cede eventually to a fragmentation shared by the (villainous) protagonist and by the structure of the text. No one central protagonist (the "head," as it were) holds the various destinies together through a masterful vision. The only "primary" character who seems to survive the death of Philippe is his brother, Joseph, the genial painter. His role was to refuse to participate in the intrigues and struggles for power, preferring to remain sequestered in his *atelier*, so that we are led to conclude that the only successful survivor is one who willingly chooses to remain incidental and marginal to the plot.

Pierrette (1840) is perhaps a more complex example of a narrative driven to explore the theoretical limits to a "strategy of endless survival," and the fate that best embodies this quest is Pierrette's own. Hers is the story of an orphan who is victimized physically and emotionally by her bachelor aunt and uncle[36]—so much so, that she is finally driven to death by them. The end of the text holds out a redemptive promise—one that offers to transform the finality of (Pierrette's) death into an immortal work. The story of Pierrette's life (and the injustice she has suffered) will never be allowed to stop, and in order to guarantee the narrative's continued existence, the narrator introduces an uplifting example.

> Pour donner à ceci d'immenses propositions, il suffit de rappeler qu'en transportant la scène au Moyen Age et à Rome sur ce vaste théâtre, une jeune fille sublime, Béatrix Cenci, fut conduite au supplice par des raisons et par des intrigues presque analogues à celles qui menèrent Pierrette au tombeau. Béatrix Cenci n'eut pour tout défenseur qu'un artiste, un peintre. Aujourd'hui l'histoire et les vivants, sur la foi du portrait de Guido Reni, condamnent le pape, et font de Béatrix une des plus touchantes victimes des passions infâmes et des factions. (III, 59)

> In order to give immense proportions to this, it suffices—by transporting the scene onto the vast theater in the Middle Ages and in Rome, to remember that a sublime young girl, Béatrix Cenci, was led to torture by reasons and causes almost analogous to those that led Pierrette to her tomb. Béatrix Cenci had as only defence an artist, a painter. Today, [based] on the testimony of the portrait by Guido Reni, history and the living condemn the pope, and make of Béatrix one of the most touching victims of vile passions and of factions.

Although the act of writing seems to promise Pierrette a form of immortality—even if this survival of death has become rather metaphorical—there is nonetheless a troubling by-product accompanying the dream that death can be overcome. The analogy with Béatrix Cenci serves to displace Pierrette from the center of the story, so that she is eclipsed; the memory of her experiences already appears rather more than slightly modified by the Italian story of incest and parricide.

Indeed, this dimension is rather more serious than the wry realization that undoing the finality of death in this novel only serves to perpetuate a victim's fate for Pierrette. As her grandmother exlaims to Pierrette's childhood sweetheart: "'Il y a,' dit la vieille, 'il y a, Brigaut, qu'ils veulent ouvrir le corps de mon enfant, lui fendre la tête, lui crever le coeur après sa mort comme pendant sa vie'" (III, 57) ["'What's happened,' said the old woman, 'what's happened, Brigaut, is that they want to open the body of my child, to split open her head, to dig out her heart after her death as [they did] during her lifetime'"]. The story of abuse and invasive penetration (the destruction of the body's boundaries) has potentially not even ended with Pierrette's demise.

The endlessness of the narrative plot of exploitation can be diverted from the continued, physical persecution of Pierrette, since Brigaut quickly seals her body in a zinc coffin in order to hide her from the gaze of her victimizers. But the narrative persecutions continue, nonetheless. Once the body has been spirited away—its absence apparently protecting the boundaries encircling its inner core—a different threat attacks its integrity. A willful misrepresentation of the subject sets in, so that the "object" of representation is "decomposed" in order to serve the (political) interests of others. During the furious political debate the story of Pierrette's suffering is curiously elided. Her story has become a pretext:

> Dans le salon de madame Tiphaine, on se vengeait des horribles médisances que le parti Vinet avait dites depuis deux ans: les Rogron étaient des monstres, et le tuteur irait en Cour d'Assises. Sur la place, Pierrette se portait à merveille; dans la haute ville, elle mourrait infailliblement; chez Rogron, elle avait des égratignures au poignet; chez madame Tiphaine, elle avait les doigts brisés, on allait lui couper un. Le lendemain, *le Courrier de Provins* contenait un article extrêmement adroit, bien écrit, en chef-d'oeuvre d'insinuations . . . et qui mettait déjà Rogron hors de cause. (III, 54)
>
> In the salon of Madame Tiphaine, one avenged oneself of the horrible scandalmongering that the Vinet party had spread for two years: the Rogrons were monsters, and the guardian would go before the Crown Court. In town [on the square] Pierrette was doing marvelously; uptown she was dying inevitably; at the Rogrons, she had scratches on her wrist; at Madame Tiphaine's her fingers were broken, one was going to cut one of them off. The following day, the *Courrier de*

> *Provins* contained an extremely shrewd, well-written article, a masterpiece of insinuations . . . that already exonerated Rogron.

Although the one account of Pierrette's sufferings seems more accurate than its opposite, both "narratives" transform Pierrette into a material possession, meant to heighten each party's chances for power. Here then are the two sides of the dilemma affected by thinking through the self's "endless survival" in *Pierrette*: either the presence of the body seems to lead to the desecration of its boundaries or its absence leads to the displacement of the self by the political interests of others. Even the "disinterested" artist, bent on fixing the immortal truth of Pierrette's sufferings, uses her story in the service of his own glory. Even for him the representation of the absent self leads to displacing the "object" of his study. By de-centering his conclusion through the reference to Béatrix Cenci, the writer implicitly reenacts the persecution of Pierrette.

There is one more strategy that we must explore, one that will help us to determine how the representation of death affects the novelistic form. Up to now we have noticed that each of the novel's "dynamics" can be interpreted as the attempt to represent different models of how a powerful and whole self might survive endlessly. Rather than imposing one dominant novelistic formulation of the problem as *the* typical Balzacian one, we should simply note at this point that any representation of the individual's experience in time—which is accompanied by the narrative challenge of defining his/her confrontation with death—seems to introduce cracks in the narrative image of total control. Either it is the narrator whose own boundaries are infiltrated or it is the text that threatens constantly to fragment itself (a threat that is perhaps not so alien to *La Comédie humaine* with its many lacunae and incomplete stories). Or we find that the "core"—meant to represent death—is displaced by conflicting, mutually annihilating accounts of it. It is in this final example that the writer himself becomes contaminated by the injustice he supposedly is attempting to unmask objectively.

The final novel which must be explored before we can turn again to the shorter narratives of Balzac's corpus is one that struggles to define a "true" and perhaps "ideal" continuity by pitting the model of a "straight line" against that of the "circle."[37] *Histoire de la grandeur et de la décadence de César Birotteau* [*History of the Rise and Fall of César Birotteau*], written in 1837, already signals in its title that the fantasies of endless survival must be reappraised. The terms "decadence" and "grandeur" (rather hyperbolic when applied to the fate of a *parfumeur*) allow us to recognize that in this novel, narrative temporality, which is associated with the protagonist, will be explored in terms of a double movement: progress and decline. The fantasy of the endless continuity of the self can no longer be understood solely as a straight, infinite line.

The text itself provides the terms that are to help depict and evaluate the temporal trajectory of the individual. The narrator, while attempting to justify the lowliness of its object of representation, remarks:

César Birotteau, qui devait se considérer comme étant à l'apogée de sa fortune, prenait ce temps d'arrêt comme un nouveau point de départ. Il ne savait pas, et d'ailleurs ni les nations, ni les rois n'ont tenté d'écrire en caractères ineffaçables la cause de ces renversements dont l'histoire est grosse. *Quand l'effet produit n'est plus en rapport direct ni en proportion égale avec sa cause, la désorganisation commence?* . . . Puisse cette histoire être le poème des vicissitudes bourgeoises auxquelles nulle voix n'a songé, tant elles semblent dénuées de grandeur, tandis qu'elles sont au même titre immenses: il ne s'agit pas d'un seul homme ici, mais de tout un peuple de douleurs. (IV, 148)

César Birotteau, who should have looked upon himself as having reached the apogee of his career, mistook the summit for the starting-point. He did not know the reason of the downfalls of which history is full; nay, neither kings nor peoples have made any effort to engrave in imperishable characters the causes of the catastrophes of which the history of royal and commercial houses affords such conspicuous examples. . . . *When the effect produced is no longer in direct relation with nor in exact proportion to the cause, disorganization sets in?* . . . Would that this story might be the Epic of the Bourgeoisie; there are dealings of fate with man which inspire no voice, because they lack grandeur, yet are even for that very reason immense: for this is not the story of an isolated soul, but of a whole nation of sorrows.[38]

The text already indicates that the traditional movement from progress to decay will be problematized; the general principle meant to explain the turn toward decline is presented in the form of a question. In addition, César's own experience of grandeur and decadence reverses the two terms. A quick glance at the narrative structure reveals to us that this questioning is not simply playful. César will be submitted to an experience of death, although, in his case, the death will occur in the middle of his life story.[39] In effect, his death, figured as a metaphor, can be survived. Again, the novelistic structure seems to promise a masterful appropriation of death; a strategy of survival seems possible.

Before we turn to the question of how one can narrate the experience of death outlived, we must consider what is at stake in the metaphorical representation of César's death. César experiences a *mort civile,* in that he loses all privileges of making any legal or economic decisions. And yet, the deathly experience is far from being simply negative: by being stripped of his social status as citizen, the narrator suggests that César's state of death almost resembles that of childhood. A certain ambivalence or undefinability is associated with being "civically dead." If the bankrupt individual is signified as completely powerless, his "nullity" also serves to provide him with the power of invisible mobility.[40]

The moment of complete destitution (represented as economic as well as moral bankruptcy) is accompanied by a rather familiar rhetoric. On the one hand, César must accept that his (already quite humble) identity be appropriated by other individuals. And it becomes quite clear in the text that this dispersal of the self cannot always be contained or controlled by laws. Both true and false creditors assemble in the hope of being able to accumulate more wealth by assuming temporarily the "name" of the bankrupt individual: "Une des plus horribles scènes de la vie de César fut sa conférence obligée avec le petit Molineux, cet être qu'il regardait comme si nul et qui, par une fiction de la loi, était devenu César Birotteau" (IV, 220) ["One of the most horrible scenes in the life of César was his obligatory conference with little Molineux, that being whom he regarded as so worthless and who, by a fiction of the law, had become César Birotteau"]. Once the "name" has been wrested from the body, it is usurped and dispersed uncontrollably.

In the metaphorical experience of death, it is not only César's "name" or identity of the self that is evacuated by being dispersed. César's *body* is also annihilated metaphorically. After his "mort civile" [civil death], César becomes quite unrecognizable. A transformation has taken place within him:

> Les négociants qui rencontraient l'employé n'y retrouvaient aucun vestige du parfumeur. Les indifférents concevaient une immense idée des chutes humaines à l'aspect de cet homme au visage duquel le chagrin le plus noir avait mis son deuil, qui se montrait bouleversé par ce qui n'avait jamais apparu chez lui, *la pensée*! (IV, 223)
>
> The merchants who met the employee did not discover any vestiges of the perfumer. Even the indifferent conceived an immense idea about the downfall of humans at the sight of this man, whose darkest sorrow had cast mourning on his face and who showed himself to be turned upside down by that which had never appeared in him—thought.

We should note here that the moment of César's metaphorical death seems, paradoxically, to mark the belief in a simultaneous change for the better. César has learned to become more thoughtful, so that his earlier nullity has been supplanted by thought and purpose. "Civil death" is accompanied by an intellectual (re-)birth.

This more hopeful belief in the possibility of learning (from experience) seems to indicate, then, that death—understood metaphorically—can be vanquished. Indeed, the novel attempts to propose that the moment of death does not need to be understood as a threat either to the individual or even to the process of narration. In fact, death can itself be analyzed and organized as a narrative; it no longer functions simply as the final, unnarratable term. This is true of César's experience and it also holds true on a more theoretical and general level. The narrator asserts:

> D'où vient la rigueur avec laquelle ce thème de croissance et de décroissance s'applique à tout ce qui s'organise ici-bas? Car la mort elle-même a, dans les temps de fléau, son progrès, son ralentissement, sa recrudescence et son sommeil. (IV, 148)

> How comes it that this argument of waxing and waning is applied so inexorably to everything thoughout the system of things?—to death as to life; for in times of pestilence death runs his course—abates, returns again, lies dormant.[41]

In order to make death more familiar, the narrator transforms it into a plot. By shifting death from the unknowable end of a causal sequence to the middle, the finality of death can be modified, even repressed temporarily. As in the case of *Pierrette* the act of writing or narrating is used to counter—albeit imperfectly—the anxiety surrounding mortality.

César's fate—discovering thought because of his destitution—causes a crucial question to surface. Which moment marks the culmination in this model of reversal? Is it César's new lucidity or the nullity of his initial (but materially more powerful) experience, where he was described as "pusillanime, médiocre, sans instruction, sans idées, sans connaissances" (IV, 144) ["cowardly, mediocre, without education, without ideas, without knowledge"]? Clearly, if we choose his previous state of nullity and wealth, we are hard pressed to explain why César's blindness has not protected him from his financial and moral catastrophe. On the other hand, if we choose the belief in "progress through (civil) death," now it is the system, where "decadence" must follow "grandeur," that is called into question. In other words, the familiar question directed at Balzac's narratives has resurfaced: does the narrated trajectory of César's experiences point to a potentially better future or does it reinforce the regret for a lost, idealized past? Is the narrative strategy in *César Birotteau* conservative or progressive? After all, by depicting "lowly characters" as well as aristocratic ones to act as protagonists, Balzac's prose could be relegated potentially to both a reactionary and to a revolutionary camp.[42]

These questions can help guide us in our reading of the ending of *César Birotteau*, where we can examine how the survival of death can be figured, and if such a survival can be sustained. The ending provides us with the image of a triumphant return: César has been able to pay back his debts to all his creditors and thereby has rearned his name and his status as bourgeois citizen. The motif of the circle (or repetition) is strong in this finale: in order to celebrate César's "return to life," his family plans a surprise party, one that will resemble completely the sumptuous feast that marked the initial climax of César's grandeur—and simultaneously, of course, the turning point in his life.

The exact repetition of the party—meant to mark the desperate attempt to annihilate the many years of mort civile—becomes unwittingly the instrument of César's death. The moment of plenitude is so great, that César's internal system breaks down radically: "En présence de ce monde fleuri, César serra la main de son confesseur et pencha sa tête sur le sein de sa femme agenouillée. Un vaisseau s'était déjà rompu dans sa poitrine, et, par surcroît, l'anévrisme étranglait sa dernière respiration" (IV, 232) ["In the presence of this world decked out in flowers, César shook the hand of his confessor and leaned his head against the breast of his kneeling wife. A vessel had already ruptured in his chest, and what is more, the aneurism was strangling his last breath"].[43] The motif of the return is present, even here through the reference to César's wife's breast. César's fall into the tomb is rewritten as the childlike nestling of the head against the breast. César's rebirth to himself is thus simultaneously marked both as birth and as death. The text does continue to question rhetorically the finality of death, but even in this novel the fantasy of survival must ultimately founder again.

The choice of depicting César's death in the context of a return, as a repeated scene of success and birth, makes interpreting the novel's linear progression rather complex. The nostalgic return to the self's lost plenitude marks, after all, both the climax of spiritual and material wholeness for César and his literal demise. "Progress" for César represents both a moving forward and a moving back. Death both precedes and follows grandeur, but it functions also as a cause of César's moral greatness. In *César Birotteau* the return from decline to grandeur undermines the system posited at the beginning of the novel but also verifies it ("Quand l'effet produit n'est plus en rapport direct ni en proportion égale avec sa cause, la désorganisation commence" [IV, 148] ["*When the effect produced is no longer in direct relation with nor in exact proportion to the cause, disorganisation sets in*"]).[44] The deliberate mixing of two threshold experiences—death and birth—at the end of the novel supports both the view that the novel's structure is essentially nostalgic (and conservative) and, equally, that such nostalgia must be lethal. The conservative thrust is thus simultaneously supported and called into question.

Even in the novels, then, where the narratives appear to be more masterful—more centered on a discourse of power and control—we can see some similarities with Balzac's shorter prose, where positions of mastery (including that of narrative authority) are destabilized. A quick glance at a few other novelistic examples should allow us to recognize that Balzac's fascination with death—his exploration of the limits of a strategy of (endless) survival—can be linked with the difficulty of even defining what might be increased power or progress. In *Le Cabinet des antiques* (1833–1836), for instance, Balzac seems to be exploring the disastrous consequences of an aristocratic upbringing that clings to the nostalgic ideal of a by-gone (but decadent) era. In *Le Père Goriot* (1834–1835), however, a more revolutionary (Parisian) formation is portrayed in terms of a self's gradual disillusionment and cynical evaluation of the present. Here the model of Rastignac's normative development is also accompanied by a shadow side that allows us to interpret the process of evolution as a movement toward moral decay.

Balzac plays with the traditional model of progress, taking pleasure in modifying it to such an extent that the concept "progress" is undone, indeed, subverted. In *Un début dans la vie [A Beginning in Life]* (1842), Balzac demonstrates how a character's formation through life leads to a gradual stripping away of (pretentious) characteristics rather than to any accumulation of knowledge and power. This is the state of affairs for the middle-aged "modern" bourgeois protagonist at the end of the narrative: "L'espèce de pitié que Pierrotin inspirait à Oscar [le protagoniste] fut la dernière faute que la vanité fit commettre au héros de cette Scène, et il en fut encore puni" (I, 342) ["The kind of pity that Pierrotin inspired in Oscar (the protagonist) was the last fault that vanity made the hero of this Scene commit, and he was punished for this again"]. Here the model of progress is simply reversed in a manner reminiscent of Kleist's "Der Zweikampf."

Eugénie Grandet (1833) represents a more complex reworking of even the possibility of progress. Here the individual's attempt to form herself, to create an original, more authentic life is blocked by the pervasiveness of an older, more established way of life.[45] In this novel the heroine attempts to defy the coercive pull of her father's narrative of life (his monomania, which determines that gold and the saving of it define where the significance of life should lie). Her attempt to narrate her own account—which turns around the generous expenditure of gold and love to a cousin, Charles Grandet, which hints at a narcissistic doubling)—provides both the illusion of her free self-determination and articulates her fundamental imprisonment within the structure of her father's account. By simply reversing the terms of her father's account of the self (as a closed system), and by opening her "economic" system to a double, she dooms herself to an existence of circularity. This sterile circularity is what the text seems to unmask in its final representation of Eugénie as a "married" spinster. She becomes the mirror image of her father, perpetuating his narrative and enforcing his avaricious, tyrannical Law. "Continuity" here becomes, then, the trap of endless, sterile, and futile repetition—a death-in-life, so that the conservative thrust appears in this novel to be especially menacing.

Although these are very schematic accounts of the narrative dilemma, they help us to perceive that the struggle to represent and to appropriate death within the novel represents a continuing, significant problematic in Balzac's prose. Although each novel pursues a different way to bring about the fantasy of an immortal, powerful character, each text reaches a limit. The attempt to reduce the threat of death seems to produce new threats. If survival is cast in spiritual terms, this "immaterial form" seems to menace the integrity of the surviving, corporeal self. If death can be translated as a characteristic of the self, this redefinition cannot block the self's vulnerability effectively. And should the finality of death be suspended by writing, even this rhetorical act cannot hope to guarantee the true memory of a character. In this, Pierrette's, case, immortality can even suggest the endlessness of suffering rather than that of mastery. And in *César Birotteau*, the representation of death becomes more overtly politicized; the metaphorical treatment of death as end and new beginning lays bare the realization that a thrust forward to a more thoughtful existence and the nostalgic movement back to the past must both lead to the individual's death.

What purpose or orientation lies behind a poetics of death must still remain shadowy at this point of the discussion. But through the analysis of the novels we can already move beyond the simple realization that for Balzac the representation of death is primary. The novels begin—on an explicit level—by positing ways in which death can be harnessed to the individual's will. Through the representation of death, however, the textual structures tend to reinforce the anxiety of powerlessness. They end up laying bare the limits of a project based on the fantasy of an endless, continuing self.

In the next chapter we will focus our attention on the shorter fiction, where we can expect to find texts less concerned with maintaining the fiction of endlessness. Let us consider how the treatment of death manifests itself in the récits and how it seems to affect Balzac's project of writing narratives—if and how the writer is able to pursue a deliberate strategy of powerlessness. We can then consider if Balzac's prose offers an alternative to an ideology based on power, control, and wealth.

Chapter Four

La pensée qui tue
Balzac's Poetics of Thought

> Observateur sagace et profond, il épiait incessamment la nature; puis, lorsqu'il l'a eu surprise, il l'a examinée avec des précautions infinies, il l'a regardée vivre et mouvoir; il a suivi le travail des fluides et de la pensée; *il l'a décomposée, fibre à fibre, et n'a commencé à la reconstruire que lorsqu'il a eu deviné les plus imperceptibles mystères de sa vie organique et intellectuelle.* En la recomposant par ce chaud galvanisme, par ces injections enchantées qui rendent la vie aux corps, il nous l'a montrée frémissant d'une animation nouvelle qui nous étonne et nous charme. (Félix Davin, "Introduction," I, 599, my emphasis)

> Shrewd and profound observer, he watched nature closely and incessantly; then, when he had surprised it, he examined it with infinite precautions, he watched it live and move; he followed the work of fluids and of thought; *he decomposed it fibre by fibre, and did not begin reconstructing it until he had guessed the most imperceptible mysteries of its organic and intellectual life.* By recomposing it through this heated galvanism, by these enchanted injections that give life to bodies, he showed to us [nature] trembling with a new animation that astounds and charms.

IMMORTALITY THROUGH THOUGHT

In Balzac's *La Peau de chagrin* [*The Fatal Skin*] (1830–31) we find a different approach to the dilemma associated with the limitations of an ideology of power seeking to master death. Near the beginning of the "philosophical tale" the antiquarian urges Raphaël, the protagonist, to withdraw from the world by renouncing all desire for possessions and success. The antiquarian dismisses the domain of experience as a fleeting "material possession" (VI, 441–42), preferring to reject the world in order to be able to conjure up his own universe:

> Voir, n'est-ce pas savoir? Oh! Savoir, jeune homme, n'est-ce pas jouir intuitivement? n'est-ce pas découvrir la substance même du fait et s'en emparer essentiellement? Que reste-t-il d'une possession? une idée. Jugez alors combien doit être belle la vie d'un homme qui, pouvant empreindre toutes les réalités dans sa pensée, transporte en son âme les sources du bonheur, en extrait mille voluptés idéales dépouillées des souillures terrestres . . . comment préférer tous les désastres de vos volontés trompées à la faculté sublime de faire comparaître en soi l'univers, au plaisir immense de se mouvoir sans être garrotté par les liens du temps ni par les entraves de l'espace. (VI, 441–42)
>
> Seeing, isn't this knowing? Oh! To know, young man, isn't this to enjoy intuitively? Isn't this discovering the substance itself of fact and essentially seizing hold of it? What remains of a possession? An idea. Judge then how beautiful must be the life of a man, who—being able to imprint all realities onto his thought—transports in his soul all the sources of happiness, [who] extracts from this a thousand ideal sensual delights stripped of worldly stains . . . how could one prefer all the disasters of your deceived wishes to the sublime faculty of making the universe appear before one, to the immense pleasure of moving without being strapped down by the bonds of time nor by the fetters of space.

When one renounces the desire to gain power over other individuals and over one's own experience, the antiquarian seems to promise, one can discover how superior are the pleasures of knowledge and the domain of ideas. It does not take a wild stretch of the imagination to discover parallels between the antiquarian's project and that of a writer like Balzac, whose intangible *Comédie humaine* rivals the Paris of the 1830s and 1840s.[1]

It does not appear to be an accident that the antiquarian's fleeting vision of control—passed over quickly by the protagonist of *La Peau de chagrin*—is given voice in the *Etudes philosophiques* [*Philosophical Studies*]. This second (of three) section(s) of the *Comédie humaine* holds out the promise that two conflicting desires can be reconciled. Both the desire to renounce control over the world and the desire to discover a different form of (authorial) power can presumably be fulfilled in a project devoted to achieving a greater, more abstract understanding of the world.[2] Rather than remaining subject to the events and "effects" of the world, Balzac chooses to articulate, if not represent, the world of invisible "causes" and "principles." In the preface to the *Etudes philosophiques* (1835) Balzac has Félix Davin explain:

> Ainsi donc, quand les *Etudes de moeurs* auront peint la société dans tous *ses effets*, les *Etudes philosophiques* en constateront *les causes*, et les *Etudes analytiques* en creuseront *les principes*. Ces trois mots sont la clef de cette oeuvre étourdissante par sa profondeur, surprenante par ses détails. (VI, 706)[3]

> Thus, when the *Studies of Customs* will have portrayed society in all its *effects*, the *Philosophical Studies* will take note of the *causes* of these, and the *Analytical Studies* will look closely at the *principles*. Those three words are the key of this work, stunning in its profundity, surprising in its details.

This description clearly seeks to establish a hierarchy, where "principles" would be considered a degree of abstract knowledge that passes beyond the stage of ascertaining causes. The concept of principle suggests either the "origin" or, according to *le Petit Robert*: "[une] proposition, notion importante à laquelle est subordonnée le développement d'un ordre de connaissance ... les vérités fondamentales sur lesquelles s'appuient tout le raisonnement" ["a proposition, an important notion which is subordinated to the development of an order of knowledge ... fundamental truths upon which all reasoning relies ..."], whereas the concept of cause—although apparently synonymous with "principle"—evokes more: "ce pourquoi un événement, une action humaine arrive, se fait" ["this reason why an event, a human action happens, takes place"].[4] The *Etudes analytiques* are meant to represent, then, the conditions or assumptions that actually permit the deciphering of "causes" that is to take place in the *Etudes philosophiques.*

Balzac takes care to justify his system as logical by reshuffling the chronology of the *Comédie humaine.* Through Davin he would have us believe that the *Etudes de moeurs* as the scientific observation of *effects* has led him to a study of the *causes* of such effects and that the distilling of *principles* marks the culmination of his project. Through Pierre Citron's documentation we are aware, however, that many of the *Etudes de moeurs* date from the late 1830s and 40s, whereas an *étude analytique* like the "Théorie de la démarche" ["Theory of the Gait/of the Process"] stems from 1833.

We should recognize from the start that a poetics of ("timeless," "immortal") ideas will only partially bypass the obstacles presented by a project pursuing more masterful, worldly strategies of power, even if it will illuminate aspects of Balzac's oeuvre. Let us begin our study of Balzac's poetics of thought by fixing on the fictional "summit" of the *Comédie humaine*, an *étude analytique.* Here it is the "Théorie de la démarche" that is primarily useful, because it promises to present a condensed form (as well as a parody) of the *Comédie humaine.* Balzac writes of his ostensible project in the "Théorie de la démarche":

> Codifer, faire le code de la démarche; en d'autres termes, rédiger une suite d'axiomes pour le repos des intelligences faibles ou paresseuses, afin de leur éviter la peine de réfléchir et les amener, par l'observation de quelques principes clairs à régler leur mouvement. En étudiant ce code, les hommes progressifs et ceux qui tiennent au système de la perfectibilité, pourraient paraître aimables, gracieux, distingués, bien élevés, fashionables, aimés, instruits, ducs, marquis ou comtes, au lieu de sembler vulgaires. . . . Et n'est-ce pas ce qu'il y a de plus important chez une nation dont la devise est *Tout pour l'enseigne*? (VII, 588)

> To codify, to draw up the code of gaits; in other terms, to compile a series of axioms for the relaxation of feeble or lazy minds in order to allow them to avoid the trouble of reflecting and to lead them, through the observation of several clear principles, to regulate their movement. By studying this code, progressive men and those who insist on the system of perfectibility, would be able to appear amiable, gracious, distinguished, well brought up, fashionable, loved, educated, dukes, marquis or counts instead of seeming vulgar. . . . And isn't this of the greatest importance in a nation whose motto is *All for the sign*?

We can note in passing that this parodic project of providing codes (of walking) helps to support Christopher Prendergast's analysis of Balzacian narrative in his *The Order of Mimesis.* Balzac seems quite aware of the negative implications that Prendergast uncovers in his critique of the system of classfication operating in the *Comédie humaine.* Prendergast writes: "Balzac's recommendations for a code of differentiation thus gives the recipe by which that code can be manipulated to produce a confusion, and a travesty, at the heart of the clarity for which the code is devised."[5] In the "Théorie de la démarche" Balzac recognizes that providing a "code de la démarche" will lead to the attempt to simulate the gait of socially higher placed individuals—leading ultimately, of course, to the inadequacy of his system to decipher the gait of one's contemporaries.

But there is more in this passage: irony is also levelled at the maxim "*Tout pour l'enseigne,*" thus calling into question the adequacy of education. In this parodic context, at least, the teaching of systems is aimed primarily at lazy or simple-minded individuals. Not only is criticism directed at the project of classification, then: It pokes fun at "progressive" individuals and at the belief in the possibility of perfecting oneself. Paradoxically, where we might expect to find praises, we find instead deep-seated reservations concerning the superiority of formation and knowledge (of codes).

In fact, Balzac explicitly calls into question the model of "education" once he ostensibly begins to do his fieldwork—once he begins to observe the movements of his fellow human beings. In his renunciation of the assumption that mankind can be perfected, he begins to resemble the Kleist of "Über das Marionnettentheater" ["On the Marionette Theater"].

> Le mouvement humain est comme le style du corps: il faut le corriger beaucoup pour l'amener à être simple. Dans ses actions comme dans ses idées, l'homme va toujours du composé au simple. La bonne éducation consiste à laisser aux enfants leur naturel, et à les empêcher d'imiter l'exagération des grandes personnes. (VII, 595)[6]

> Human movement is like the style of the body: one needs to correct it a lot in order to lead it to being simple. In his actions like in his ideas, man always goes from the composite to the simple. Good education consists in leaving children to their nature and in hindering them from imitating the exaggeration of adults.

The amusing cynicism of this passage may mask the fact that here the argument of the "Théorie de la démarche" has undercut itself. The narrator only finds animals able to move gracefully, without revealing any vices (VII, 594), and this fact shows that his initial goal of establishing a code that might express "les lois du beau idéal en fait du mouvement" (VII, 586) ["the laws of ideal beauty with regard to movement"] is thwarted. Not only is the code of ideal movements replaced by a catalogue of vices (VII, 594), this code (as the product of noting the connection between internal causes and external effects) also does not permit the narrator greater access to shaping internal causes. The narrator recognizes the gap between his power of observation and the effects of such perspicacity. Essentially, since he permits "courtisans and cheats" to imitate nobler characters, his system will only encourage vice rather than check it.

Balzac's "Théorie de la démarche" is not simply an exercise in the futility of scientific discourse. One brief look at the (almost arbitrary) structure of the argument reveals that the topic of physical movement functions in part as a pretext for another, more fundamental preoccupation: the obsession with *la pensée* as thought and as the faculty of thinking. There are five sections to the "Théorie," each corresponding to a particular subject matter.

The preface attempts to situate the discussion of movement in its historical context and notes that no physiological, psychological, transcendent, or philosophical discourse exists on the topic of walking. This leads the narrator to exult in his new idea, upon which he confers demiurgic powers: "Une idée neuve est plus qu'un monde: elle donne un monde" (VII, 582) ["A new idea is more than a world: it creates a world"]. The narrator next goes on to discuss the development of new ideas, and we should consider that here again it is the "meta-topic" thought rather than the subject of walking that seems to capitivate the writer. He discovers that the development of a thought has three ages: "enthusiasm; fatigue; and maturation."[7]

The third stage of the argument marks the writer's fatigue with his new idea. However, rather than being frustrated with the dimensions of his task to observe the different walking styles of his contemporaries, he begins to question the adequacy of rational discourse by wondering what distinguishes mad forms of knowledge from more "legitimate," scientific ones:

> Un fou est un homme qui voit un abîme et y tombe. Le savant l'entend tomber, prend sa toise, mesure la distance, fait un escalier, descend, remonte. . . . Puis il vit en famille. Le fou reste dans sa loge. Ils meurent tous deux. Dieu seul sait qui du fou, qui du savant, a été le plus près du vrai. Empédocle est le premier savant qui ait cumulé. (VII, 583)

> A madman is a man who sees an abyss and falls into it. The scientist hears him fall, takes his gauge, measures the distance, makes a staircase, descends, climbs up again. . . . Then he lives with his family. The madman stays in his hut. Both die. Only God knows who was closer to truth—the madman or the scientist. Empedocles is the first scientist who was both.

The flippant tone of the passage may seem to hint that the narrator's dilemma is a false one and yet, he does apply the danger to himself: "Ici je serai toujours entre la toise du savant et le vertige du fou. . . . Je me place au point précis où la science touche à la folie, et je ne puis mettre de garde-fous" (VII, 583) ["Here I will always be between the gauge of the scientist and the vertigo of the madman. . . . I place myself at the precise point where science touches madness, and I cannot put up any barriers"]. For the narrator "description" is potentially equivalent to "experience." For instance: despite their differences both the madman and the scientist experience the abyss. And how does this anecdote apply to the narrator's situation? The lack of consciousness explicit in the experience of movement is recreated—in a magnified form—by the excessive and therefore fruitless attempt to delimit the significance of that movement.

It is not surprising that the decision to anchor the study in facts and observation follows the stage of despair. And yet, this fourth moment also forces the writer to perceive the futility of his project. As we noted earlier, rational perspicacity leads to the belief in human decadence rather than to the affirmation of human progress. The essay ends, then, with the denunciation of thought. The end result of the movement of ideas is not the maturation of one particular idea but rather the realization that all thought is "the power that corrupts our movement" and that acts as "the dissolvant of the human species" (VII, 595). We realize, then, that it is the obsession with thinking rather than with walking that dominates in the "Théorie."

Curiously, rather than ending with the resonant: "*Rien* sera la perpétuelle épigraphe de nos tentatives scientifiques" (VII, 596) ["*Nothing* shall be the perpetual epigraph of our scientific attempts"], Balzac chooses to conclude with two sayings that seem rather discontinuous with the rest of the argument:

> Celui qui a dit: "Le premier pas que fait l'homme dans la vie est aussi le premier vers la tombe," obtient de moi l'admiration profonde que j'accorde à cette délicieuse ganache que Henry Monnier a peinte, disant cette grande vérité: "Otez l'homme de la société, vous l'isolez." (VII, 596)

> He who said: "The first step that man takes in life is also the first toward the tomb," obtains from me the profound admiration that I grant the deliciously foolish figure that Henri Monnier cut when he stated this great truth: "Remove man from society, [then] you isolate him."

The first connection that can be made between this enigmatic ending and the essay is possible if one recognizes that the two statements are tautological, highlighting the inadequacy of both descriptions. What do these sayings tell us but that a moment that appears to be a beginning actually marks a dead end? It little seems to matter whether the beginning is an empirical birth or an ideological (Rousseauist) break with society.

A second connection becomes visible if we juxtapose the two proverbs with the last (and unresolved) task that the narrator sets for himself. His hope is to be able to "know the precise point at which movement is beneficial ["bienfaisant"] and where it is fatal (VII, 596). In other words: the question must be to determine when, in a given sequence, an act is oriented toward progress or already toward decline. And here, the concluding paragraph permits us to see that there is no crucial turning point. No movement can be divorced from its eventual fatal consequences—whether that movement is empirical or ideological. For Balzac—as for Kleist—the crisis of knowledge turns on the (impossible) problem of defining crucial distinctions. But whereas Kleist seems to struggle with the impossibility of keeping opposite concepts separate, Balzac struggles with the impossibility of controlling the causality of a sequence. For Balzac in his "Théorie de la démarche" the "death of meaning" seems to reside in the impossibility of fixing the significance of one movement and, more importantly, the impossibility of defining the moment that separates progress from decline.

THE DEATH OF MEANING ACCORDING TO BALZAC'S CRITICS

The "Théorie de la démarche" marks one example where the "idea" or "thought" is represented, in that the subject matter concerning the tangible world (of walking) cedes to an "invisible" world, where the genesis, maturation, and ultimately, evaluation of thought become the focus of the study. It is safe to say that the "Théorie de la démarche" does not bear out the antique dealer's assumption in *La Peau de chagrin* that the world of knowledge permits greater control. The preoccupation with analyzing experience does not protect the narrator from the vertigo of undifferentiated experience. This is due to the narrator's inability to determine fully the significance of a particular gesture and it is also due to his discovery that self-conscious knowledge—far from protecting the beauty of movement—actually helps to corrupt it. The analysis of theoretical knowledge does not, then, permit the analyst to determine causes more effectively; even his self-reflexive language is still immersed in the empiricism of temporality ["une idée a trois âges," that is, "an idea has three ages"]. In the final analysis, a text that preoccupies itself with the condition for meaning ultimately seems to discover that the representation of ideas must remain tautological.[8]

A poetics of thought might seem to put us at quite a remove from a study of death in Balzac's short prose. And yet, the link between "thinking" and death for Balzac is twofold. Added on to the metaphorical treatment of death as the "limit of thought" comes Balzac's preoccupation with thought as a corruptive, deadly force. This insight can be supported by Maurice Bardèche's discussion of Balzac's career as a novelist. Bardèche chooses 1830 as a crucial turning point in Balzac's writing, by noting that the author fuses his three essential talents—the ability to observe, to write, and to "philosophize." Bardèche sees Balzac discovering his primary task in 1830, a task that will continue to orientate the project of the *Comédie humaine*:

> Le romancier va explorer la vie sociale guidé par l'idée qu'il vient de découvrir, la puissance destructrice de la pensée.[9]
>
> The novelist is going to explore social life, guided by the idea that he has just discovered, [which is] the destructive power of thought.

It is in the *Etudes philosophiques*, however, that the poetics of thought is particularly focused: the quest to discover the causes underlying the "effects of society" is accompanied, almost even overshadowed by the task to unmask the deadliness of thought. In the preface to the *Etudes philosophiques* (supervised by Balzac) we learn that one axiom provides the common denominator of the diverse texts in this section:

> "La vie décroît en raison directe de la puissance des désirs ou de la dissipation des idées." . . . il [Balzac] montre *l'idée* exagérant *l'instinct*, arrivant à la passion, et qui, incessamment placée sous le coup des influences sociales, devient désorganisatrice. (VI, 704)

> "Life diminishes in direct proportion to the power of desires and the dissipation of ideas." . . . he [Balzac] shows the *idea* engendering *instinct*, reaching passion, and which—placed unceasingly in the grip of social influences—becomes disruptive.

Although it may be reassuring to have discovered an underlying theme, which promises to guarantee the logical coherence of the *Etudes philosophiques*, it cannot be overlooked that the concepts *idée* and *pensée* remain empty, undefined terms. If we search for definitions in the preface, we can discover a list detailing *examples* of ideas. What seems to distinguish the "idea" from appearance or experience is simply the level of theoretical abstraction involved. Among other examples we find the idea of happiness, of heredity, of maternal love and paternity, of avarice, art, and even of crime. The final example, *Louis Lambert*, augments the degree of abstraction, since in this philosophical study we find "thought killing the thinker" (VI, 704–5). With the exception of the last example, each of the characterizations of the "idea as harbinger of death" is rooted in the world of experience. Whereas earlier the idea was associated with temporality, here the idea is translated into a particularly intense form of experience. And indeed, a few years later—in 1842—"thought" potentially becomes a new, ethereal substance, so that the original disjunction between matter and intellect is close to being undone:

> Si, par des faits incontestables, la pensée est rangée un jour parmi les fluides qui ne se révèlent que par leurs effets et dont la substance échappe à nos sens même aggrandis par tant de moyens mécaniques, il en sera de ceci comme de la sphéricité de la terre. . . . Notre avenir restera le même. (I, 54)

> If, through indisputable facts, thought is one day classified among the fluids that only reveal themselves through their effects and whose substance escapes even our senses augmented by mechanical means, this will be like the sphericity of earth. . . . Our future will stay the same.

More interesting than the deconstructive realization that the primary antithesis between thought and substance is unraveling is the realization that Balzac's attempt to define the "idea" is itself determined by historical context. The Balzacian definition of the idea, which stresses its material and spiritual characteristics, results from a primary choice aimed at determining which condition of meaning might guarantee the quality of knowledge. Even Balzac seems quite aware of the relativity of his own knowledge; his is a "science" that will continually develop and seek to perfect itself.

The intersection of thought and death in Balzac's narratives is an important one, and it has more far-reaching consequences than the realization that assuming a philosophical or scientific stance does not provide any more power or stability than the more familiar masterful roles. More interesting in the connection between a poetics of ideas and of death is the possibility of anchoring Balzac's own epistemological anxieties more firmly in his own historical context—and this has been a strategy undertaken by many of the critics intent on deciphering what might constitute the primary epistemological concepts in the *Comédie humaine.*

Two dominant schools of thought become perceptible at this point. Critics either choose a structural or more static model, or they select a dynamic principle as the key guaranteeing the coherence of Balzac's many narratives. For the first approach the representation of thought becomes the illustration of one key concept in the *Comédie humaine: the unity of composition* (I, 51) or, as the fictional Balthasar Claës will call it, the "Absolute." Although Claës sees in the discovery of the unitary principle the possibility of harnessing all its energy (and competing ultimately with God [VI, 636]), the novelist sets himself a less ambitious task. His belief that "there is only one animal" (I, 51) grants his entire project a common denominator. The diversity of his text will reside in noting the intersection of changing, external circumstances and the "one animal."

The boundaries of such an all-encompassing concept are temporal. If one emphasizes the unity of a far-reaching project, one seems at the same time to be stressing the necessary closure of that system. Theoretically, at least, the openendedness (or future) of the project seems threatened. Critics such as Bernard Leuilliot deny that limit by insisting that "wholeness" is imposed after the fact; it must be understood retrospectively.[10] Leuilliot argues that a retrospective "auto-contemplation" reshapes a project, granting it "unity of composition," and he concludes: "Ainsi *la digression est la condition de possibilité de l'unité de composition. Elle est ce qui fait que tous les livres puissent n'en former qu'un*" ["Thus, *digression is the condition for the possibility of the unity of composition. Because of [digression], all books can form only one [work]*"].[11] Leuilliot is certainly right to emphasize that for Balzac the return of the characters ["le retour des personnages"] constitutes a form of digression meant to reinforce the impression of wholeness in the *Comédie humaine.* Nonetheless, his study helps to reveal the difficulty of distinguishing "unity" from digression, once "wholeness" becomes a retrospective category. Most significantly, if the governing principle is simply "unity of composition," the project—by not easily appropriating new elements—seems unable to maintain a forward thrust. Here, then, is one oblique form of the deadliness of an "idea."

Françoise Gaillard emphasizes the historical debate of Balzac's time over defining what might be the "unity of composition," and she, even more clearly, notes the "temporal" limits of the concept. At stake in the scientific model is the debate between the scientists, Cuvier and Saint-Hilaire:

> Cuvier partait d'un donné: les espèces, et ne s'intéressait qu'à montrer que chacune obéissait à une nécessité interne, *formelle* . . . dans la théorie de Geoffroy Saint-Hilaire le changement n'affecte que les formes, donnant naissance aux espèces, et laisse l'animal, unité originelle, inchangé en son fond, *conservé*.[12]

> Cuvier proceeded from a given: the species, and was only interested in showing that each obeyed an internal, *formal* necessity . . . in the theory of Saint Hilaire, the change only affects the forms, giving birth to species, and leaves the animal unchanged, *conserved* in its core.

Balzac clearly does choose Saint-Hilaire's model over Cuvier's (I, 51), and Gaillard allows us to perceive the significance of this choice. Here the denial of change and, ultimately, of time is at stake. Nostalgia for the past governs the desire to believe in the reversibility of history.[13] Again, the representation of the structural idea of wholeness relies, then, on refusing to look forward.

It might seem that selecting a dynamic principle as the dominant idea to be represented in the *Comédie humaine* will mark a contradiction of the findings of both Leuilliot and of Gaillard. Nevertheless, Peter Brooks in his discussion of *La Peau de chagrin* does discover an important scientific obsession of Balzac's time, which lends more weight to this dynamic principle: the nineteenth-century obsession with motors: "The self-contained motor, working through combustion . . . also corresponds to the emerging conception of human desire."[14]

But even here the search for self-propelling movement cannot be interpreted as a figure of progress. When Brooks juxtaposes the scientific model with the dynamics of narrative, he discovers, paradoxically, that—in narrative, at least—the drive forward does not necessarily point to the affirmation of a more perfect future. In fact, in narrative the thrust forward is accompanied by a continual displacement of naming, by the (dilatory) need to delay satisfaction—a need that Brooks associates elsewhere with a narrative "death instinct."[15] Brooks concludes:

> Narratives portray the motors of desire that drive and consume their plots, and they also lay bare the nature of narration as a form of human desire: the need to tell as a primary human drive that seeks to seduce and to subjugate the listener, to implicate him in the thrust of a desire that never can quite speak its name—never can quite come to the point—but that insists on speaking over and over again its movement toward that name.[16]

According to Brooks, this deferral of meaning as naming seems particularly well exemplified in Balzac's *étude philosophique, La Peau de chagrin*, even though the line separating the *refusal* from the *ability* to name is quite effaced. We can conclude then: While we find "meaning" with no forward movement in a (structural) system of closure, we find in the dynamic model "movement" accompanied by a continued suspension of meaning.

Interpreting at least the *Etudes philosophiques* in the *Comédie humaine* as a massive project devoted to representing one particular thought will permit us to perceive in what way a poetics of ideas holds within it the inescapability of narrative death. In the spatial model the "deadliness" takes the form of repetitiveness. The texts cannot progress beyond the circularity implied by the "unity of composition." And in the dynamic model narrative death takes the form of "loss or indefinite suspension of meaning."

When one studies how thought is to be represented, the stress must also be laid on the second term, on the limits of representation or of language. In fact, much of the critical focus has been on the question of how language subverts meaning in Balzac's narratives. Critics seem to fall into two camps in their discussion of how the coherence of Balzacian language is threatened. The first group tends to argue that Balzac retains his authorial control. Both Janet Beizer and, perhaps more familiarly, Roland Barthes argue that a crisis of meaning is staged in the Balzacian text, but that the possibility of thematizing such "textual decomposition" actually reinforces the continued mastery of the author. Janet Beizer uses *Le Père Goriot* as her example of "thematized textual disintegration," noting that the abdication of two paternal plots (Goriot's and Vautrin's)—while producing a "mad proliferation of familial and social relationships, "[17] does not fully entrap Rastignac in a subordinate position by the end of the novel. It is more important to recognize that the text succeeds in representing the crisis—the recognition that "over-determination, accumulation, and excess" of signification cannot act as substitutes, when "distinction and order" have been relinquished.[18]

In *S/Z*, the analysis of *Sarrasine*, Roland Barthes notes that the intersection of three different levels—financial, sexual, and rhetorical—repeats the same crisis of meaning and thus helps, once again, to thematize and thereby contain the *trouble de la représentation.*

> Les trois voies [rhétorique, de la castration, économique] conduisent à énoncer un même trouble de classement: il est mortel, dit le texte, de lever le trait séparateur, la barre paradigmatique qui permet au sens de fonctionner.[19]

> The three methods [rhetorical, of castration, economic] converge to express a similar confusion of classification: it is fatal, says the text, to lift the separating trait, the paradigmatic bar which allows meaning to function.

Both Barthes and Beizer attribute to Balzac a rather conservative strategy—one, in which the potential disintegration of society and, implicitly, language is acknowledged but suppressed. The crisis facing Balzacian language—by being thematized—is thus apparently overcome. Here, in contrast to Kleist, the narrative voice does not succumb to the anxiety surrounding the arbitrariness and therefore the infinite possibilities of uncontrolled substitution of one sign for another.

Barthes seems to suggest that if there is a crisis of language (or artistic representation), it is experienced primarily by the protagonist, Sarrasine himself. Sarrasine's anxiety lies in the relation between signifier and signified. The concern is for an "adequate" representation—and the condition for adequacy is equated with the work's ability to represent its model "totally." In *Sarrasine* this model is the "perfect woman":

> Partagée, écartée, la femme n'est qu'une sorte de dictionnaire d'objets-fétiches. Ce corps déchiré, déchiqueté . . . l'artiste . . . le rassemble en un corps total, corps d'amour enfin descendu du ciel de l'art, en qui le fétichisme s'abolit et par qui Sarrasine guérit. . . . Malice du langage: une fois rassemblé pour se *dire*, le corps total doit retourner à la poussière des mots, à l'égrenage des détails, à l'inventaire monotone des parties, à l'émiettement: le langage défait le corps, le renvoie au fétiche.[20]

> Divided, spread apart, woman is only a sort of dictionary of fetish-objects. The artist . . . reassembles this torn, mutilated body . . . into a total body, a body of love finally descended from the heaven of art, in which fetishism is abolished and by which Sarrasine is cured. . . . Malice of language: once reassembled in order to speak *itself*, the total body must return to the dust of words, to the picking off of details, to the monotonous inventory of parts, to being frittered away: language undoes the body, returns it to the fetish.

Barthes' description of Sarrasine's dilemma allows us to perceive echoes of Balzac's own preoccupations, as these are articulated in his "Avant-Propos" of 1842. The limit of a project devoted to "total representation"—whether this be of a woman or of Society in its entirety—resides potentially in the fragmentation of the reproduced image. Opposed to a strategy of "wholeness" or "completion" is not the slippery substitution of one term by another (cf. Kleist's crisis of meaning) but rather the sign as fragmented image, pointing simultaneously to the unbridgeable gap between the sign and its model.

Although very few of the critical studies of Balzac's narratives touch directly upon the crisis implicit in fragmentation, most of them provide different descriptions (and even evaluations) of how narrative shattering takes place.

The crisis presented by fragmentation can be approached "sociologically," although in such accounts the evaluation tends to be primarily a negative one. In this line of inquiry it is the "public" that loses its identity as a whole community. Or, as Christopher Prendergast puts it, Balzac essentially presents the dangers of "individuation." Prendergast goes on to define the implications of this crisis:

> As signs multiply, meanings fluctuate, the "public" fragments, the question that presses itself upon Balzac is how to gather up this heterogenous, mobile and often deceptive material into a unified and coherent whole: what stands for what, what is the "measure" of things, what might qualify as a "common" language?[21]

For Prendergast the fragmentation of the public leads ultimately to the fragmented word. There is no longer any central meaning upon which a community can agree.[22]

Prendergast sees Balzac skirting "linguistic anarchy" by recognizing the dangers of "polysemy."[23] But where Prendergast identifies polysemy, others simply see "plurality." For critics like Martin Kanes the loss of a fixed, central perspective simply leads to the necessity of constantly juxtaposing and modifying (subjective) interpretations concerning the significance of the "world as text." For him "fragmentation (of subjective perspectives)" acts as a call to creativity, insisting on the relativity of points of view and on the need to generate words.[24]

Nonetheless, with or without negative connotations, Kanes and Prendergast connect the existence of a fragmented public with the loss of stable, ordered signification. Narrative death understood as fragmentation can take the form of overabundant, shattered perspectives annihilating the possibility of fixing, let alone communicating meaning.

Aside from affecting the "referent," fragmentation is seen to touch upon the signifier as well as upon the signified. The study of the fragmented form (or language) leads to a heightened level of metatextuality. A form is chosen by Balzac that appears to be quite traditional, but the simplicity of Balzac's choice is misleading.

Prendergast in his study of melodrama in Balzac's prose identifies the figure of Hulot (in *La Cousine Bette*) as an initially "traditional" persona who begins to lose his social contours, thus implicitly calling into question the adequacy of that convention known as "character."[25] But it is Fredric Jameson's study of Balzac's descriptive language that reveals perhaps most clearly how Balzac uses a form against itself in order to shatter its appeal to self-evident meaning.

Jameson notes that Balzac makes use of several codes at once to draw attention to the inadequacy of all three descriptive forms. He divides the Balzacian portrait into three sections by analyzing the status of one detail: the whiteness of the protagonist's linen. In the first reading the detail invites the reader to interpret the protagonist's social standing—whiteness is equivalent to aristocratic elegance—while the second code, that of sexuality, identifies the character as a virile man, always at the ready. The final, financial, code undoes the accuracy of the first two codes or, as Jameson puts it, "unmasks" their "illusions" by providing the rather prosaic explanation that the protagonist is boarding with a laundress.[26] Jameson goes on to comment on the significance of this overabundance of codes:

> The illusory richness of the older codes is demystified, and stripped of its capacity to mislead, but at the same time nothing replaces it but the abstract system of financial cause and effect itself.[27]

The deliberate lack of coherence between the three levels (or codes) of meaning highlights the possibility that Balzac may be experimenting with acts of narrative destruction. He is demonstrating, as it were, the inadequacy of formal conventions (such as character or genre). The wholeness as well as the effectiveness of form is shattered by the disjunction between form and content (in the earlier examples) or by an excess of narrative signals.

"Fragmentation" is, then, discussed either as a trap to be avoided—subverting the possibility of meaningful language—or as an affirmative, subversive strategy—forcing a necessary reworking of outdated forms. Once the discussion turns away from the relation between word and word to the relation of signifier and signified, we find again that critics are divided on how to evaluate the disjunction between description and vision. Janet Beizer, for one, interprets this disjunction in terms of an anxiety. She notes the inadequacy of language to capture sufficiently the extent of an author's "vision." That symbol of inadequacy acts as a reminder of the proximity of the death of language and the death of meaning. Lucien Dällenbach, on the other hand, emphasizes the creativity (of multiple readings) generated by the disparity between word and signified.[28]

Balzac's preoccupation with "thought" in his corpus highlights, on the one hand, the different ways in which ideas are also subject to the principle of death—either by being subject to temporality themselves or by introducing a paralyzing closure or even by evoking a dynamic open-endedness that works to undermine the possibility of meaning. On the other hand, once the focus turns to the question of *representing* thought, the nature of the crisis seems to change and, as the different critical studies show, the crisis seems to turn around the prevalence of the "fragment" as the (deathly) limit of Balzacian narrative. Nonetheless, the shattering of form is not necessarily perceived as a limitation brought on by the historical context. Several critics attempt to see in fragmentation a strategy meant to explore newer codes of creativity. The self-destruction of a text—on the level of its narrativity—becomes the precondition for a new form. The despair with older (scientific) as well as narrative models becomes, potentially, the dynamic thrust helping to produce a new, more elusive object of representation. It is at this point that Davin's 1835 account of Balzac's originality—although meant to illuminate the methodology of the *Etudes de moeurs*—sheds light on the question how the pursuit of narrative self-destruction can become the source of a new creative style:

> Observateur sagace et profond, il épiait incessamment la nature; puis, lorsqu'il l'a eu surprise, il l'a examinée avec des précautions infinies, il l'a regardée vivre et se mouvoir; il a suivi le travail des fluides et de la pensée; *il l'a décomposée, fibre à fibre, et n'a commencé à la reconstruire que lorsqu'il a eu deviné les plus imperceptibles mystères de sa vie organique et intellectuelle.* (I, 599, my emphasis)
>
> Shrewd and profound observer, he watched nature closely and incessantly; then, when he had surprised it, he examined it with infinite precautions, he watched it live and move; he followed the work of fluids and of thought; *he decomposed it fibre by fibre, and did not begin reconstructing it until he had guessed the most imperceptible mysteries of its organic and intellectual life.* By recomposing it through this heated galvanism, by these enchanted injections that give life to bodies, he showed to us [nature] trembling with a new animation, that astounds and charms us.

OVERCOMING NARRATIVE DEATH; OR, THE STRATEGY OF FRAGMENTATION: A STUDY OF *LOUIS LAMBERT*

It is in Balzac's short prose where "textual decomposition" seems most prevalent. A shorter text deliberately restricts its narrative flow, by imposing "external" limits on its length. But—typically for Balzacian récits—narrative splintering seems also to characterize their internal structure. We need only to think of *L'Auberge rouge* (1831), *Maître Cornélius* (1831), *La Grande Bretèche* (1830) (incidentally only part of another narrative text: *Etude de femme* and referred to again in *La Muse du département*), *L'Elixir de longue vie* (1830), *Gobseck* (1830), *Le Colonel Chabert* (1832), *Adieu* (1830), *Gambara* (1837), *Honorine* (1843), and *Louis Lambert* (1833)—the list is not exhaustive. Often in these tales an initial first-person narrator must reconstruct or solve an enigma by seeking out various dispersed (sometimes self-contradictory) storytellers. The brevity of the short narrative does not always protect its coherence.

There is one text among these examples that highlights two of our central preoccupations in this chapter: *Louis Lambert*. First, this récit represents an example of a "fragmented" text and, indeed, this fragmentation is even thematized.[29] It becomes a topic that is both explored and experienced by the narrator. *Louis Lambert* is also, we may recall, the story of a "thinker destroyed by thought," so that in many ways we may expect to discover in the récit a poetics of the idea pushed to its limit. It is the narrator's attempt to order the facts of Lambert's life—to plot and explain the trajectory of his progress or ultimate decay—that both drives the text forward and leads to the intersection of the poetics of the idea and the process of splintering present in the récit.

Lambert's death occurs at the end of the text, and yet the significance of this moment remains highly ambiguous, since the text's structure renders problematic the interpretation of this ending. Although the narrator begins confidently with a traditional description of the origins of the gifted protagonist, he soon is forced to deviate from this "omniscient," continuous narrative by inserting Lambert's letters and, later, fragments of the protagonist's letters. Eventually, he must transcribe fragments of Lambert's final discontinuous utterances. This visible breakdown of a coherent story seems to point to a crisis in narrative. At this point it is not clear, however, whether the narrative splintering is being used to demonstrate the general limits of linear, causal description or whether it is simply the narrator, who has been contaminated by his subject matter—Louis gradually refusing (continuous) speech.

The narrator's reliability cannot, perhaps, be guaranteed, since he admits to a feeling of great kinship with Lambert. Together as children they constituted, after all, the team *le Poète-et-Pythagore.* Indeed, the unnamed narrator does directly note the magnetic pull of Lambert's ecstatic, mad vision upon him. He is afraid to cede to that exaltation and thus does not return to visit Louis at the end of the story.

> Je redoutai de me retrouver dans cette atmosphère énivrante où l'extase était contagieuse. Chacun aurait éprouvé comme moi l'envie de se précipiter dans l'infini, de même que les soldats se tuaient tous dans la guérite où s'était suicidé l'un d'eux au camp de Boulogne. (VII, 323)

> I was afraid to place myself again in that heavy atmosphere, where ecstasy was contagious. Any man would have felt as I did, a longing to throw himself into the infinite, just as one soldier after another killed himself in a certain sentry box where one had committed suicide in the camp at Boulogne.[30]

Paradoxically, however, it is this articulated awareness, this refusal to participate in Louis's ecstatic vision, that lends the narrator a certain air of authoritative objectivity and credibility.

The complexity of *Louis Lambert* does not only revolve around the question of the narrator's reliability. The greater knot is the evaluation of Lambert himself—whether his story is that of a genius turned mad or of a genius achieving inarticulable, intellectual freedom from physical constraints. Lambert's discontinuous utterances can be interpreted either as a loss of causal thought, culminating in complete silence and aphasia or as the laconic but brilliant utterances of a thinker able to bypass the slower intellectual processes more common to "philosophers," bound by the laws of temporality.

The narrator, while still a young boy, prefers the second explanation. He notes that after long contemplations, "Louis ne me disait qu'un mot, mais ce mot annonçait une immense rêverie" (VII, 295) ["Louis only told me one word but that word indicated an immense meditation" (my translation)]. The fragment is not necessarily a symptom of disintegrating speech, but can be interpreted as the condensed sign of an entire system of thought. This is also the argument set forward by Pauline, Louis's fiancée near the end of the récit. For her, Louis's mental ability is so far advanced that he chooses in part not to communicate the sequence of his ideas:

> Souvent, après avoir parlé d'un objet frivole, innocent point de départ de quelque rapide méditation, un penseur oublie ou tait les liaisons abstraites qui l'ont conduit à sa conclusion, et reprend la parole en ne montrant que le dernier anneau de cette chaîne de réflexions. Les gens vulgaires à qui cette vélocité de vision mentale est inconnue, ignorant le travail intérieur de l'âme, se mettent à rire du rêveur, et le traitent de fou . . . Louis est toujours ainsi: sans cesse il voltige à travers les espaces de la pensée. (VII, 321)

> Which of us has not often known what it is to think of some futile thing and be led on to some serious reflection through the ideas or memories it brings in its train? Not infrequently, after speaking about some trifle, the simple starting point of a rapid train of reflections, a thinker may forget or be silent as to the abstract connection of ideas leading to his conclusion, and speak again only to utter the last link in the chain of his meditations. Inferior minds, to whom this swift mental vision is a thing unknown, who are ignorant of the spirit's inner workings, laugh at the dreamer . . . and regard him as a madman. Louis is always in this state; he soars perpetually through the spaces of thought. (L, 264–65)

This refusal to accept Louis's madness reveals more than sheer perversity. Louis's story does not simply provide the reader with another literary example of madness. He potentially becomes exemplary of a new form of progress, where increased social and linguistic control is seen to be less desirable than the gradual withdrawal from the physical world.[31] Indeed, before his madness has struck him, Lambert is quoted describing a new pattern of progress:

> Il avait tâché de lier les phénomènes moraux entre eux par une chaîne d'effets, en suivant pas à pas tous les actes de l'intelligence, commençant par les simples mouvements de l'instinct animal qui suffit à tant d'êtres . . . puis, allant à l'agrégation des pensées, arrivant à la comparaison, à la réflexion, à la méditation, enfin à l'extase et à la catalepsie. Certes, Lambert crut avec la naïve conscience du jeune âge avoir fait le plan d'un beau livre en échelonnant ainsi ces divers degrés des puissances intérieures de l'homme. (VII, 319)

> He had been trying to link mental phenomena together by a series of results, following the processes of the intellect step by step, from their beginnings as those simple, purely animal impulses of instinct, which are all-sufficient to many human beings . . . then going on to the aggregation of ideas and rising to comparison, reflection, meditation, and finally ecstasy and catalepsy. Lambert, of course, in the artlessness of youth, imagined that he had laid down the lines of a great work when he thus built up a scale of the various degrees of man's mental powers. (L, 258)

Louis's early projection of his own fate helps to problematize the orientation of the *Etudes philosophiques.* Lambert represents "the thinker killed by his thinking," but at the same time this fate seems to be of his own choice and making. For him his catalepsis or voluntary paralysis constitutes an ideal of intellectual progress. True knowledge, by moving beyond causal or continuous thought, seems only attainable at the cost of the voluntary suspension of life.

Louis's intellectual pursuits do not appear to be completely arbitrary. They are echoed implicitly in the narrative structure. First, the narrator attempts to stay within the constraints of temporality and logic by trying to explain "how a so-well-organized mind could have lost its way" (VII, 319, my translation). The explanation draws on Louis's life and on his new engagement in order to reconstruct the situation, which might have brought on the "crisis." However, the rational reconstruction—although logical—falls short of providing solace to the listener, here Louis's uncle. The causal description does not fill the void left by Louis.

Equally, if we consider the goals of the narrator, we can see that he wishes to make us understand the "intellectual history" of Lambert and that he must draw on Lambert's true "interior life" in order to achieve his goal. He hopes to be able to "organize" again the life of Lambert, by simply substituting more traditional events with Lambert's "intellectual experiences" (VII, 311). But the narrator is quick to note that a text devoted to the "internal world" can no longer be completely bound by chronology. The "disorganization" of the text constitutes at the same time its superiority to more familiar narrative forms.

> Il laissait, suivant son expression, *l'espace derrière lui.* Mais je ne veux pas anticiper sur les phases intellectuelles de sa vie. Malgré moi déjà, je viens d'intervertir l'ordre dans lequel je dois dérouler l'histoire de cet homme qui transporte toute son action dans sa pensée, comme d'autres placent toute leur vie dans l'action.

> He left *space behind him,* to use his own words. But I will not here anticipate the intellectual phases of his life. Already, in spite of myself, I have reversed the order in which I ought to tell the history of this man, who transferred all his activities to thinking, as others throw all their life into action. (L, 161; my emphasis)

Through the subject matter, the traditional method of causality used to link disparate sections of a narrative cedes to a structure where a greater, simultaneous interconnectedness or unity seems to provide the coherence of the account.

Even if parallels exist between Lambert's intellectual quest and the narrative structure, the one argument that undermines the supremacy of Louis's fragmentation and silence is his recorded death. This ending potentially seals off any discussion that in *Louis Lambert* we may have found a new form of intellectual progress. It could be argued that Lambert experiences several forms of death in the récit. The most final of deaths occurs at the end of the text, where Louis's physical death is accompanied by the death of his memory. No written text marks the place of his burial; Louis's story is meant to die with his body. The tombstone as opaque fragment seems to indicate that the history of Lambert's struggles are outside mainstream considerations.[32]

> Son tombeau consiste en une simple croix de pierre, sans nom, sans date. Fleur née sur le bord d'un gouffre, elle devait y tomber inconnue avec ses couleurs et ses parfums inconnus. Comme beaucoup de gens incompris, n'avait-il pas souvent voulu se plonger avec orgueil dans le néant pour y perdre les secrets de sa vie! (VII, 324)

> His tombstone is a plain stone cross, without name or date. Like a flower that has blossomed on the margin of a precipice, and drops into it, its colors and fragrance all unknown, it was fitting that he, too, should fall. Like many another misprized soul, he had often yearned to dive haughtily into the void, and abandon there the secrets of his own life. (L, 274)

Whether this "outside" must be translated as "falling short of the mark" rather than as "moving beyond normal perspectives" is left unanswered by the text.

Another figurative form of death takes place shortly before he is to undertake his marriage to Pauline. Louis attempts to castrate himself (VII, 319). Here his intellectual withdrawal from the world can be understood as a precipitous flight from (sexual) reality. Nevertheless, if his action is not completely the fruit of profound meditation, it does not result solely from intense, sexual repression. His experience is that of the incompatibility of knowledge and experience. His insights seem to poison the moments of vital plenitude. In fact, his early, wild cases of lifelessness ["... chaque sens se détend ... l'imagination s'éteint, les désirs meurent, et ma force humaine subsiste seule" (VII, 315) ("... each sense becomes slack ... the imagination fades, desires die, and only my human force lives on") (my translation)] seem to be generated by his recognizing the human condition:

> Il [le génie raisonneur/le démon impitoyable] flétrit la plus belle oeuvre en m'en montrant le principe, et me dévoile le mécanisme des choses en m'en cachant les résultats harmonieux. En ces moments terribles ... je souhaite la mort en y voyant un repos. (VII, 315)

> He [the reasoning genius/pitiless demon] mars the fairest work by showing me its skeleton, and reveals the mechanism of things while hiding the beautiful results. At those terrible moments ... I long for death to give me rest. (L, 245)

There is, at least, one other representation of (figurative) death in this text that applies to Lambert. The paralysis experienced by Lambert—supposedly voluntary—reduces his body to a near cadaver. His mental retreat from the world leaves a decrepit, feminized body, one reminiscent of an earlier historical epoch. ["Ses cheveux, aussi longs que ceux d'une femme, tombaient sur ses épaules, et entouraient sa figure de manière à lui donner de la ressemblance avec les bustes qui représentent les grands hommes du siècle de Louis XIV" (VII, 320) ("His hair was as long as a woman's, falling over his shoulders and hanging about his face, giving him a resemblance to the busts of the great men of the time of Louis XIV") (L, 262)]. Lambert no longer belongs to his own time. Moreover, the loss of sensation familiarly associated with the experience of death is focused in Louis's eyes. The narrator exclaims upon seeing him:

> Hélas! déjà ridé, déjà blanchi, enfin déjà plus de lumière dans ses yeux, devenus vitreux comme ceux d'un aveugle.... C'était un débris arraché à la tombe, une espèce de conquête faite par la vie sur la mort, ou par la mort sur la vie. (VII, 320)

> Alas! he was wrinkled, white-headed, his eyes dull and lifeless as those of the blind. . . . He was a wreck snatched from the grave, a conquest of life from death—or of death from life! (L, 263)

The detail of the eyes hardly seems fortuitous, although it does mark a moment of ambivalence in the text. Louis's lack of physical sight may be hinting at his loss of intellectual vision, and yet it also places him indirectly in a literary tradition—that of the blind seer endowed with prophetic vision.

In each of these representations of death, then, a certain ambivalence exists—an ambivalence that helps to make Lambert's story less one-dimensional, indeed, which characterizes death in a slightly more positive light. The refusal to participate in life becomes the condition for greater wisdom and knowledge, and in this scheme of things the actual moment of death marks a victory of the internal self over the external one. The narrator even is unable to discern which principle—life or death—has won the upper hand; the two terms have become almost indistinguishable. The youthful Lambert—following Swedenborg—has, in fact, redefined "selfhood" in order to transform death into a moment of intellectual and spiritual rebirth.

> Selon Swedenborg, l'ange serait l'individu chez lequel l'être intérieur réussit à triompher de l'être extérieur. . . . Si, faute d'avoir une vue translucide de sa destinée, il fait prédominer l'action corporelle au lieu de corroborer sa vie intellectuelle, toutes ses forces passent dans le feu de ses sens extérieurs, et l'ange périt lentement par cette matérialisation des deux natures. Dans le cas contraire, s'il substante son intérieur des essences qui lui sont propres, l'âme l'emporte sur la matière et tâche de s'en séparer. Quand leur séparation arrive sous cette forme que nous appelons la Mort, l'ange, assez puissant pour se dégager de son enveloppe, demeure et commence sa vraie vie. (VII, 296)

> According to Swedenborg, the angel is an individual in whom the inner being conquers the external being. . . . If, for lack of a lucid appreciation of his destiny, he allows bodily action to predominate, instead of confirming his intellectual being, all his powers will be absorbed in the use of his external senses, and the angel will slowly perish by the materialization of both natures. In the contrary case, if he nourishes his inner being with the ailment needful to it, the soul triumphs over matter and strives to get free. When they separate by the act of what we call death, the angel, strong enough then to cast off its wrappings, survives and begins its real life. (L, 187–88)

Following this description Lambert's fall into catalepsy and death becomes the external (but misleading) manifestation of his internal blossoming. The fragment of his body—although unreadable to those unfamiliar with the "Swedenborgian code"—bears mute testimony to the desirability of physical death. At this point we see, then, that the representation of ideas *is* deadly, but that this deadliness constitutes the goal toward which Lambert has been mentally striving.

If physical death has become desireable, then "narrative death"—in the form of internal shattering—would seem to grant the "fragment" positive values as well. And indeed, the text does set out to show how the "fragment" provides access to knowledge that the more constrained logical sequences cannot hope to uncover. A first example of the treasures of fragmentation is presented near the beginning of the récit. The narrator first points to Louis's ability of total recall. No knowledge is ever lost to him—neither places, words, things, faces, or even thoughts. Disparate elements can be reassembled by him in order to reconstruct exactly past experience.

> Cette puissance s'appliquait également aux actes les plus insaisissables de l'entendement. Il se souvenait, suivant son expression, non seulement du gisement des pensées dans le livre où il les avait prises, mais encore des dispositions de son âme à des époques éloignées. Par un privilège inouï, sa mémoire pouvait donc lui retracer les progrès et la vie entière de son esprit. (VII, 288)

> And this power he could exert with equal effect with regard to the most abstract efforts of the intellect. He could remember, as he said, not merely the position of a sentence in the book where he had met with it, but the frame of mind he had been in at remotest dates. Thus his was the singular privilege of being able to retrace in memory the whole life and progress of his mind. (L, 160)

The process of fragmentation—Louis's pursuing a remembered word or name—allows him the escape from his present situation. Fragmentation thus marks an escape from traditional temporal limits; Louis, at least, is not bound by linear, one-directional chronology.

In *Louis Lambert* this process of fragmentation, which shatters the coherence of the present in its search to reconstruct as perfectly as possible the past, is also equated with the work of the narrator. Although the constant interruption of his voice—while calling his personal authority into question—grants greater authenticity to his narrative reconstruction of Lambert's story, this hardly seems to be the only motivation behind the fragmentary structure. At the end of the récit, for instance, the narrator freely admits that he prefers depicting his "impressions" of Lambert rather than providing a more "poetic" development of "visions" concerning Lambert's "incomplete" being (cf. VII,

323). His motivation for this decision comes at an earlier stage. He speaks of the care he has used in handling the palimpsests of Lambert's letters:

> une lettre dont on se souvient toujours, dont chaque phrase est le fruit d'une rêverie, dont chaque mot excite de longues contemplations, où le sentiment le plus effréné de tous comprend la nécessité des tournures les plus modestes. . . . (VII, 312)

> a letter he will never forget, each line the result of a reverie, each word the subject of long cogitation, while the most unbridled passion known to man feels the necessity of the most reserved utterance. . . . (L, 238)

The presence of such fragments within the narrative defers the finality of the narrator's own interventions. The text remains open to the sensitivity and, ultimately, to the interpretation of each new reader. The shattered linear continuity of the narrative does, then, permit a greater creativity and flexibility in the reconstruction of personal narratives.

But in Louis's case the preoccupation with fragmentation also transcends the personal. Lambert's captivation by the freedom of "internal life" is prepared by his fascination with isolated words. He reads dictionaries and meditates upon disparate words in order to reconstruct imaginatively a cultural history of ideas. In short, the word as fragment generates a flight of imaginative thought:

> "Souvent," me dit-il, en parlant de ses lectures, "j'ai accompli de délicieux voyages, embarqué sur un mot dans les abîmes du passé. . . . La plupart des mots ne sont-ils pas teints de l'idée qu'ils représentent extérieurement? . . . L'assemblage des lettres, leurs formes, la figure qu'elles donnent à un mot, dessinent exactement, suivant le caractère de chaque peuple, des êtres inconnus dont le souvenir est en nous." (VII, 287)

> "Often," he said to me when speaking of his studies, "often have I made the most delightful voyage, floating on a word down the abyss of the past. . . . Are not most words colored by the idea they represent? . . . The combination of letters, their shapes, and the look they give to the word are the exact reflection, in accordance with the character of each nation, of the unknown beings whose traces survive in us." (L, 158)

The creativity of reconstruction goes beyond the Cratylist fantasy, where the word might share the qualities of the referent it represents. The word characterizes the speaker rather than its referent—and it is the residual history of speakers originating from different epochs, places, and cultures that becomes accessible to a thinker like Lambert. Through discontinuous fragments Louis hopes ultimately to discover an etymologically based history of the world.

Lambert's redefinition of time—which includes perfect reconstructions of past experience and thought as well as the rewriting of the cultural heritage, transcending the boundaries of temporality—marks a quest that ultimately will undo all time. Despite the constant emphasis on reconstruction—on the part of the narrator as well as of Louis—it is not the "myth" or plot that is privileged in *Louis Lambert* but rather the isolated word and its evocative power. At the end of Louis's quest—coinciding perhaps with his final removal from time and corporeality—is the desire for "Flesh becoming the Word" again ["Fragment XXI—'Et la Chair Se Fera LE VERBE, ELLE DEVIENDRA *LA PAROLE DE DIEU*' (VII, 323)]. The fragment ultimately becomes, then, the symbol for the lost, original Word, now lost by being fractured into numerous languages and writings.

> L'antique peinture des idées humaines configurées par les formes zoologiques n'aurait-elle pas déterminé les premiers signes dont s'est servi l'Orient pour écrire ses langages? Puis *n'aurait-elle pas traditionellement laissé quelques vestiges dans nos langues modernes, qui toutes se sont partagé les débris du verbe primitif des nations*, verbe majestueux et solennel, dont la majesté, dont la solennité, décroissent à mesure que vieillissent les sociétés; dont les retentissements si sonores dans la Bible hébraïque, si beaux encore dans la Grèce, *s'affaiblissent à travers les progrès de nos civilisations successives?* (VII, 287, my emphasis)

> Was it not the ancient mode of representing human ideas as embodied in the forms of animals that gave rise to the shapes of the first signs used in the East for writing down language? Then *has it not left its traces by tradition on our modern languages, which have all seized some remnant of the primitive speech of nations*, a majestic and solemn tongue whose grandeur and solemnity decrease as communities grow old; whose sonorous tones ring in the Hebrew Bible, and still are noble in Greece, but *grow weaker under the progess of successive phases of civilization?* (L, 159, my emphasis)

A poetics of death—that includes the denial of the body in its search to represent the "idea"—coincides in *Louis Lambert* with the quest for atemporality. The theoretical rediscovery of the "primitive word"—perhaps experienced by Lambert—would permit all languages and meaning to be simultaneously present. For *Louis Lambert* within the framework of such a quest the "fragment" in its shattering of the text, in its freedom from the one-directionality of linearity becomes the most adequate symbol of such an original Word.

EXPERIMENTING WITH NARRATIVE FRAGMENTATION

Louis Lambert seems to mark a turning point in Balzac's career. According to Pierre Citron's chronology, the year 1833 represents the moment when Balzac begins to turn more and more away from his philosophical tales to the *Etudes de moeurs.* He also begins to reassemble his texts in order to construct a more systematic, nearly whole corpus.[33] The pursuit of a narrative strategy that might emphasize the representation of ideas—and forms of (literary) atemporality—seems, by this development, to have been abandoned.

Nonetheless, Balzac does continue to write short prose, and this short fiction is still characterized by fragmented narrative structures. *Louis Lambert* can be distinguished from these later "fragmented" texts in that the later narratives tend to introduce framed stories. The preliminary story is generally interrupted by other tales; the text no longer seems to confront the impossibility of its being narrated.

The dilemma facing the narrator of *Louis Lambert* focuses on the inadequacy of sequence; both the continuous series of events in the narrating of Lambert's life and the logical order of ideas constituting thought become more and more problematical. In the later short prose, however, it is the relation between the narrator and his textual product that replaces the earlier, more troubling narrative crisis. The artistic narrators discover that the narrative does not necessarily stand in a relation of continuity with the writer. An explanation for the need to shatter that illusory relation arises from the juxtaposition of *Un drame au bord de la mer* (1835) with *Albert Savarus* (1842). In the latter short novel, the desire to write one's own story simply by masking the proper names leaves the writer vulnerable to manipulation by another character easily able to decipher the text. This "reader," eager to continue the writer's story—through knowledge gleaned from the transparently autobiographical text—is able to stage the downfall of Albert, the first author. In *Un drame au bord de la mer,* the act of writing is used in an opposite way in order to free the listener-cum-writer from the horror of a tale of infanticide. The voracious, murdered child begins to resemble the narrator's own written text, since both child and récit threaten to enthrall and paralyze the "parent" or writer.

Three positions are, in effect, examined in *Un drame au bord de la mer:* the vulnerability of the self before "entering fully into life" (before producing either children or texts) is supplemented by the vision of destruction produced by the devouring consumption of the "enfant terrible," which, in turn, is followed by the vision of powerlessness that the paternal hermit, having punished his progeny with death, seems to occupy on the edge of the sea. The hermit is speechless, characterized only by his burning gaze.

The narrator's response to this general hopelessness and paralysis is, essentially, to repeat the gesture of the murderer. He turns to writing in the hope that by becoming a narrator he will be successful in casting off his own text (his self-image of hopelessness):

> J'étais si cruellement tourmenté par les visions que j'avais de ces trois existences [père, mère et fils], qu'elle [Pauline] me dit:—Louis, écris cela, tu donneras le change à la nature de cette fièvre.
>
> Je vous ai donc écrit cette aventure, mon cher oncle; mais elle m'a déjà fait perdre le calme que je devais à mes bains et à mon séjour ici. (VII, 103)

> I was so cruelly tormented by the visions I had of these three existences [father, mother and son] that [Pauline] told me: Louis, write it down. You will probably fool the nature of this fever.
>
> I have thus written this adventure for you, my uncle; but it has already made me lose the calm that I owe these baths and my stay here!

The hope of mastering the identity crisis through writing—and the vision that such a disjunction will permit the self to return to its initial belief in its own creative ability—is, curiously, a "model" imposed by another (the loving companion, Pauline). The act of writing understood as separation, or even as a symbolic infanticide, and used as the means to return to a "whole" and "masterful" self, is thus undermined, partially because this return to wholeness is situated outside the self, but primarily because the decision marks a potential doubling of the hermit's destructive gesture. Here the narrative act only helps to fix the writer (incidentally a younger "Louis Lambert") in a bleak present. The atemporality generated by writing is experienced here chiefly in negative terms—as the loss of a future.

The text that seems to stretch to its limits a discontinuous structure[34] while reexamining a poetics of thought is *Gambara*, written in 1837. In contrast to *Louis Lambert* we can find in this text explicit denunciations levelled at the (here musical) goal of representing ideas. Gambara, the (ostensibly mad) composer, is told:

> Si au lieu de viser à exprimer des idées, et si au lieu de pousser à l'extrême le principe musical, ce qui vous fait dépasser le but, vous vouliez simplement réveiller en nous des sensations, vous seriez mieux compris, si toutefois vous ne vous êtes pas trompé sur votre vocation. Vous êtes un grand poète. (VI, 608)[35]

> If instead of aiming to express ideas, and if instead of pushing the musical principle to its extreme—which makes you overshoot the goal, you simply wanted to awaken sensations in us, you would be better understood—that is, if you are not mistaken about your vocation. You are a great poet.

As in *Louis Lambert* it is difficult to determine whether the protagonist is indeed mad. On the one hand, it is his metatextual reflections that lead him to compose cacophony rather than harmony, thus living out in the musical domain the same destiny as Frenhofer does in the world of painting in *Un chef-d'oeuvre inconnu.*[36]

The composer is happily oblivious to the chaos of his creation; he is too bound up with the theoretical content of his work, with its "subject matter," to perceive the anarchy of sounds he has produced. Gambara's opera is about the life of Mahomet, a motif which can be interpreted as the (at least partially) successful appropriation of divine immortality by a mere mortal. Here is Gambara's own commentary of his work:

> Le troisième [acte] présente Mahomet dégoûté de tout, ayant épuisé la vie, et dérobant le secret de sa mort pour devenir un Dieu, dernier effort de l'orgueil humain. . . . Ne trouvez-vous pas . . . dans cette musique vive, heurtée, bizarre, mélancolique et toujours grande, l'expression de la vie d'un épileptique enragé de plaisir, ne sachant ni lire ni écrire, faisant de chacun de ses défauts un degré pour le marchepied de ses grandeurs, tournant ses fautes et ses malheurs en triomphe? (VI, 599–600)

> The third [act] presents Mahomet, disgusted with everything, having depleted his life and concealing the secret of his death in order to become a God, last effort of human pride. . . . Don't you find . . . in this lively, jerky, bizarre, melancholy and always great music, the expression of the life of an epileptic, mad about pleasure, neither knowing how to read nor write, making of each of his faults a step on the stepladder of his grandeur, turning faults and unhappinesses into triumphs?

The musical text recovers partially the strangeness of its "epileptical and analphabetic" model. But the real goal of the musical text is, as it were, overshot. The opera was meant to capture the (happy) appropriation of defaults, even of death, in order to affirm the mastery (and immortality) of the self; instead, the opera reveals an ironic truth, an irony that is played out at the expense of the composer and one that he never manages to unravel.

The narrative context of the scene allows the reader, however, to decipher the irony. Gambara is performing his opera for the select audience of his wife and her future lover, Andrea Marcosini. With his reference to the suffering, self-effacing wife who dies (unacknowledged by her husband) in the process of sustaining his greatness, the opera enacts the drama of Gambara's own *ménage*. Both Marianina, his wife, and Andrea recognize the accuracy of the "self-portrait," and Gambara, mistakenly interpreting their emotion as a sign of their musical approbation, calls out triumphantly: "Vous me comprenez enfin" (VI, 600) ["You finally understand me"]. The truthful but unperceived depiction of Gambara's own situation is reduced to the arbitrary, cast-off, never-recognized product of an otherwise misguided and "failed" art form. The opera thus is an example of the complete disjunction between authorial intention and its product.

Gambara's compositions—by transcending the restrictions imposed by a more traditional musicology—are judged to be idiosyncratic, even mad. A cure is proposed: the reintegration of Gambara must lie in annihilating the (innovative) consciousness, which seems to be deforming his musical work. This suspension of the conscious self is represented in *Gambara* as intoxication. Only in his drunken creativity is Gambara able to "perform" beautifully and, more significantly, is he able to participate in a generally understood discourse about music. He is able for instance, to comment lucidly on the strengths and faults of Meyerbeer's *Robert-le-Diable*.[37]

Gambara's suspension of consciousness connects the poetics of death with the experience of fragmentation. The disjunction between author and his text can be understood here as a loss—a form of "authorial death." On the one hand, of course, the "intoxication" that Gambara unwittingly submits to, represents a metaphorical enactment of the death of the artist's consciousness in order that he might create. On the other hand, however, the initial dilemma of the artist's "lucid" madness—as idiosyncratic, noncommunicable language—which precedes intoxication, might be construed as a more fundamental kind of death. *Gambara*, in effect, has doubled in upon itself, creating two forms of a self's death (intoxication vs. madness) and two brands of lucidity (traditional discourse vs. the artist's translation of the principles governing his opera, *Mahomet*). Which death is the fertile one? Which lucidity is the crippling one?

This moment of interpretative crisis is reminiscent of the enigma posed by Kleist's "Die Heilige Cäcilie," where the ironic interconnection of the self's death and its "mad" vision transformed the core of the text (the "miraculous" concert) into an unreadable, even unlocatable center. In Balzac's story, Gambara chooses a position. He refuses the cure offered to him and pursues his own vision rather than allowing himself to be appropriated by the coercive and dismissive gaze of Society. At the end of the récit a sober Gambara proclaims:

> Ma musique est belle, mais quand la musique passe de la sensation à l'idée, elle ne peut avoir que des gens de génie pour auditeurs, car eux seuls ont la puissance de la développer. Mon malheur vient d'avoir écouté les concerts des anges et d'avoir cru que les hommes pouvaient les comprendre. (VI, 610)
>
> My music is beautiful, but when music passes from sensation to ideas, it can only have people of genius as listeners, for only they have the power to develop it. My misfortune comes from having heard the concerts of angels and from having believed that man would be able to understand them.

Gambara prefers the madness of his idiosyncrasy to the intoxication of tradition, although he loses his wife and his operas by pursuing his own course.

Although Gambara continues to believe in the idea as superior "object" of representation, his fate in the récit seems to call his vision into question. Gambara experiences three forms of artistic fragmentation in addition to the dissolution of his marriage. He is reduced to performing fragments of his own work to the public in order to scrape a living together. More seriously, even this truncated performance brings him no recognition. The excellence of his compositions is attributed to Rossini (VI, 610); even the authorial signature is wrested from him. Not only is public acclaim withheld from Gambara, he finally must participate in the dissemination of his written work. The paper over which he has labored becomes more valuable than his transcribed operas. The manuscript is literally fragmented—torn to pieces:

> Ainsi, trois grands opéras dont parlait ce pauvre homme . . . avaient été disseminés dans Paris et dévorés par les éventaires des revendeuses. (VI, 609–10)
>
> Thus, three great operas about which this poor man was speaking . . . had been disseminated in Paris and had been devoured by the stalls of second-hand dealers.

On the one hand, Gambara's fragmented texts still do circulate in the city of Paris. And yet, the fragment—as vehicle for represented ideas—seems in contrast to *Louis Lambert* to be stripped of its potential to evoke a more intense experience or a more complex, imaginatively restored, historical reality. Even the discontinuous narrative control experienced by the narrator in *Gambara* is integrated less directly into the dynamics of the text. Rather than hinting at the greater insights of the creator, the process of fragmentation in *Gambara* is seen to threaten the integrity and survival of the created texts.

HISTORICAL CONSIDERATIONS

Although Balzac asserts that the *Etudes philosophiques* are primarily concerned with the representation of *causes*, it seems that over time he distances himself from a "poetics of the idea." The representation of thought—that allows him to stretch the forms of narrative sequence as well as of cultural constructs of progress and power—supplants the anxiety over decline with the anxiety over the proximity of madness and genius. We can note, then, where Kleist uses narrative scenes of death in order to demonstrate the impossibility of maintaining any binary oppositions, Balzac's preoccupation with narrative enactments of death highlights first the impossibility of separating progress from decline and, then, in his quest for alternatives to the traditional models of progress, the threat of madness, incoherence, and incommunicability. The threat of the death of meaning thus also reinscribes itself in Balzac's oeuvre. Kleist and Balzac's works bear the mark of an anxiety over literal and metaphorical death, although both define this anxiety in different ways.

There is one last cultural consideration to be pursued in Balzac's anxious fascination with the fragment. If we juxtapose the texts in the *Etudes philosophiques* without considering how the *pensée qui tue* is depicted in these stories, we can note an alternate thematic pattern that helps to undermine the purely philosophical bent of the tales. Within the framework of the *Etudes philosophiques* there seems to be an overwhelming preoccupation with France's national boundaries. The concern with England (through *Melmoth reconcilié*), with Flanders (through *Maître Cornélius, Jésus Christ en Flandres,* and *La Recherche de l'Absolu*), with Italy (*Les Proscrits* and *Gambara*), and with Germany (*L'Auberge rouge*) seems to highlight those limits that represented points of strife in France's own preoccupation with determining its national shape during the Middle Ages. By describing the struggle of nations to determine their particular cultural center, the writer seems to articulate indirectly his creative anxiety over his own identity, indeed over his separate authority.

Although it might be tempting to draw parallels between the anxiety generated by the struggle to define cultural identity and authorial originality, it is more to the point to recognize simply how the preoccupation with the fragment in Balzac's corpus goes beyond literary or even epistemological concerns. Indeed, critics attempting to define the significance of Balzac's historical context tend to agree that the political repercussions associated with the fragment (interpreted as a process of fracturing) tend to be overwhelmingly negative rather than dynamic, as one might expect after considering the emergence of a partially fragmented French national identity. The phenomenon of "fragmentation" in the nineteenth century can be perceived in social terms, as Christopher Prendergast argues, and is linked with democratization (or, to use Prendergast's term, with "individualism"). Here fragmentation is understood chiefly as the dissolution of a homogenous, clearly identifiable French society—a dissolution that leads gradually to the loss of a "common language" and ultimately to the instability of meaning.[38] Or, to follow Roland Barthes' line of argument, fragmentation can be understood in economic terms. It results from the suppression of origin (associated with the shift from a "landed" to an "industrial" monarchy).[39] From this historical perspective Barthes also emphasizes the negative connotations associated with fragmentation understood temporally as loss of origin:

> En passant de la monarchie terrienne à la monarchie industrielle, la société a changé de Livre, elle est passée de la Lettre (de noblesse) au Chiffre (de fortune), du parchemin au registre, mais elle est toujours soumise à une écriture. La différence qui oppose la société féodale à la société bourgeoise, l'indice au signe, est celle-ci: l'indice a une origine, le signe n'en a pas; passer de l'indice au signe, c'est abolir la dernière (ou la première) limite, l'origine, le fondement, la butée, c'est entrer dans le procès illimité des équivalences, des représentations que rien ne vient plus arrêter, orienter, fixer, consacrer.[40]

> By passing from the landed monarchy to the industrialized monarchy, society changed Books; it passed from the Letter (of nobility) to the Figure (of fortune), from the parchment to the ledger, but it always submits to writing. The difference which opposes feudal society to bourgeois society, the index to the sign, is this one: the index has an origin; the sign does not; to pass from the index to the sign is to abolish the last (and the first) limit, the origin, the foundation, the end wall; it is to enter into the unlimited process of equivalences, of representations that nothing comes any longer to stop, orient, fix, consecrate.

Françoise Gaillard adds another dimension, when she points out that historical time marked by rupture poses another, equally grave threat. She notes that a fragmented temporal sequence points to the irreversibility of historical events, to the impossibility of returning to a more stable, conservative past.[41]

Each of these accounts emphasizes the nostalgic thrust behind Balzac's awareness of history. Janet Beizer's account is clearest here, when she refers to Balzac's longing for a lost paternal law:

> Nineteenth-century revivals of the father's laws are not, however, limited to thematic stagings of it. The realist aesthetic, with its emphasis on mimesis and its reliance on observation, omniscience, documentation, and control, may well be a nostalgic paternalistic fantasy, the broadest manifestation of the attempt to recuperate, in the novel, the authority and power of a by-gone age.[42]

At stake in all these accounts—whether it is evoked overtly or not—is Balzac's nostalgia for a lost monarchy, the lost paternal king, Louis XVI.

Each of these historical accounts, which interprets Balzac's preoccupation with a fragmented continuum, stresses the loss of meaning, loss of origin or destruction of paternal law and, consequently, leaves aside the more creative potential attributed to the literary fragment. We can see that the status of the fragment does fluctuate in Balzac's corpus. In *Louis Lambert*—when the role of the creative mind is represented—the fragmentary form hints at the possibility of passing beyond, indeed transcending, the shackles of logic and, ultimately, of life. In *Gambara*, of course, the process of fragmentation is represented as affecting predominantly the composer's texts, and in this account the fracturing of a continuum loses its creative aura.

In *Honorine* the strivings of the (shattered) creator depicted in *Louis Lambert* are juxtaposed with the destiny of the fragmented texts represented in *Gambara*; the two plots (along with the conflicting evaluations of the fragment) are held together in an uneasy tension. The ungovernable displacements in *Honorine* make it difficult to judge whose victimatization more nearly resembles that of the deposed father and whose is due, rather, to the annihilating tyranny of the father. And it is through its indeterminate, mutually unbalancing voices that *Honorine* rewrites and focuses a historical dilemma facing the generation of the 1830s and 1840s—one that is no longer oriented only by the trauma of a decapitated king. There is, after all, another, equally troubling figure in French history. As the officer Genestas points out in *Le Médecin de campagne*, France (or at least its military) has lost its father (VI, 149) with the imprisonment and death of Napoleon. It is also well known that Balzac sought both to emulate and to supplant the figure of Napoleon Bonaparte—so that even in this historical relation, the role of model and double becomes unstable. M. I. Sicard documents Balzac's own double relation to Napoleon as "continuateur" and "rival:"

> Dans la pièce où travaillait Balzac rue Cassini, se trouvait une statue de Napoléon, d'un demi-mètre de haut, avec cette inscription de la propre main d'Honoré: "Ce qu'il n'a pu achever par l'épée, je l'accomplirai par la plume."[43]

> In the room on Cassini Street, where Balzac worked, was located a statue of Napoleon, half a meter in height, with the inscription [written] by the own hand of Honoré: "What he was able to complete by the sword, I shall accomplish by the feather" [pen].

Balzac as Napoleon's double pursues in the *Comédie humaine* a guarded respect and critical judgment toward the strengths and weaknesses of the "self-made Emperor" and his creation. This rewriting of Napoleon's achievements emphasizes both Balzac's aggressive fascination by the Emperor's image and the ambivalent awareness that the Emperor has perhaps been betrayed by the inertia and resistance of his Empire.[44]

Napoleon's creation—the shaping of a new national identity of France as Empire rather than as Kingdom—is also destroyed by the resistance (and autonomy) that stems from his "fragmented" creation. Let us note, however: whereas in *Le Cabinet des antiques* Balzac anxiously unmasks the splintering of Napoleon's new creation produced by the opposition of the old aristocracy, in *La Vendetta* he criticizes Napoleon's vision, primarily on the grounds that Napoleon has failed to determine his own originality and atemporality. In the latter text Balzac points to Napoleon's continued and crippling adherence to the old Corsican tradition of the feud. It is this permissive adherence to tradition that allows the "throttling" of young energy needed to supplant the old order.

This "logic of the fragment"—of the creation turning against the creator, and the creator betraying the originality of his creation—allows us to reconsider the struggle at stake in Balzac's project. Through the example of Napoleon we can note that the construction of a national myth or of a narrative must be understood as the piecing together of the often self-contradictory and even invading narrative voices needed to make visible a narrative enigma; yet these also ultimately undermine a narrator's mastery.

This logic of the fragment—Balzac's own calling into question of progress and the discourse of power—can be applied to the entire *Comédie humaine*, since it also is marked by internal fragmentation in its abundance of titles and incomplete texts and by the novels that are themselves often structured as a sequence of fragmented sections. The troubled structure of mirroring, the shattering of the system holding creator and text (as double) in a stable relation makes perceptible the anxiety of finding both the narrator's and narrated object's positions contaminated by a destructive violence. Rather than marking simply the jubilant acceptance of self-displacement advocated in *La Cousine Bette*, the experience of the narrating self's displacement by his/her discourse can actually be read as the anxiety driving the Balzacian text forward. At stake might be the search for an alternative to the inevitable simultaneity of textual infanticide and parricide implicit in the act of narration.

NOTES

INTRODUCTION

1. Michel de Montaigne, *Essais, Tome I* (Paris: Garnier-Flammarion, 1969), p. 35. Henceforth, references to the essays of Montaigne come from volumes I, II, and III of the edition above and are indicated in my text by roman numeral (volume) and arabic number (page).

2. All translations from the French and German are mine, unless otherwise indicated.

3. Charles Baudelaire, "La Mort des artistes" in his *Les Fleurs du mal*, in *Oeuvres complètes, Bibliothèque de la Pléiade* (Paris: Gallimard, 1975), p. 127.

Here is the sonnet in its entirety:

Combien faut-il de fois secouer mes grelots
Et baiser ton front bas, morne caricature?
Pour piquer dans le but, de mystique nature,
Combien, ô mon carquois, perdre de javelots?

Nous userons notre âme en de subtils complots,
Et nous démolirons mainte lourde armature,
Ayant de contempler la grande Créature
Dont l'infernal désir nous remplit de sanglots!

Il en est qui jamais n'ont connu leur Idole,
Et ces sculpteurs damnés et marqués d'un affront,
Qui vont se martelant la poitrine et le front,

N'ont qu'un espoir, étrange et sombre Capitole!
C'est que la Mort, planant comme un soleil nouveau,
Fera s'épanouir les fleurs de leur cerveau!"

4. This interpretation is indebted in part to Professor Victor Brombert's seminar on nineteenth-century French poets, offered in the fall of 1982. In this seminar Professor Brombert analyzed the existence of two poetic projects in the nineteenth century: that of the apostle and that of the "génie." According to Professor Brombert's theory, Baudelaire, by refusing to act as the mouthpiece of a god, represented a particularly salient example of a rebellious poet, who opposed his creation to a more traditionally divine one.

5. Christa Wolf, *Kassandra* (Darmstadt: Luchterhand, 1984), p. 5.

6. Ibid., p. 27.

7. Here one is led to think, along with Kristeva and Freud, about the unrepresentable quality of death (cf. Julia Kristeva, *Black Sun, Depression and Melancholia* [New York: Columbia University Press, 1987–89], p. 138).

8. Wolf, *Kassandra*, p. 27.

9. Franz Kafka, *Tagebücher, 1910–1923*, edited by Max Brod (Frankfurt a.M.: Fischer, 1984), p. 262.

10. The officer describes the mechanism of the harrow to the explorer:

> Sowohl das Bett, als auch der Zeichner haben ihre eigne elektrische Batterie; das Bett braucht sie für sich selbst, der Zeichner für die Egge. Sobald der Mann festgeschnallt ist, wird das Bett in Bewegung gesetzt. Es zittert in winzigen, sehr schnellen Zuckungen gleichzeitig seitlich, wie auch auf und ab. . . . nur sind bei unserem Bett alle Bewegungen genau berechnet; sie müssen nämlich peinlich auf die Bewegungen der Egge abgestimmt sein. Dieser Egge aber ist die eigentliche Ausführung des Urteils überlassen.
>
> Unser Urteil klingt nicht streng. Dem Verurteilten wird das Gebot, das er übertreten hat, mit der Egge auf den Leib geschrieben.

Franz Kafka, "In der Strafkolonie" in his *Sämtliche Erzählungen*, edited by Paul Raabe (Frankfurt a.M.: Fischer, 1980), p. 103.

11. Kurz writes in his *Traum-Schrecken*:

> Sein "Ekel" vor dem Schmutz, vor dem "widerlichen Filz" (E110, 116), sein Sauberkeitswahn sind Symptome dafür, daß er die Maschine von dem sauberhalten will, was doch nach seinen eigenen Worten ihre Bestimmung ist. Die Maschine ist für ihn daher ein "Lebenswerk" (E111) in einem ganz anderen Sinn, insofern sie eine Verdrängung des Todes darstellt. . . . Insgeheim und untergründig lehnt der Offizier den alten Kommandanten, der für Todesnähe und Lebensverneinung steht, ab. Weil er sich gegen den Tod wehrt, ist daher auch sein eigener Tod keine Erlösung, kein 'Spiel'."

Gerhard Kurz, *Traum-Schrecken, Kafkas literarische Existenzanalyse* (Stuttgart: J. B. Metzlersche Verlagsbuchhandlung, 1980), p. 54–55.

12. Franz Kafka, "In der Strafkolonie," p. 120.

13. Ibid., p. 123.

14. Ibid., p. 113.

15. Ibid., p. 121.

16. Interestingly enough, Julia Kristeva also hints at the subversive thrust linked with the representation of death when she comments on Holbein's representation of the dead Christ:

> The unadorned representation of human death, the well-nigh anatomical stripping of the corpse convey to viewers an unbearable anguish before the

> death of God, here blended with our own, since there is not the slightest suggestion of transcendency. What is more, Hans Holbein has given up all architectural or compositional fancy. The tombstone weighs down on the upper portion of the painting, which is merely twelve inches high, and intensifies the feeling of permanent death: this corpse shall never rise again. The very pall, limited to a minimum of folds, emphasizes, through that economy of motion, the feeling of stiffness and stone-felt cold.

Julia Kristeva, "Holbein's Dead Christ" in her *Black Sun, Depression and Melancholia*, p. 110.

17. Plato, *Phaedrus*, translated by R. Hackforth, F.B.A. (Cambridge: Cambridge University Press, 1979), p. 157.

18. Elizabeth Bronfen and Sarah Goodwin, "Introduction" in *Death and Representation* (Baltimore: Johns Hopkins University, 1993), p. 17.

19. D. A. Miller, *The Novel and the Police* (Berkeley: University of California, 1988), p. 28.

20. Richard Terdiman, *Discourse/Counter-Discourse. The Theory and Practice of Symbolic Resistance in Nineteenth-Century France.* (Ithaca: Cornell University Press, 1985), p. 107.

21. Roddey Reid, *Families in Jeopardy. Regulating the Social Body in France, 1750–1910.* (Stanford: Stanford University Press, 1993), p. 5.

22. D. A. Miller, pp. 17, 27–28.

23. Kleist's disillusionment with an immortal, objective truth is expressed at various intervals in his letters. One example of this is his letter, dated March 22, 1801, on page 633 in H. Sembdner's edition, volume II.

24. Not only the "Avant-Propos" borrows scientific jargon, concerned with zoology and the classification of species. Even Balzac's prose explores the new scientific discoveries. *Ursule Mirouët* is a particularly clear example of this preoccupation, as is *La Recherche de l'absolu.*

25. All references to Balzac's *Comédie humaine* are drawn from Balzac, *La Comédie humaine, Tomes I-VII* (Paris: Aux Editions du Seuil, 1966). Subsequent references to Balzac's works will be incorporated in the text marked by the Roman numeral to indicate the volume, followed by the page number. The passage in question here is from *Le Médecin de campagne*, VI, 202.

26. Kleist, *Katechismus der Deutschen*, volume II, p. 350. Moreover, in his *Hermannsschlacht* the difficulty of defining cultural identity informs the entire play.

27. Ibid., p. 360.

28. Ibid., p. 737.

29. Robert Alter also discusses the impact of Napoleon on literature and emphasizes how he represents a figure in European history that "destroyed old orders and called into question most received values." Alter's thesis, while aware of negative,

threatening currents, tends to emphasize the more powerful connotations associated with the Napoleonic figure; Alter uses him to explain the shift to a more "realistic" as opposed to "self-conscious" style of writing:

> The literary question, then, was no longer of the ontological status of literature but of literature's more or less efficient function as a means. How was the novelist to represent the disturbing protean potential of the individual human being and at the same time realize or enact that potential through the exercise of the shaping power of fiction over an imagined, real-seeming world? Both challenged and threatened by the Napoleonic phenomenon, the novelist himself determines to set his impress on a world that he can reconstitute, combining or purposely confusing mimesis and poesis, imitation and making. Fictional invention for the self-conscious novelists of the pre-Napoleonic era is a process of intellection, simultaneously critical of its own operations and of the nonliterary objects toward which it is directed. For the nineteenth-century novelists, fictional invention often seems virtually a mode of action and as such cannot afford the luxury of self-criticism.

Robert Alter, "The Self-Conscious Novel in Eclipse" in his *Partial Magic. The Novel as a Self-Conscious Genre* (Berkeley: University of California Press, 1975), pp. 101–2.

30. I should mention, perhaps, that my original goal was to develop a strategy for reading short prose and that I chose the representation of death in short narrative as a way to trace the "discontinuous" or self-suspending elements that help to distinguish short texts from novels. Although the "genre-orientation" of my study gave way to a more historical study aimed at isolating the critique of writers directed at predominant ideologies of their time as well as at their own mimetic projects, I kept the focus on short texts, since in them the disruptive force of death scenes upon the narrative structure seems particularly vivid.

31. This structural detail was commented upon in length by Professor Brombert during his lectures on great European writers in the fall of 1989.

32. Leo Tolstoy, *The Death of Ivan Ilych and Other Great Stories*, translated by Aylmer Maude (New York: Signet, 1960), p. 154.

33. "A man would come, for instance, wanting some information. Ivan Ilych, as one in whose sphere the matter did not lie, would have nothing to do with him: but if the man had some business with him in his official capacity, something that could be expressed on officially stamped paper, he would do everything, positively everything he could within the limits of such relations" (p. 117).

34. This imagery stems from letters Kleist writes to his fiancée, Wilhelmine von Zenge. The clearest example is again the letter on p. 633 in volume II of Sembdner's edition.

35. Tzvetan Todorov, "Poetics and Criticism" in *The Poetics of Prose* (Ithaca: Cornell University Press, 1977), p. 32.

36. Robert Alter's description of Balzac's realism is particularly useful here: "The fundamental impulse in Dickens and Balzac is to expand spatially, and so syntactically their writing often tends to fall into large series of juxtaposed objects or multiplied

instances of the same general phenomenon, using repetitive or parallel structures. Fielding, on the other hand, is quite uninterested in the spatial expansion of the represented scene. His own elaboration moves back along a temporal axis into cultural history, and the syntactical form it takes is an intricate structure of subordination in which one senses the arch intelligence of the narrator controlling the disparate members, manipulating not only fictional objects but our judgment of men and society, our awareness of the linguistic categories with which we judge" (Robert Alter, "The Self-Conscious Novel in Eclipse" in *Partial Magic*, p. 102).

37. Again in the second volume of Montaigne's *Essais* we can find the following self-description: "A mesme que mes resveries se presentent, je les entasse; tantost elles se pressent en foule, tantost elles se trainent à la file. Je veux qu'on voye mon pas naturel et ordinaire, ainsin détraqué qu'il est" (II, 79).

38. Cf. Montaigne, *Essais* II, 423; III, 53.

39. Montaigne's rhetoric of loss could even be extended to his eventual definition of "life," which transformed life into a series of deaths. Suddenly death becomes the primary trait, leading potentially to a loss of difference between the two terms: "//Mais, conduicts par sa main [de la nature], d'une douce pente et comme insensible, peu à peu, de degré en degré, elle nous roule dans ce miserable estat et nous y apprivoise; si que nous ne sentons aucune secousse, quand la jeunesse meurt en nous qui est en essence et en verité une mort plus dure que n'est la mort entiere d'une vie languissante, et que n'est la mort de la vieillesse." (I, 136).

Other examples of a "rhetoric of loss" can be found in the numerous descriptions of "famous deaths," where Montaigne hopes to discover models of how to die "properly." These descriptions ultimately end with a shift of narrative focus—a loss of the topic. The account of the death loses itself in an analysis of what constitutes "honour" or "virtue" (II, 340; II, 406–13; III, 48–49).

40. Initially, of course, a reversal of mastery can be perceived in the metatextual notes of the writer. "///Je n'ay plus faict mon livre que mon livre m'a faict, livre consubstantiel à son autheur . . ." (II, 326) is the more familiar sentence, but a clearer description of this modified relation can be discovered in "De la vanité": "//Je sens ce proffit inesperé de la publication de mes meurs qu'elle me sert aucunement de regle. Il me vient par fois quelque consideration de ne trahir l'histoire de ma vie. Cette publique declaration m'oblige de me tenir en ma route, et à ne desmentir l'image de mes conditions" (III, 193). Here it is the work that begins to act as the measure of authority for the writer's actions. It is the concrete reality of the text functioning as Montaigne's memory that seems to reverse the relation of mimetic model to "essai."

And yet, the *Essais* are not the new dominant term, since Montaigne begins even to be alienated from this, his own work. In "De l'Experience," for instance—although it may seem that the sybilline leaves (or personal notes) which hold the history of Montaigne's bladder pains provide consolation to the patient—they still remain "sybilline," that is, enigmatic to the writer. If they can replace a faulty memory, they become both the sign of a rediscovered memory and of the barrier between the self and a spontaneous self-knowledge. The unbound sheaves always point simultaneously to the loss and to the retrieval of memory (cf. III, 303).

41. Philippe Lacoue-Labarthe, "Typographie" in S. Agacinski, J. Derrida, S. Kofman, Ph. Lacoue-Labarthe, J.-L. Nancy, and B. Pautrat, *Mimesis des articulations* (France: Aubier-Flammarion, 1975), p. 222.

42. Ibid., pp. 218, 220.

43. Christopher Prendergast, "Balzac: Narrative Contracts" in *The Order of Mimesis, Balzac, Stendhal, Nerval, Flaubert* (New York: Cambridge University Press, 1986), p. 96.

44. Perhaps the most famous of such studies is Albert Béguin's *Balzac visionnaire*. Béguin writes:

> Pourtant, dans les romans où des destinées communes se déroulent en pleine société moderne, la vision n'est pas autre chose qu'une vue en transparence, qu'un regard qui charge d'une signification insolite des êtres, des objets, des événements laissés à leur place habituelle et dans la cohérence du quotidien. Tandis que les contes sont visions en un sens plus fort du mot; ils pourraient être, ou bien ils sont la transcription de songes, d'hallucinations, le relevé de faits hors nature, le compte rendu d'histoires fantastiques.

Albert Béguin, ". . . arracher des mots au silence, et des idées à la nuit" in *Balzac visionnaire* (Genève: Albert Skira, 1946), pp. 183–206, p. 186.

45. Here Davin's preface to Balzac's *Etudes de moeurs* is helpful: "Observateur sagace et profond, il épiait incessamment la nature; puis, lorsqu'il l'a eu surprise, il l'a examinée avec des précautions infinies, il l'a regardée vivre et se mouvoir; il a suivi le travail des fluides et de la pensée; il l'a décomposée, fibre à fibre, et n'a commencé à la reconstruire que lorsqu'il a eu deviné les plus imperceptibles mystères de sa vie organique et intellectuelle" (*La Comédie humaine, I*, p. 599).

46. In his letter Kleist expresses his anxiety most clearly: "Aber zu schnell wechseln die Erscheinungen im Leben und zu eng ist das Herz, sie alle zu umfassen, und immer die vergangnen schwinden, Platz zu machen den neuen—Zuletzt ekelt dem Herzen vor den neuen, und matt gibt es sich Eindrücken hin, deren Vergänglichkeit es vorempfindet—Ach, es muß öde und leer und traurig sein, später zu sterben, als das Herz" (KB, 661).

47. Ronald Schleifer, "Afterword. Walter Benjamin and the Crisis of Representation: Multiplicity, Meaning, and Athematic Death" in E. Bronfen and S. Goodwin, *Death and Representation* (Baltimore: Johns Hopkins University, 1993).

48. Martin Heidegger, Skt. 53. "Existenzialer Entwurf eines eigentlichen Seins zum Tode" in *Sein und Zeit* (Tübingen: Max Niemeyer Verlag, 1984), p. 266.

Gianni Vattimo in his *Introduction à Heidegger* (Chapitre VII: "Etre-là et temporalité; L'être-pour-la-mort," from his *Introduction à Heidegger*, 1971) helped me to grasp the implications of Heidegger's arguments:

> La mort possibilise les possibilités, elle les fait apparaître véritablement en tant que telles et, par là, elle les met en possession de l'être-là qui ne s'attaque à aucune d'entre elles de manière définitive mais les insère dans le contexte tou-

> jours ouvert de son propre projet d'existence. Nous pouvons dire à présent que c'est seulement et précisément dans la mesure où il anticipe sa propre mort comme possibilisation de la possibilité que l'être-là a une histoire, c'est-à-dire un dévéloppement unitaire au-delà du fragmentaire et de la dispersion. (p. 58)

> L'anticipation de la mort est possibilisation de toutes les possibilités, ce qui implique toutefois une sorte de suspension temporaire de l'adhésion à ces possibilités, une espèce de dégagement des intérêts et de la manière péremptoire dont ils s'imposent dans leur présence de fait. Etre dispersé dans l'adhésion à telle ou telle possibilité constitue précisément un des traits de l'inauthenticité. (p. 60)

49. By using "death" rather than "desire" as the touchstone of my study, I tend to analyze the text as a response to *anxiety*, as an attempted response to the invisible and unnameable rather than as the playful experimentation with fantasy and desire. Thus, Leo Bersani's discussion of desire in the literary text might at first glance seem diametrically opposed to my analysis of death. And yet, there do seem to exist points of intersection, especially if one considers Bersani's critique of the phenomenon of desire within the context of Balzac's narratives. Desire is here described as a disruptive, even destructive force:

> The fear of desire in Balzac can be discussed as a fear of psychological fragmentation. Desire dynamites the Balzacian view of character—the "essentialist" psychology which allows Balzac to present characters in terms of a fixed, intelligible, and organizing passion. It threatens, in short, those coherent portraits of personality which are an important part of Balzacian expositions, and which characters' subsequent behavior will mainly illustrate and confirm. Can desire be contained by the ordering strategies of a descriptive narrative? If they cannot, narrative itself risks being fragmented into the mere juxtaposition of images of energy like those which assail Raphaël in the antique shop. . . . The Balzacian narrator is, precisely, the godlike presence who imposes a kind of providential order on his own fictional histories. And the rigid structure of a Balzac narrative is both menaced and energized by desires which may destroy characters, but which the narrative manages to contain at least formally.

Leo Bersani, "Realism and the Fear of Desire" in *A Future for Astyanax. Character, Desire in Literature* (New York: Columbia University Press, 1984), p. 73. Bersani uses Balzac's *Comédie humaine* as a foil to Proust's narratives. Both share a terror of desire, but Proust's Marcel "lacks" a competely definable or continuous character and is thus able to experiment more fully with partial, fragmentary selves—with (potential?) self-dissolution (ibid., pp. 86–87). In Balzac's case it is certainly true that the character's "portrait" (also Balzac's fascination with the world of thought or mental states) help to define the individual. Nonetheless, the complexity of Balzac's narrative situations, as well as his own critique of the storyteller's mastery, seems to be underplayed, even sacrificed, through the contrast with Proust's *A la recherche du temps perdu.*

CHAPTER 1. KLEIST'S *ERZÄHLUNGEN:* A NARRATIVE STRATEGY OF DEATH

1. Heinrich von Kleist, *Sämtliche Werke, Band II,* edited by Helmut Sembdner, p. 634. All subsequent references to Kleist's letters will be identified as KB, page no. Unless otherwise specified, all translations out of the French and German are my own.

2. In the letter written in March 1801, Kleist attempts to express his awareness that no one objective truth exists. It is a little paradoxical, however, to note that Kleist needs to represent *one* moment of death in order to signify the impossibility of the singular in the face of the plural (Truth being effaced by mortal truths).

3. Kleist writes: "*Bildung* schien mir das einzige Ziel, das des Bestrebens, *Wahrheit* der einzige Reichtum, der des Besitzes würdig ist. . . . Mir waren sie so heilig, daß ich diesen beiden Zwecken, Wahrheit zu sammeln, und Bildung mir zu erwerben, die *kostbarsten* Opfer brachte . . ." (KB, 633).

For Kleist the two terms *Wahrheit* and *Bildung* seem quite interdependent. One might add here that in its definition of *Bildung* the *Wahrig* dictionary places the stress on "vielseitige Kenntnis, verbunden mit Geschmack, Urteil, Sinn für Welt; Anstand; Takt und Herzensgüte" as well as on "geistige und innere Formung." However, as with any key cultural term, *Bildung* is better treated as a dynamic term, redefined again and again over the course of centuries. This is Rolf Selbmann's strategy in his *Der deutsche Bildungsroman;* he notes, for instance, the medieval, religious beginnings of the concept, where through "formatio" the individual is to be led back to a lost state of innocence (1). While the Enlightenment privileges the development of individualism—guaranteeing an autonomous space for an open-ended, personal evolution—Selbmann argues that the nineteenth century is marked by a skepticism, if not pessimism, regarding the potential of *Bildung.* Moreover, during the nineteenth century, the concept becomes, increasingly, a political tool, meant to subordinate the individual to norms outlined by the State. Gradually, the goal of *Bildung* is to create a defining barrier, separating a prosperous bourgeoisie from the lower classes (6). Rolf Selbmann, *Der deutsche Bildungsroman* (Stuttgart: Metzler, 1984).

4. Consider Peter Brooks's adaptation of Freud's *Jenseits des Lustprinzips,* in *Reading for the Plot: Design and Intention in Narrative* (New York: Random Books, 1984).

5. The limitations of the principle of adequatio are clearly expounded by Jean Beaufret in his analysis of truth in Martin Heidegger's work: "Dans la deuxième partie du *Discours de la Méthode,* Descartes définit la vérité par l'ajustement de nos opinions au niveau de la raison. Il y a donc vérité chaque fois que se réalise l'adéquation de la pensée à un niveau, qu'il faut entendre ici au sens instrumental . . . comme l'équerre ou, d'un mot plus abstrait, la norme qui 'juge' de la rectitude du jugement"(p. 355). Beaufret goes on to argue that the norm making judgment possible can itself never be tested. The norm itself possesses no greater norm to prove its accuracy. Heidegger, by redefining truth as *aletheia,* attempts to break free of the sterile circle associated with adequatio. Jean Beaufret, "Martin Heidegger et le problème de la vérité," 1967, pp. 353–73.

6. Erich Auerbach emphasizes the wide range of the mimetic project, intent on subsuming *stream of consciousness* in its category:

> Beneath the conflicts, and also through them, an economic and cultural leveling process is taking place. . . . And it [a common life of mankind] is most concretely visible now in the unprejudiced, precise, interior and exterior representation of the random moment in the lives of different people. So the complicated process of dissolution which led to fragmentation of the exterior action, to reflection of consciousness, and to stratification of time seems to be tending toward a very simple solution. (pp. 552–53)

Erich Auerbach, "The Brown Stocking" in *Mimesis* (Princeton: Princeton University Press, 1973), pp. 525–53.

7. Henri Birault, "Le Problème de la mort dans la philosophie de Sartre" in *Autour de Jean-Paul Sartre: littérature et philosophie* (Paris: Gallimard, 1981), pp. 183–215, p. 187.

8. Heinrich von Kleist, "Die Heilige Cäcilie, oder die Gewalt der Musik" in *Sämtliche Werke und Briefe, Zweiter Band*, edited by Helmut Sembdner (München: Carl Hanser Verlag, 1961), p. 228. All further references to this story will be included in the body of the text and will be marked as C.

9. The crisis of naming, as it is bound up with the uncontrollable series of substitutions, is particularly clear in Kleist's *Amphitryon.* In the famous confrontation scene between Jupiter and Alkmene in Act II (according to Sembdner, this scene constitutes one of Kleist's deviations from his Molieresque model, *Sämtliche Werke, Erster Band*, p. 927), Alkmene is accused of blasphemy. Instead of attempting to approach Jupiter directly in her prayers (which, Alkmene argues, would mean praying to a blank marble wall [A, l. 1456]), she is accused of using Amphitryon's image as a method of mediating the relationship between herself and the divine. Jupiter argues that it is this act that has initiated the play of doubling, which is ostensibly destroying Alkmene's (and Amphitryon's) world.

In the fourth and fifth scenes of Act II the crisis of language is, in effect, acted out between Alkmene and Jupiter. The dangerous structure is the mimetic, purely doubling or copying one, and it is perceptible in all the encounters between Alkmene and Amphitryon, but especially so, once Jupiter is forced to refer to himself as his own "Abgott" (A, l. 1288) or idol. The divine (unique) centre of stable meaning has itself been sucked into the doubling substitution. There is no longer a single, fixed point of reference, a fact that also destroys the authority of Alkmene's word (her oath). Precisely in that Jupiter, by imitating Amphitryon, is separate from his divine being, he is forced to break the power of her oath (which vows the destruction of the imposter, none other than Jupiter himself). This marks a crucial moment. The word that safeguards honor and one that guarantees the equation of truth with life—by breaking the oath, after all, Alkmene makes herself susceptible to the Furies—this word has been separated from its meaning; in Jupiter's terms, it has been "fragmented" (A, ll. 1328ff.). All references to *Amphitryon* are from Helmut Sembdner's *Sämtliche Werke, Erster Band* (München: Carl Hanser Verlag, 1961) and are referred to as A.

10. Consider John Ellis's discussion of the narrator in Kleist's *Erzählungen*, in particular in "Das Erdbeben in Chili." Ellis writes:

> In the 'Erdbeben' there is constantly a struggle to interpret the events on the part of the narrator, and of the characters of the story; and so previous interpretations achieve a special interest for a story whose very theme is interpretation. This is because the point of the story lies not in the meaning of the events themselves but in the attempts made by the narrator and the characters to give them meaning." (p. 49)

John Ellis, "Kleist: 'Das Erdbeben in Chili,'" in his *Narration in the German Novelle: Theory and Interpretation* (New York: Cambridge University Press, 1974), pp. 46–76.

11. One could consider that the displacement to a past historical context allows Kleist to repress his anxiety over the current situation of Germany. In his *Hermannsschlacht*, for instance, he chooses the conflict between the Roman state and the Germanic tribes in order to discuss elliptically the conflict between France and Germany.

12. The antithesis between a Lutheran and an institutional attitude is already problematized by the historical figure of Luther himself, as Paul M. Lützeler points out in his historicizing study of "Michael Kohlhaas":

> Die Situation, in der sich der [sächsische] Kurfürst befindet, ist äußerst heikel: Einerseits will er nichts gegen eine bis zur Intimität mit ihm befreundete Adelsfamilie unternehmen, eine Familie, die immerhin die Vertreter höchster Staatsämter stellt; andererseits kann er nicht den Wunsch Luthers ignorieren, eines Mannes, der jene moralische Macht verkörpert, welcher sein Fürstenhaus ein gut Teil Legitimität verdankt. . . ." (pp. 227–28)

Paul Michael Lützeler, "Heinrich von Kleist: *Michael Kohlhaas* (1810)" in *Romane und Erzählungen der deutschen Romantik. Neue Interpretationen*, edited by P. M. Lützeler (Stuttgart: Reclam, 1981), pp. 213–33.

13. Heinrich von Kleist, "Michael Kohlhaas" in Helmut Sembdner, *Heinrich von Kleist: Sämtliche Werke und Briefe, Band II* (München: Carl Hanser Verlag, 1961), p. 49. All further references to the text will be included in the body of the chapter and will be referred to as MK.

14. Martin Luther, *Reformatorische Schriften in acht Bändchen*, edited by Otto v. Gerlach (Berlin: G. Eichler Verlag), Band 4, p. 64.

15. Ibid., Band 3, p. 172.

16. Ibid., Band 3, p. 186.

17. Ibid., Band 4, p. 36, my emphasis.

18. Helga Gallas also stresses the importance of the logic of substitution in "Michael Kohlhaas," especially pointing out that the problematic gypsy's note is very much a part of the narrative, since it is an episode purely of Kleist's invention. She notes, in fact, a far more complex network of substitution, in which even the plot sequences reduplicate one another. Her analysis is compelling:

> Die zweite Sequenz ist also eine Wiederholung der ersten aber mit vertauschten Rollen. Die hervorgehobenen Plätze, die Orte der Struktur sind offenbar: ein Herausforderer, ein Gedemütigter und ein Objekt, um das sich alles dreht, die Pferde. Einen dritten Platz besetzen Lisbeth und Knecht Herse, denen eine Vermittler—bzw. Helferrolle zukommt; beide richten nichts aus, werden verletzt, beide sterben. (p. 65)

She adds that the object of annihilation ("Junker Wenzel") is replaced by Kohlhaas, as is the object of persecution (Kohlhaas by the elector of Saxony) and the female mediator. Her interpretation emphasizes the trajectory of desire, as it follows the movement of the signifier. She highlights the triviality of a substitution that does not depend on the substance of a desired object, but only on its position. The note around Kohlhaas's neck, for instance, only is coveted by Kohlhaas, once the elector of Saxony desires it. Inherently, it has no value (and therefore is not described physically in the narrrative).

The significance of substitution to the narrative, according to Gallas, does not reside in the way it might reflect on Kleist's poetics. She is interested in tracing the path of the signifier, retelling, as it were, a Saussurian and Lacanian narrative. Her reading, as she insists herself, is less interested in recuperating a meaning in the text than in enacting a psychoanalytical principle; she traces the way desire functions in the text. As a result, the slippage of the signifier has created in her analysis a signified that tends to leave the particularity of Kleist's historical and literary context unexplained. Helga Gallas, *Das Textbegehren des "Michael Kohlhaas." Die Sprache des Unbewußten und der Sinn der Literatur* (Reinbek bei Hamburg: Rowohlt, 1981).

19. Chase's deconstruction of Kleist's anecdote is rather subtle:

> Each story within the narrative *performs* in a manner consistent with the cognition it offers, namely that cognition is not consistent with performance. Each story functions in a way consistent with what it figures: for its function, like what it figures, is the failure to function, to persuade, to take calculable effect; yet if what the story figures is precisely the *inconsistency* between figure and function, then in the very process of consistency with that figure, the story functions in a manner inconsistent with it. (p. 155)

Cynthia Chase, "Mutilated Doll, Exploding Machine" in *Decomposing Figures, Rhetorical Readings in the Romantic Tradition* (Baltimore: Johns Hopkins University Press, 1986), pp. 141–56.

20. Kleist's lack of success as an officer, his struggle to reconcile *Pflicht* and *Neigung* support the reading that he is searching for a synthesizing, third term. Nonetheless, as one can clearly see in *Amphitryon* or in *Prinz Friedrich von Homburg*, where the drama of feeling and duty seems to be resolved by the end of the play, an analysis of the structure of the two plays again undermines such a dialectical mediation. In *Amphitryon*, the example of Hercules, who must first live the life of a human before he can become divine, clearly separates the two antithetical values (human and divine). Hercules never becomes the synthesis of the two values; he depends both on the work of time and on Jupiter for the transition from human to divine. Or in *Prinz Friedrich*, the happy resolution depends on a series of reversals generated by the *deus ex machina* technique. The active intervention of the characters in achieving an ideal synthesis is especially minimal in the later play.

21. Conrady is struck by the original title of Kleist's collection of short prose (*Moralische Erzählungen*) and follows this lead by attempting to discover the effect of Cervantes' exemplary tales on Kleist's narratives. Conrady does emphasize the *process* of moral reflection and stresses that writer and reader experience a certain quest (*Suchen*) within the narrative. Still, he does emphasize the moral model: ". . . Aufleuchten einiger Richtpunkte für menschliches Verhalten, aber ohne den steten Lohn des Ausgangs und ohne die Sicherheit von christlich-religiös oder gesellschaftlich-gebundenen überzeitlichen oder auch zeitgebundenen Werten . . ." (p. 713). Karl Otto Conrady, "Das Moralische in Kleists Erzählungen. Ein Kapitel vom Dichter ohne Gesellschaft" in *Wege der Forschung. Heinrich von Kleist*, pp. 709–35.

22. Walter Müller-Seidel, "Die Struktur des Widerspruchs in Kleists 'Marquise von O . . . ,' in *Wege der Forschung, Heinrich von Kleist*, pp. 244–68.

23. Klaus Müller-Salget, "Das Prinzip der Doppeldeutigkeit" in *Wege der Forschung. Kleists Aktualität*, pp. 167–92; Wolfgang Kayser, "Kleist als Erzähler" in *Wege der Forschung. Heinrich von Kleist*, pp. 230–43.

24. Two of the critics, while pursuing studies of language, focus primarily on narrative voice. John Ellis, for instance, emphasizes the narrative strategy Kleist adopts in his "Erdbeben in Chili." In this story, Ellis argues, the limitations of subjective perception are being dramatized. Not even the narrator is granted omniscient status, with the result that the story enacts the individual's impotence to understand or explain events in the world. Following John Ellis's lead and equally struck by the phenomenon that each constructed explanation is lamed by the continuing onslaught of catastrophes, Norbert Altenhofer notes how the reader is actually presented with all the significant details. The reader thus transcends a purely subjective vision, only to find that the exhaustive accumulation of authoritative information leads to Authority itself being relativized. A juxtaposition of the two critics' interpretation leads to an ironic invalidation of both positions. By appealing to the narrative perspective as the criterion to determine why Kleist's stories refuse to submit themselves to a moral or cognitive order, the two critics fall into the same trap set by all of Kleist's narratives. The strategy they analyze seems to posit simultaneously that the inadequacy of subjectivity and the paralysis created by an excess of objectivity are to blame for the absence of any mimetically meaningful interpretation.

John Ellis writes: "In this tension between the narrator's desire to see coherence in the story and his wish merely to relate what actually happened, letting this speak for itself, lies its most characteristic quality. . . . The meaninglessness of the story is something which we experience, but only as a disappointment after a search for meaning and thus the tension which the 'getürmte Unglücksfälle' bring is the tension between alternative meanings, not tension instead of meaning" (John Ellis, pp. 70–71). John Ellis, "Kleist: 'Das Erdbeben in Chili,'" in *Narration in the German Novelle: Theory and Interpretation* (New York: Cambridge University Press, 1974). pp. 46–76.

Norbert Altenhofer's reading follows: "Das poetische Skandalon liegt in einer 'Skizzenhaftigkeit', die das Genre der moralischen Erzählung so weit radikalisiert, daß dem Leser kein Ereignis, kein Gedanke, kein Gefühl verschwiegen und ihm dennoch alle Arbeit moralischer Urteilsbildung und metaphysischer Sinnkonstruktion zugemutet wird" (p. 53).

And then he writes: "Die moralische Erzählung beansprucht selbst keine Autorität mehr; sie zitiert nur noch Autoritäten (darunter die des Genres, dem sie sich zuordnet, ohne es zu erfüllen) und autorisiert den Leser zur Auslegung eines Sinns, der im Text nur in der Form des Rätsels erscheint" (p. 53). Norbert Altenhofer, "Der erschütterte Sinn. Hermeneutische Überlegungen zu Kleists 'Das Erdbeben in Chili,'" in David Wellbery, *Positionen der Literaturwissenschaft. Acht Modellanalysen am Beispiel von Kleists 'Das Erdbeben in Chili'* (München: Beck'sche Elementarbücher, 1985), pp. 39–53.

25. Friedrich Kittler, "Ein Erdbeben in Chili and Preußen" in Wellbery, *Positionen der Literaturwissenschaft*, pp. 24–38.

26. Ibid., p. 37.

27. Girard writes: "Das Paradox des mimetischen Begehrens besteht darin, daß es entzweiend und konfliktsschwanger ist, solange es auf Objekten hin polarisiert ist, welche die Antagonisten sich aneignen wollen. Sobald es sich aber auf die Antagonisten selbst bezieht und die Vernichtung des anderen zum Ziel hat, kann es wieder kumulativ werden, denn Zerstörung kann, im Gegensatz zu Aneignung, mit anderen geteilt werden. Durch einen Akt der Zerstörung und Ausschliessung kann daher eine gewisse Einheit der Gruppe wiedererlangt werden" (p. 137). René Girard, "Mythos und Gegenmythos: Zu Kleists 'Das Erdbeben in Chili,'" in Wellbery, *Positionen der Literaturwissenschaft*, pp. 130–48.

28. It is easy to project the reversal of the third example. The permission to marry Natalie is inverted twice: first, by the prince's conjecture that it is this fulfillment of his desire that has precipitated his death sentence and second, by his ready renunciation of his bride-to-be.

29. Heinrich von Kleist, *Prinz Friedrich von Homburg*, ll.361–63. All other references to the play will be included in the body of the chapter and will be marked as P, line number.

30. Heinrich von Kleist, *Plays*, edited by Walter Hinderer (New York: Continuum, 1982), p. 286.

31. Ibid., p. 291.

32. Ibid., p. 294.

33. The series of reversals that separate forcibly word from will and make it impossible for us to recognize a linear, causal development might seem to force us to assume that the logic governing the "Schauspiel" is "tragic"—as it is for Hölderlin in his "Anmerkungen zur Antigonae." Hölderlin writes: "Die tragische Darstellung beruhet . . . darauf, daß der unmittelbare Gott, ganz Eines mit dem Menschen (denn der Gott eines Apostels ist mittelbarer, ist höchster Verstand in höchstem Geiste), daß die *unendliche* Begeisterung *unendlich*, das heißt in Gegensäzzen, im Bewußtseyn, welches das Bewußtseyn aufhebt, heilig sich scheidend, sich faßt, und der Gott, in der Gestalt des Todes, gegenwärtig ist." Friedrich Hölderlin, "Anmerkungen zur Antigonae" in the *Stuttgarter Hölderlin-Ausgabe. Band 5*, edited by F. Beissner (Stuttgart: Scheufele, 1952), p. 269.

The Hölderlinian paradox that allows God to represent himself in the figure of death: clearer, that transforms God into the condition of human existence, that is, of temporality and, consequently, of human mortality, is evaded by Kleist. The latter, following a logic of reversal, can still allow the "Kurfürst" to lose his power vis-à-vis the state (consider the mutiny of his officers) and allow the prince to *articulate* his "unbeugsamer Wille" to die in order to achieve the happy "inverted" resolution. Hölderlin's text and the logic of tragic paradox was discussed in Philippe Lacoue-Labarthe's seminar on "Tragedy and Philosophy" during the spring of 1986 at the Université de Strasbourg II.

34. Kleist, "Über das Marionettentheater" in Sembdner, *Sämtliche Werke, Zweiter Band*, p. 345. All subsequent references to Kleist's anecdotes or literary essays will be included in the body of the chapter and will be referred to as II, page no.

35. This distinction is most clearly described by Helga Gallas. Language, she notes, can be interpreted as "articulation" rather than as "representation," if Saussure's linguistics are applied: "'Denn damit die 'undifferenzierte, amorphe Masse' des Denkens sich in bestimmten Gedanken—d.h. überhaupt in Gedanken—artikuliert, müssen die verschiedenen Gedankenelemente sich voneinander absetzen, sich unterscheiden, differenzieren: sie müssen sich aufeinander beziehen, sich zueinander als *Signifikanten verhalten, um Signifikate zu werden*" (pp. 38–39). Helga Gallas, *Das Textbegehren des "Michael Kohlhaas." Die Sprache des Unbewußten und der Sinn der Literatur* (Reinbek bei Hamburg: Rowohlt, 1981).

36. Hans-Peter Hermann, "Zufall und Ich. Zum Begriff der Situation in den Novellen Heinrich von Kleists" in *Wege der Forschung. Heinrich von Kleist* (pp. 367–411), p. 397.

37. Stierle writes: "Der Sprechende spricht im Fortgang sprachlicher Kontinuität, während in dieser selbst das Rätsel des reinen Jetzt, die abgründige Sicherheit des hevorbrechenden Gegenwärtigen zur Erscheinung kommt" (p. 66). Karlheinz Stierle, "Das Beben des Bewußtseins. Die narrative Struktur von Kleists 'Das Erdbeben in Chili,'" in Wellbery, *Positionen der Literaturwissenschaft*, pp. 54–68.

38. Hans-Peter Hermann writes: "Mit der formalen Bindung an den zeitlichen Ablauf der Sprache reduziert Kleist auch die inhaltlichen Aussagemöglichkeiten seines Stils. Zeitloses darzustellen, überschreitet sein Vermögen; so ist er außerstande, Erfahrungen aufzubewahren, Gesetzmäßigkeiten zu entwickeln, einen menschlichen Charakter als Entelechie zu entfalten. Deutungen zu geben, fehlt ihm die nötige Distanz; so bleibt die Wirklichkeit für die Menschen und bleiben die Menschen für einander ein Rätsel."

["Kleist also reduces the possible expression of content in his style through the formal bond to the temporal development of language. To represent atemporal elements goes beyond his ability; thus he is incapable of storing experiences, of developing principles, of unfolding a human character as entelechy. He lacks the necessary distance to provide interpretations; thus, reality and themselves remain an enigma to the people."] Hans-Peter Hermann, "Zufall und Ich," p. 403.

39. Hermann, p. 409.

40. Helmut Schneider, "Der Zusammensturz des Allgemeinen" in Wellbery, *Positionen der Literaturwissenschaft* (pp. 110–29), p. 129.

41. Ibid., p. 129.

42. "Der Text zeugt von einer Problematisierung des Narrativen, die den kulturellen Vorgang des Erzählens in Frage stellt. Dies wird vor allem an der Handhabung des Zufalls sichtbar, die die narrative Kontinuität aufhebt und innerhalb der Narration selbst die Wirksamkeit einer ihr fremden Macht erkennen läßt. Die Predigt des Chorherrn, die wir als Verdrängung des Zufalls durch die Narration bezeichnet haben, stellt gleichfalls eine kritische Selbstreflektion innerhalb der Erzählung dar" ["The text bears witness to a problematization of the narrative, which calls into question the cultural process of the tale. This is especially visible in the handling of chance, which undoes the narrative continuity and which makes recognizable within the narrative itself the effectiveness of its foreign power. The sermon of the canon, which we have read as the repression of chance through narrative, equally represents a critical self-reflection within the story"]. David Wellbery, "Semiotische Anmerkungen zu Kleists 'Das Erdbeben in Chili,'" in *Positionen der Literaturwissenschaft* (pp. 69–87), p. 86.

43. The Derridean echo is unmistakable. Two especially salient sources for such an analysis can be found in *Of Grammatology*, translated by Gayatri Chakravorty Spivak:

> But the supplement supplements. It adds only to replace. It intervenes or insinuates itself *in-the-place-of*; if it fills, it is as if one fills a void. If it represents and makes an image, it is by the anterior default of a presence. Compensatory [*suppléant*] and vicarious, the supplement is an adjunct, a subaltern instance which *takes-(the)-place* [*tient-lieu*]. As substitute, it is not simply added to the positivity of a presence, it produces no relief, its place is assigned in the structure by the mark of an emptiness. Somewhere, something can be filled up *of itself*, can accomplish itself, only by allowing itself to be filled through sign and proxy. The sign is always the supplement of the thing itself. (p. 145)

> Reason is incapable of thinking this double infringement upon Nature: that there is *lack* in Nature and that *because of that very fact* something is *added* to it. Yet one should not say that Reason is *powerless to think this*; it is constituted by that lack of power. It is the principle of identity. It is the thought of the self-identity of the natural being. It cannot even determine the supplement as its other, as the irrational the nonnatural for the supplement comes *naturally* to put itself in Nature's place. The supplement is the image and the representation of Nature. The image is neither in nor out of Nature. The supplement is therefore equally dangerous for Reason, the natural health of Reason. (p. 149)

Jacques Derrida, "From/Of Blindness to the Supplement," *Of Grammatology*, translated by Gayatri Chakravorty Spivak (Baltimore: Johns Hopkins University Press, 1974), pp. 144–52.

44. Werner Hamacher, "Das Beben der Darstellung" in Wellbery, *Positionen der Literaturwissenschaft* (pp. 149–73), p. 191.

45. Ibid., p. 172.

46. The deadliness of the mirror or of doubling is enacted especially clearly in *Amphitryon.* Refer to note 9 for an explanation of the connection between doubling and the death of meaning.

CHAPTER 2. *BILDUNG* AND MORTALITY: KLEIST'S SEARCH FOR A POETICS OF DEATH

1. Garrett Stewart, "Points of Departure" in *Death Sentences. Styles of Dying in British Fiction* (Cambridge, Mass.: Harvard University Press, 1974), pp. 1–52, p. 7.

2. Curiously, Kleist's career as a writer seems to begin under the sign of death. The first letter in Helmut Sembdner's *Sämtliche Werke* is written after Kleist has lost his mother and is dated March 13, 1793. Kleist seems to find it difficult to write of his mother's death to his aunt:

> Der Gedanke an Ihnen, beste Tante, erpreßt mir Tränen, indem ich zugleich an eine verlorne zärtliche Mutter denke, und der Gedanke an Ihre Wohltaten tröstet mich indem ich nun keine *verlaßne* Waise zu sein glaube. Dies alles, Tantchen, Schmerz und Freude, ist bei der Neuheit dieses unglücklichen Vorfalls natürlich; die beste Trösterin aller Leiden, die Zeit, wird nach und nach auch *mich* trösten, aber vergessen werd ich die Ursach nie. (KB, 468)

The argument that this letter coincidentally survived, where other earlier letters didn't, can be supplemented by another, more compelling point. One could conceivably argue that Kleist begins to write letters, now that he has left his home to begin his career as an officer. But even the beginning of his military life seems only to be necessary because of the death of his mother:

> [Cap.v.Franckenberg] . . . glaubte mich nicht so früh zu sehen, doch freut' es ihm [sic]. Seine Verwundrung nahm aber ab, als ich ihm sagte, daß *Frankfurt a. O.* für mich, seitdem ich keine Mutter besitze, kein Aufenthalt der Freude mehr sei. Er nahm wahren Anteil an meinen Verlust und wünschte mir Glück, wenigstens keine *verlassene* Waise zu sein, und versprach sich meiner nur um desto mehr anzunehmen. (KB, 466)

Kleist's Bildung resembles Rousseau's account of his own Bildung in *Les Confessions.* Both seem to be propelled toward consciousness because of the death of the mother. But whereas Rousseau has constructed his narrative of his own life to highlight this initial loss (which could then be supplemented by the world of books), Kleist seems to be enacting a similar beginning quite unconsciously. It can only remain a conjecture to consider how significant the mother's death is to this beginning of Kleist's Bildung and his career as a writer.

3. Consider Joseph Frank's *The Widening Gyre,* in which he shows that the famous Lessing distinction between poetry and painting emphasizes the link between medium and aesthetic form, between medium and the condition of human perception. Lessing's radical contribution to literary criticism is described as follows:

> No longer was aesthetic form confused with mere externals of technique or felt as a strait jacket into which the artist, willy-nilly, had to force his creative

> ideas. Form issued spontaneously from the organization of the art work as it presented itself to perception. Time and space were the two extremes defining the limits of literature and the plastic arts in their relation to sensuous perception; and following Lessing's example, it is possible to trace the evolution of art forms by their oscillations between these two poles.

Joseph Frank, "Spatial Form in Modern Literature" in *The Widening Gyre. Crisis and Mastery in Modern Literature.* (Bloomington: Indiana University Press, 1963), p. 309.

4. Rolf Selbmann, in his *Der deutsche Bildungsroman*, outlines the transformations of the concept *Bildung*. The following quotation highlights nicely some of the tensions affecting the evolution of the term:

> "Bildung" als Individualitäts-und Entwicklungsbegriff setzt sich auch sozialgeschichtlich ab von der Staatserziehung als Normentradierung zur Einpassung in eine eben ständisch vorgegebene Gesellschaft, sondern zielt auf die Instandsetzung eines Individuums unter Gewährung eines persönlichen Spielraums, freilich mit dem Risiko, das Ende des Bildungsprozesses nicht mehr exakt vorherbestimmen zu können. (p. 20) (Also see endnote 3, chapter 1.)

Rolf Selbmann, *Der deutsche Bildungsroman* (Stuttgart: J. B. Metzler, 1984).

5. Two of the critics quick to note the link between Bild and Bildung are Jean-Luc Nancy and Philippe Lacoue-Labarthe. In their study of Early German Romanticism, they write:

> C'est l'imagination transcendentale, l'*Einbildungskraft*, la fonction qui doit former (*bilden*) l'unité et qui doit la former comme *Bild*, comme représentation et tableau . . . comme phénomène. . . . Ce que forme ou construit l'imagination transcendentale, c'est donc bien un objet saisissable dans les limites de l'intuition *a priori*, mais rien qu'on puisse penser sous le concept d'*eidos* ou d'Idée. (p. 44)

The connection is presented under the heading of the self that cannot represent itself to itself. The lack of "substantiality" makes necessary the construction of an image, thereby mediating the formation of a coherent self. Jean-Luc Nancy and Philippe Lacoue-Labarthe, "L'Ouverture—le système-sujet" in *L'Absolu littéraire* (Seuil), pp. 40–52.

6. The sense of Bildung that seems most pertinent in the late eighteenth and early nineteenth centuries is the one outlined by Rolf Selbmann in *Der Deutsche Bildungsroman* (Stuttgart: J. B. Metzler, 1984). Please refer especially to pp. 2–3, as well as pp. 42ff.

7. After deciding to break with the theatrical company, Wilhelm continually seems to meet with characters who are not totally unfamiliar to him and who make him question his formation, not to mention his ideals. As a result, Wilhelm begins to worry about the shape of his life:

> War jene Aussicht, jener Ausweg nach der Bühne bloß einem unordentlichen, unruhigen Menschen willkommen, der ein Leben fortzusetzen wünschte, das ihm die Verhältnisse der bürgerlichen Welt nicht gestatteten, oder war es alles anders, reiner, würdiger? Und was sollte dich bewegen können, deine dama-

> ligen Gesinnungen zu ändern? Hast du nicht vielmehr bisher selbst unwissend deinen Plan verfolgt? (p. 258)

Johann Wolfgang von Goethe, *Wilhelm Meisters Lehrjahre* (Berlin: Aufbau Verlag, 1962). All subsequent references to the text will be included in the chapter and referred to as WML, page no.

8. Heinrich von Kleist, "Das Bettelweib von Locarno" in Helmut Sembdner, *Sämtliche Werke, Zweiter Band*, p. 196.

9. At this point we should recall "Die Heilige Cäcilie, oder die Gewalt der Musik," where music acts both as the miracle which suspends the planned destruction of the cathedral, but retains its own violent power as well; the *Gewalt* robs the four brothers of their identity as well as of their will.

10. Of the three sentences that constitute the "Todeslitanei" (written in November 1811, just preceding Kleist's suicide), here are the first and last ones:

> Mein Jettchen, mein Herzchen, mein Liebes, mein Täubchen, mein Leben, mein liebes süßes Leben, mein Lebenslicht, mein Alles, mein Hab und Gut, meine Schlösser, Äcker, Wiesen und Weinberge, o Sonne meines Lebens, Sonne, Mond und Sterne, Himmel und Erde, meine Vergangenheit und Zukunft, meine Braut, mein Mädchen, meine liebe Freundin, mein Innerstes, mein Herzblut, meine Eingeweide, mein Augenstern, o, Liebste, wie nenn ich Dich? . . . Ach Du bist mein zweites besseres Ich, meine Tugenden, meine Verdienste, meine Hoffnung, die Vergebung meiner Sünden, meine Zukunft und Seligkeit, o, Himmelstöchterchen, mein Gotteskind, meine Fürsprecherin und Fürbitterin, mein Schutzengel, mein Cherubim und Seraph, wie lieb ich Dich! (I, 46)

Credit should go to August Sauer for the title of Kleist's poem to Henriette von Vogel. He seems to be the only one interested in comparing Kleist's poem to Henriette with her poem dedicated to the writer. The study is a short one: August Sauer, *Kleists Todeslitanei.* (*Prager Deutsche Studien, Heft 7*) (Prag: Carl Bellmann Verlag, 1907).

11. The youths sing: "Auf, wir kehren ins Leben zurück. Gebe der Tag uns Arbeit und Lust, bis der Abend uns Ruhe bringt, und der nächtliche Schlaf uns erquickt" (*Wilhelm Meisters Lehrjahre*, p. 617).

12. Friedrich Schlegel, *Lucinde*, p. 111.

13. In his description of the idealistic nature of both "Die Marquise von O . . ." and "Der Zweikampf," Müller-Seidel makes reference to the importance of the antithesis: *Versehen-Erkennen.* The following analysis elucidates the earlier story, but it also applies, within the framework Müller-Seidel establishes, to "Der Zweikampf."

> Nie aber ist die tragische Spannung um ihrer Selbst willen—so wenig wie der Widerspruch—der letzte Aspekt, sondern das Dritte jenseits aller Widersprüche. Kleist nennt es das Gefühl. *Seine* Wahrheit ist dem Zweideutigen nicht mehr unterworfen. Aber die Widerspruchslosigkeit reicht schon ins Wunderbare, ins Überweltlich-Göttliche hinein. (pp. 263–64)

Walter Müller-Seidel, "Die Struktur des Widerspruchs in Kleists 'Die Marquise von O . . .'" in *Wege der Forschung. Heinrich von Kleist*, pp. 244–68.

14. Heinrich von Kleist, "Der Zweikampf" in Helmut Sembdner, *Sämtliche Werke, Zweiter Band*, p. 236. All subsequent references to the text will be included in the body of the chapter and will be referred to as Z, page no.

15. Friedrich, the chamberlain, begins to trace the arrow back to the murderer, who (unbeknownst to the reader) is Jakob. In the process of this search, the arrow begins to be treated as a legible, even if coded, text:

> Der Pfeil schien für die Rüstkammer eines vornehmen und reichen Mannes verfertigt zu sein, der entweder in Fehden verwickelt, oder ein großer Liebhaber von der Jagd war; und da man aus einer, dem Knopf eingegrabenen, Jahreszahl ersah, daß dies erst vor kurzem geschehen sein konnte: so schickte die Herzogin, auf Anraten des Kanzlers, den Pfeil, mit dem Kronsiegel versehen, in alle Werkstätten von Deutschland umher, um den Meister, der ihn gedrechselt hatte, aufzufinden, und, falls dies gelang, von demselben den Namen dessen zu erfahren, auf dessen Bestellung er gedrechselt worden war. (Z, 231)

16. Heinrich von Kleist, *The Marquise of O—and Other Stories*, translated by Martin Greenberg (New York: Frederick Ungar, 1973), p. 289.

17. Ibid., p. 303.

18. Ibid., p. 316.

19. Ibid., p. 299.

20. Another example of such a symbolic annihilation is Helene's (Friedrich's mother's) response to Friedrich's failure to kill Jakob. She perceives this failure as a direct sign of Littegarde's guilt and declares that the worst kind of punishment is a complete silence. She literally turns her back on Littegarde, so that her gesture symbolizes that she does not even recognize Littegarde's existence: "Entrüstung, die sie der Worte würdigt, ehrt sie; unsern Rücken mag sie erschaun, und vernichtet durch die Vorwürfe, womit wir sie verschonen, verzweifeln!" (Z, 252).

21. Perhaps the clearest example of such madness is her outcry: ". . . meine Sinne reißen . . ." (Z, 251).

22. Kleist, *The Marquise of O—and Other Stories*, p. 311.

23. The clearest example of this self-sacrifice occurs in the last scene. Amphitryon declares:

> Jetzt einen Eid selbst auf den Altar schwör ich,
> Und sterbe siebenfachen Todes gleich,
> Des unerschütterlich erfaßten Glaubens,
> Daß er Amphitryon ihr ist.
> (A, ll. 2287–90)

24. "Betrachtungen über den Weltlauf" consists primarily of two sentences that are perfect inverted mirror images of one another. The second half of the essay explains how time leads to a decline rather than to progress:

Diesen Leuten dient zur Nachricht, daß alles, wenigstens bei den Griechen und Römern, in ganz umgekehrter Ordnung erfolgt ist. Diese Völker machten mit der *heroischen* Epoche, welche ohne Zweifel die höchste ist, die erschwungen werden kann, den Anfang; als sie in keiner menschlichen und bürgerlichen Tugend mehr Helden hatten, *dichteten* sie welche; als sie keine mehr dichten konnten, erfanden sie dafür die *Regeln*; als sie sich in den Regeln verwirrten, abstrahierten sie die *Weltweisheit* selbst; und als sie damit fertig waren, wurden sie *schlecht.* (II, 326–27)

25. Heinrich von Kleist, *Penthesilea*, in Helmut Sembdner, *Sämtliche Werke, Erster Band*, ll. 3037–43.

26. Heinrich von Kleist, *Plays*, edited by Walter Hinderer and translated by Humphrey Trevelyan (New York: Continuum, 1982), p. 268.

27. Such a reworking will not surprise readers of Freud too much. In his essay entitled "The Three Caskets," Freud describes tendencies that emerge in the representation of death. Either the notion of death is represented simply as *dumbness* in dreams (p. 67) or it is experienced as a *displacement.* He writes: "Such a displacement will astonish us least of all in relation to the Goddess of Death, since in modern thought and artistic representation . . . death itself is nothing but a dead man" (p. 69).

28. Consider, for instance, the structure of Freud's *Drei Abhandlungen zur Sexualtheorie*, which reconstructs the child's development by emphasizing the continuity of flow of that growth (p. 69). Sigmund Freud, *Drei Abhandlungen zur Sexualtheorie (1904–1905)* (Frankfurt a. M.: Suhrkamp, 1983).

29. In *Jenseits des Lustprinzips* one of the footnotes reads:

Der Gegensatz zwischen Ich- und Sexualtrieben wandelte sich in den zwischen Ich- und Objekttrieben, beide libidinöser Natur. An seine Stelle trat aber ein neuer Gegensatz zwischen libidinösen (Ich- und Objekt-) Trieben und anderen, die im Ich zu statuieren und vielleicht in den Destruktionstrieben aufzuzeigen sind. Diese Spekulation wandelte diesen Gegensatz in den von Lebenstrieben (Eros) und von Todestrieben um. (p. 269)

Sigmund Freud, *Jenseits des Lustprinzips* in *Psychologie des Unbewußten. Band III.* (Frankfurt a.M.: 1975), pp. 213–72.

30. Ibid., p. 271.

31. Ibid., pp. 247–48.

32. Freud's hypothetical account of the beginning of life and the interplay between life-sustaining and life-destroying impulses makes it a little difficult to explain the persistence of the life force. We find the following statement in *Jenseits des Lustprinzips*: "Eine lange Zeit hindurch mag so die lebende Substanz immer wieder neu geschaffen worden und leicht gestorben . . ." (p. 248).

33. Peter Brooks focuses on *Beyond the Pleasure Principle*, but does so primarily in order to dwell on the dilatory function produced by the intersection of the two drives, the pleasure drive and the death drive. Although he is interested in developing a narrative theory that can show how death is central to the narrative structure, the represen-

tation of death in his critical theory also suffers from displacement. Remarks such as: "the organism must discover its own perfect death" remain rather mystical, since the shift is still away from the dominance of death; the pleasure principle is still valorized primarily.

34. *Jenseits des Lustprinzips*, p. 247.

35. Michel de M'Uzan describes the ambivalence inherent to the creative object: "De cette haine toujours indécise dans son orientation, prête à se diriger vers l'extérieur ou à se retourner contre le sujet lui-même et par là souvent, proche du crime, l'oeuvre vraie garde toujours la marque, même dans ses aspects les plus volontairement réconciliés" (p. 10). Michel de M'Uzan, "Aperçus sur le processus de la création littéraire" (1964), in *De l'art à la mort. Itinéraire psychanalytique* (Paris: Gallimard, 1977), pp. 3–27.

36. Ibid., p. 8.

37. Ibid., pp. 7–8.

38. Not surprisingly, this relation to death is necessitated by the structure of the individual psyche —by its radical emptiness. Lacan notes: "Il est un élément indispensable de l'insertion de la réalité symbolique dans la réalité du sujet, il est lié à la béance primitive du sujet. En cela, en son sens originel, il est dans la vie psychologique du sujet humain l'apparition la plus proche, la plus intime, la plus accessible, de la mort" (p. 245). Jacques Lacan, "Questions à celui qui enseigne" in *Séminaire II. Le moi dans la théorie de Freud et dans la technique de la psychanalyse* (Paris: Seuil, 1978), pp. 241–57.

39. Gallas writes: "Um begehrt zu sein, muß ich für den anderen begehrlich sein; und das bin ich, wenn ich beim anderen einen Mangel ausfülle." (p. 76) The child, by functioning as the mother's "phallus," is able to fill the lack of the mother and is therefore desired by her. This argument is, incidentally, not so far removed from the one advocated by Freud in his essay "On Femininity." Helga Gallas, *Das Textbegehren des 'Michael Kohlhaas'*.

40. Here Gallas provides us with a tangible example of a death couched in psychoanalytical terms: ". . . er [Kohlhaas] muß auf Gewinnung von des Vaters Recht (auf die Mutter) aus sein, was allerdings seinen Tod als geschlechtlich identisches Subjekt bedeutet (weil er der Instanz der 'Mutter' unterworfen bleibt)" (p.81). According to Gallas this occurs in *Michael Kohlhaas* symbolically, when Kohlhaas swallows the capsule that the elector of Saxony desires. The capsule is an object of symbolic power. No detail surrounds it, and it causes both the collapse of the figure of paternity (the "Kurfürst of Sachsen") and seals Kohlhaas's doom to be beheaded.

41. Although this synopsis is quite obviously modeled on Saussure's *Course of General Linguistics*, I have summarized it by referring to Helga Gallas: ". . . ein Laut muß sich erst von anderen Lauten unterscheiden, um als Signifikant wirken zu können, ein Gedanke wird erst zum Signifikat durch den Gegensatz zu anderen Gedanken" (p. 36).

42. Ibid., p. 37.

43. Again I use Gallas, who gives credit to Samuel Weber for noting that the signified mimics the movement of the signifier: "Denn damit die 'undifferenzierte, amorphe

Masse' des Denkens sich in bestimmten Gedanken—d.h. überhaupt in Gedanken—artikuliert, müssen die verschiedenen Gedankenelemente sich voneinander absetzen, sich unterscheiden, differenzieren: sie müssen sich aufeinander beziehen, sich zueinander als *Signifikanten verhalten, um Signifikate zu werden* (pp. 38–39).

44. Ibid., p. 50.

45. Melanie Klein's analysis of a little child's introduction to language demonstrates this principle in a pragmatic context. Refer to Jacques Lacan, "La topique de l'imaginaire" in *Le Séminaire. Livre I. Les écrits techniques de Freud* (Paris: Seuil, 1975), pp. 95–103.

The voluntary suppression of an initial desire can seem, at best, only a symbolic enactment of death. Other explanations, attempting to articulate the interdependence of death and speech, leave the "scientific" realm of child development and linguistics for the (more Freudian) world of myth. Shoshana Felman, for instance, uses *Oedipus at Colonus* as the mythical key to equate the child's voluntary displacement from the centre of its mother's desire with its death.

In the Sophocles play, Oedipus must accept his death in order to pass from "story into history." The child, by accepting that its self-image (as "King") and its self-consciousness are transformed by the voluntary identification with the Father's prohibitive Law, undergoes a similar experience. The initiation of the child to language is thus staged as a mythical death. This "radical de-centerment" or "self-expropriation" is the necessary precursor to speech and narration, and its centrality is most clearly articulated by Oedipus's question, frequently cited both by Lacan and Felman: "Is it now that I am nothing, that I am made to be a man?" Shoshana Felman, "Beyond Oedipus: The Specimen Story of Psychoanalysis" in *MLN 98* (1983): 1021–53, p. 1029.

Felman's analysis of *Oedipus at Colonus* is especially cogent. She writes:

> [Oedipus] *assumes the Other*—in himself, he assumes his own *relation* to the discourse of the Other . . . ; he assumes, in other words, his radical de-centerment from his own ego, from his own self-image (Oedipus the King) and his own (self)-consciousness. And it is this radical acceptance, and assumption, of his own *self-expropriation* that embodies, for Lacan, the ultimate meaning of Oedipus's analysis, as well as the profound Oedipal significance of analysis as such. (p. 1028)

Felman also describes the task of psychoanalysis in terms of expropriation:

> Colonus thus embodies, among other things, not just Lacan's own exile, Lacan's own story of expropriation from the International Psychoanalysis Association, but Lacan's dramatic, tragic understanding that psychoanalysis is radically *about expropriation*, and his *assumption* of his story, his assumption, that is, all at once of his own *death* and of his own *myth*—of the *legacy* of this expropriation—as his truly destined psychoanalytic legacy and as his truly training psychoanalytic question: "Is it now that I am nothing, that I am made to be a man?" (p. 1041)

This is a radical reworking of an intuition outlined in Freud's *Totem and Taboo*, where Freud argues that the confrontation with death sets the survivors on a trajectory, which brings them theory (pp. 92–93) and the ambivalence of social customs. (That ambivalence is most clearly outlined in Freud's fictional myth of a Father and his sons.

The sons kill the Father in an attempt to appropriate power but find themselves even more enthralled by their Father after his death. All social customs, which entail both a celebration of their freedom as well as a conciliatory gesture toward the dead Father, simultaneously bears the mark of their crime and of their subjection to the Father's Law [pp. 142ff.].) Sigmund Freud, *Totem and Taboo* in *The Standard Edition of the Complete Psychological Works of Sigmund Freud. Volume XIII*, translated by James Strachey (London: Hogarth Press).

Stuart Schneiderman selects *Antigone* as the key example of the primacy attributed to death in Lacanian psychoanalysis, but aside from that difference, he essentially also stresses the importance of identification with the Other (here: the gods and/or the dead) as the subject's heroic encounter with its own death:

> Antigone's action is ethical; she makes the desire of the gods into her own. She acts according to her desire, and that desire is the desire of the Other. Note that she does not pose the question of what good would accrue to her, what worldly goods will be hers. Her act is disinterested in the largest sense; she does not consider the claims of her ego for happiness.

Just as Felman attempts to show how in Lacan's life mythical self-expropriation is the necessary stance of the analyst, Schneiderman dwells on Lacan's analytical techniques in order to show how the symbolic experience of death is thrust upon the analysand in order to help his or her development. Schneiderman mentions the "short session," a psychoanalytic session that is suspended without warning and arbitrarily, it seems, by the analyst. During the "short session" the analysand is not permitted to construct a coherent and self-gratifying image of his/her own ego. The control of one's conscious ego is shattered in order to allow the unconscious—the Other—to be articulated. Stuart Schneiderman, *Jacques Lacan. The Death of an Intellectual Hero* (Toronto: University of Toronto Press), pp. 166–67.

46. Schneiderman, p. 69.

47. Ibid., p. 103.

48. Lacan, "Le Désir, la vie et la mort" in *Séminaire II*, p. 267.

49. Lacan describes the reaction of a six-month-old infant before the mirror:

> Il y suffit de comprendre le stade du miroir *comme une identification* au sens plein que l'analyse donne à ce terme: à savoir la transformation produite chez le sujet, quand il assume une image, —dont la prédestination à cet effet de phase est suffisamment indiquée par l'usage, dans la théorie, du terme antique d'*imago*.
>
> C'est que la forme totale du corps par quoi le sujet devance dans un mirage la maturation de sa puissance, ne lui est donnée que comme *Gestalt*, c'est-à-dire dans une extériorité où certes cette forme est-elle plus constituante que constituée, mais où surtout elle lui apparaît dans un relief de stature qui la fige et sous une symétrie qui l'inverse, en opposition à la turbulence de mouvements dont il s'éprouve l'animer. (pp. 94–95)

Jacques Lacan, "Le stade du miroir comme formateur de la fonction du Je telle qu'elle nous est révélée dans l'expérience psychanalytique" in his *Ecrits* (Paris: Seuil, 1966), pp. 93–100.

50. Once the difference of desire is established, as *le désir de rien,* it is less difficult to see why the death drive replaces the more familiar (sexual) desire in explaining the narrative movement of a text.

51. Lacan, "Le Désir, la vie, la mort," pp. 261–62.

52. Lacan, "Questions à celui qui enseigne," p. 250.

53. Heinrich von Kleist, "Die Verlobung in Santo Domingo" in Helmut Sembdner, *Sämtliche Werke, Zweiter Band,* p. 160. Henceforth all references to this story will follow the quotation directly and will be marked as V.

54. Heinrich von Kleist, *The Marquise of O—and Other Stories,* p. 194.

55. Ibid., p. 46.

56. For the reference, see "Die Verlobung," p. 177.

> Die Alte, während sie den sonderbaren Ausdruck des Mädchens betrachtete, sagte bloß mit bebenden Lippen: daß sie erstaune. Sie fragte, was der junge Portugiese verschuldet, den man unter dem Torweg kürzlich mit Keulen zu Boden geworfen habe? Sie fragte, was die beiden Holländer verbrochen, die vor drei Wochen durch die Kugeln der Neger im Hofe gefallen wären? Sie wollte wissen, was man den drei Franzosen und so vielen andern einzelnen Flüchtlingen, vom Geschlecht der Weißen, zur Last gelegt habe, die mit Büchsen, Spießen und Dolchen, seit dem Ausbruch der Empörung, im Hause hingerichtet worden wären?

Babekan's justification lies in the list of murders already committed. Revolution takes the place of conscience in her case, and even the direct avowal that her victims had no personal guilt does not lead to any thoughtful revision of her position. Revenge justifies all acts.

57. Kleist dramatizes his dilemma in another letter written to Wilhelmine von Zenge in January 1801:

> Vielleicht hat die Natur Dir jene Klarheit, zu Deinem Glücke, versagt, jene traurige Klarheit, die mir zu jeder Miene den Gedanken, zu jedem Worte den Sinn, zu jeder Handlung den Grund nennt. Sie zeigt mir alles, was mich umgibt, und mich selbst, in seiner ganzen armseligen Blöße, und der farbige Nebel verschwindet, und alle die gefällig geworfnen Schleier sinken und dem Herzen ekelt zuletzt vor dieser Nacktheit. (KB, 621)

58. Jürgen Schröder's excellent analysis of "Der Findling" illustrates Kleist's crisis of belonging nowhere very lucidly. Schröder also emphasizes that "Der Findling" is about the poet's own project of writing. On the one hand, Kleist is interested in exploiting the logic of substitution he has analyzed in "Allerneuester Erziehungsplan." As a result, the narrative is very much a self-reflexive, self-referential text.

> An die Stelle der fehlenden und versagenden menschlich-moralischen Ordnungen und Sinnsysteme ist eine naturgesetzliche Ordnung getreten, die über die Menschen wie über lebendige Marionetten verfügt. Kleist hat in dieser Novelle Ernst gemacht mit dem Vorschlag des 'Allerneuesten Erziehung-

> splans,' das Gesetz der Experimentalphysik, in dem Kapitel von den Eigenschaften elektrischer Körper, auf die 'moralische Welt' zu übertragen und anzuwenden. . . . Der Findling ist dementsprechend auch eine Versuchsfigur, ein 'unelektrischer (neutraler) Körper,' der durch eine Aufnahme in die Familie Piachi in die Atmosphäre elektrischer Körper gebracht wird und die 'entgegengesetzte Elektrizität' annimmt. (p. 121)

Jürgen Schröder, "Kleists Novelle 'Der Findling': Ein Plädoyer für Nicolo" in *Kleist-Jahrbuch 1985*, edited by Hans Joachim Kreutzer (Berlin: Erich Schmidt Verlag, 1985), pp. 109–27.

Schröder emphasizes the "death drive" of the text—the attempt of the characters to reestablish the preliminary stability, so that Piachi's vengeful act of thrusting the unjust mandate in his adoptive son's mouth is the desperate attempt to reduce Nicolo again to the "vacuum" he was before.

Equally compelling is Schröder's interest in Kleist's self-perception; he seems himself to be like the foundling with no real place in society. Kleist, then, is "herausgedrängt aus allen möglichen Identifikationen." (p. 127)

59. Kleist, *The Marquise of O—and Other Stories*, p. 208.

60. Ibid., p. 194.

61. Gustav had denounced the French Revolution publicly and during politically troubled times. Through this speech act he effectively condemns himself to death. Although the death sentence is mediated first by Mariane and then by Toni, Gustav finally assumes the death for himself.

The suppressed love scene is interesting for another reason: it is presented in a sense as a rape both of Toni and of Gustav. Both do not seem to take responsibility for the event. Toni is quite passive and seems the true victim, whereas Gustav argues that the act is inexplicable. He even shifts the blame to Toni for his lack of discipline. If one agrees with Maurice Blanchot that death is the encounter with the impersonal and with one's own complete impotence, this sexual encounter becomes an example of a cloaked death scene.

62. Kleist, *The Marquise of O—and Other Stories*, p. 217.

63. Ibid., p. 226.

64. Ibid., p. 227.

65. Ibid., p. 209.

66. Ibid., p. 215.

67. Ibid., pp. 220–21.

68. The Russian count first attempts to die on the battlefield in order to redeem the honor of the marquise, which has been lost through his rape of her. This movement of self-abnegation is echoed by the retreat of the marquise (her near murder by her father) and by the final stipulation—that the count give up all claims on his "wife." Such sacrifice becomes the condition for his happiness at the end of the narrative. In fact, the gesture that leads to his reintegration into the society of the marquise is the symbolic acceptance of his death to society—his voluntary giving up of his last will and testament:

> Er warf unter den Geschenken, womit die Gäste den Neugebornen bewillkommten, zwei Papiere auf die Wiege desselben, deren eines, wie sich nach seiner Entfernung auswies, eine Schenkung von 20 000 Rubel an den Knaben, und das andere ein Testament war, in dem er die Mutter, falls er stürbe, zur Erbin seines ganzen Vermögens einsetzte. (p. 143)

Heinrich von Kleist, "Die Marquise von O . . . " in Helmut Sembdner, *Sämtliche Werke, Zweiter Band*, pp. 104–43.

69. Kleist, *Penthesilea*, in Helmut Sembdner, *Heinrich von Kleist, Volume I*, l. 2607.

70. Kleist, *Plays*, p. 267.

CHAPTER 3. IN PURSUIT OF POWER: A STUDY OF BALZAC'S NARRATIVES IN HIS *COMÉDIE HUMAINE*

1. Honoré de Balzac, *The Works of Honoré de Balzac, Volume XI* [*Cousin Betty*], introduced by George Saintsbury (Freeport, New York: n.d.), pp. 204–5.

2. All references to Balzac's *Comédie humaine* are drawn from Balzac, *La Comédie humaine, Tomes I–VII* (Paris: Aux Editions du Seuil, 1966). Subsequent references to Balzac's works will be incorporated in the text marked by the Roman numeral to indicate the volume, followed by the page number. The passage in question here is from *Les Proscrits*, VII, 281.

3. In the opening pages of *Facino Cane* the narrator explains his ability to "empathize" completely with individuals on the street. This ability explains the confidence of the protagonist Facino Cane, and his willingness to communicate with the narrator. Whether the narrator has complete mastery or abdicates his own control is left ambivalent, as is the conclusion itself, since we never do learn whether Facino's narrative is true, fabricated, or simply mad. Here is the passage describing the narrator's ability to "identify" completely with passers-by on the street:

> Quitter ses habitudes, devenir un autre que soi par l'ivresse des facultés morales, et jouer le jeu à volonté, telle était ma distraction, A quoi dois-je ce don? Est-ce une seconde vue? est-ce une de ces qualités dont l'abus mènerait à la folie? Je n'ai jamais cherché les causes de cette puissance; je la possède et m'en sers, voilà tout. Sachez seulement que, dès ce temps, j'avais décomposé les éléments de cette masse hétérogène nommée le peuple, que je l'avais analysée de manière à pouvoir évaluer ses qualités bonnes et mauvaises. (*Facino Cane*, IV, 257–58)

4. In another *Etude philosophique* written in 1831, we find that movement and the arabesque are associated with pure (poetic) fantasy. The following passage is drawn from *L'Enfant maudit*:

> Avec l'instinct que donne la paternité le vieillard choisissait toujours ses cadeaux parmi les oeuvres dont les ornements appartenaient à ce genre fantasque nommé arabesque, et qui, ne parlant ni aux sens ni à l'âme, s'adressent seulement à l'esprit par les créations de la fantaisie pure. (VII, 31)

This form of poetry is supposed to bypass both the senses and the soul in order to affect only the spirit. Within the context of the story it becomes clear that such distinctions begin to blur; in fact, the delicate character to be protected from the senses and from the exhileration of the soul still finds her way to such intoxicating experiences.

5. Gaëtan Picon documents Balzac's own sense of exile as a writer in a letter to Zulma Carraud. Picon writes: "Pour vivre—plus tard—pour jouir—enfin—il doit supprimer ce qu'on appelle *vie.* 'J'ai, pendant un mois, à ne pas quitter ma table, où je jette ma vie comme un alchimiste son or dans un creuset" (A Zulma, 1832).

Gaëtan Picon also refers to another letter written to Zulma Carraud in 1831:

> 'Je vis sous le plus dur des despotismes: celui qu'on se fait à soi-même. Je travaille nuit et jour. Je suis venu ici me réfugier au fond d'un château, comme dans un monastère. . . . L'égoïsme de l'homme qui vit par la pensée est quelque chose d'affreux. Pour être un homme en dehors des autres, il faut commencer par s'en mettre réellement en dehors. N'est-ce pas un martyre pour un homme qui ne vit que par l'épanchement des sentiments, qui ne respire que tendresse, et qui a besoin de trouver sans cesse près de lui une âme pour asyle, de méditer, de comparer, d'inventer, de chercher sans cesse, de voyager dans les espaces de la pensée, quand il aime à aimer?

These references are drawn from Gaëtan Picon, *Balzac* (Paris: écrivains de toujours/seuil, 1956), pp. 15, 18.

6. Gaëtan Picon, *Balzac* (Paris: écrivains de toujours/seuil, 1956), p. 158.

7. Ibid., p. 168.

8. Ibid., p. 168.

9. Ibid., p. 32.

10. Picon, p. 138. We should keep in mind at this point that Balzac apparently did not disassociate himself completely from his work. His numerous corrections of his proofs are almost legendary, according to Peter Brooks and Christopher Prendergast.

11. Ibid., p. 98.

12. Jean-Jacques Rousseau, *Les Confessions, tome II* (Paris: Garnier-Flammarion, 1968), p. 99.

13. Please refer to chapter 4, in which Félix Davin's preface is analyzed. There it becomes clear that Balzac "decomposes" and then "reconstructs" his object of representation; he is not portrayed as a simple "photographer" of his time.

14. Ibid., p. 78.

15. The eponymous hero of *Maître Cornélius* (1831) commits suicide as a result of his desire never to submit to sleep, to be in control at all times. His avarice extends to the point that he plays both the role of the thief and that of the victim; in his sleep he steals the money that he has accumulated during the day. In order to block this theft of himself, he begins to take strong antinarcotics. It is his lack of sleep that finally drives him to kill himself: "Enfin, cet homme si puissant, ce coeur endurci par la vie politique et la vie commerciale, ce génie obscur dans l'histoire, dut succomber aux horreurs du

supplice qu'il s'était créé. Tué par quelques pensées plus aiguës que toutes celles auxquelles il avait résisté jusqu'alors, il se coupa la gorge avec un rasoir" (VII, 125).

16. Pierre Citron makes mention of this letter in his own preface to the *Etudes philosophiques*: "Une lettre d'octobre 1834 à Mme Hanska précise que les *Etudes de moeurs* peindraient les sentiments et la vie, les *Etudes philosophiques* 'pourquoi les sentiments, pourquoi la vie'. Dans les premières, les 'individualités typisées'. Dans les secondes, 'les types individualisés.' Mais le sens de l'oeuvre ne nous apparaît pas exactement, avec le recul, celui qu'y mettait Balzac" (VI, 413).

17. We can speak of Wenceslas's "lucid analysis," albeit ironically, since he passes for a great man in social circles because of his ability to formulate his insights ["dessiner son plan par la parole"] (V, 81).

We might also note here that both Balzac and Kleist seem to share a skepticism vis-à-vis preformed ideas or inspiration. One need only juxtapose this passage in *La Cousine Bette* with Kleist's *Über die allmähliche Verfertigung des Gedankens beim Reden* in order to perceive that both writers seem to situate a certain hopefulness in the spontaneous production of words or artworks.

18. Honoré de Balzac, *The Works of Honoré de Balzac, Volume XI* [*Cousin Betty*], introduced by George Saintsbury (Freeport, New York: n.d.), pp. 204–5.

19. Here one can insert Balzac's own description of the creative process as it is set down in the *Traité des excitants modernes* (1838), which finds its place in the *Etudes analytiques*. He pursues another articulation of the necessary suspension of the narrative will. Through the fictional self-construction of a "je," Balzac describes the process that accompanies his work in the night. He speaks of his all-important stimulant, coffee, that acts as the material base to his intellectual pursuits:

> les plexus s'enflamment, ils flambent et font aller leurs étincelles jusqu'au cerveau. Dès lors, tout s'agite: les idées s'ébranlent comme des bataillons de la grande armée sur le terrain d'une bataille, et la bataille a lieu. Les souvenirs arrivent au pas de charge, enseignes déployées; la cavalerie légère des comparaisons se développe par un magnifique galop; l'artillerie de la logique accourt avec son train et ses gargousses; les traits d'esprit arrivent en tirailleurs; les figures se dressent; *le papier se couvre d'encre*, car la veille commence et finit par des torrents d'eau noire, comme la bataille par sa poudre noire. (VII, 601, my emphasis)

In this metaphorical depiction, the writer's abdication of mastery is portrayed through the implicitly violent image of a battle that rages in the creator's mind night after night, as he struggles to compose. Primarily, though, it is the separateness of the "memories," as well as of the rhetorical and fictional figures from the writing self that expresses the potential death of authorial control. The act of writing seems quite passive, especially if we consider that the paper seems to cover itself with ink, rather than being inscribed purposefully by a writing subject.

20. This line of questioning could be considered an offshoot of Terry Eagleton's remarks in his book *Literary Theory. An Introduction* (Minneapolis: University of Minnesota Press, 1983). He writes:

> Its [critical discourse's] apparent generosity at the level of the signified is matched only by its sectarian intolerance at the level of the signifier. Regional dialects of the discourse, so to speak, are acknowledged and sometimes tolerated, but you must not sound as though you are speaking another language altogether. To do so is to recognize in the sharpest way that critical discourse is power. To be on the inside of the discourse itself is to be blind to this power, for what is more natural and nondominative than to speak one's own tongue? (p. 203)

Although Eagleton is writing about the language of literary criticism here rather than that of literature (a distinction that he tends, moreover, to call into question), his argument helps us to recognize how significant the intersection of narrative discourse and power actually is. At this point it is too early to begin speculating on how adequately Balzac calls into question the institutions of his time, notably wealth as well as political and social success. Nonetheless, he does concern himself with power. He often stages the power of the author (and his loss of authority) in his récits.

21. Pierre Citron explains the historical context of *Honorine* in his preface to the récit in the Seuil edition:

> Cette longue nouvelle, qui eut peut-être comme premier titre prévu *la Séparation*, fut écrite en trois jours, à la fin de décembre 1842, selon une confidence de Balzac à Mme Hanska; sans doute le romancier ne voulait-il parler que de la première rédaction: il la revit et la corrigea en février 1843, et la fit paraître dans la *Presse* du 17 au 29 mars 1843, puis, en volume, en 1844. L'oeuvre prit place en 1845 dans *la Comédie humaine*, au tome IV des *Scènes de la vie privée*." (I, 559)

It is curious to note a singular lack of commentary on this text. The only two references I found were Franc Schuerewegen, "Pour effleurer le sexe: A propos d'*Honorine* de Balzac" in *Studia Neophilologica*, 1983 (55–62), pp. 183–97, and Hava Sussmann, "Un avatar du mythe de Tristan et Yseut" in *L'année balzacienne*, 1981 (2), pp. 297–99.

In the latter article Sussmann simply emphasizes that Balzac has woven several motifs and episodes of the Tristan legend into his récit. Sussmann concludes: "Faut-il comprendre que la folie, la démesure, la passion meurtrière étaient l'apanage des temps à jamais révolus? C'est, semble-t-il, ce que Balzac suggère en faisant coïncider le dénouement de l'histoire avec la révolution de Juillet. . . . Ainsi, profondément modifié par Balzac, le mythe de Tristan et Yseut débouche, non sans ironie, sur le réel contemporain" (p. 299). Please see endnote 28, below, for comments on Franc Schuerewegen's article.

22. Honoré de Balzac, *Modeste Mignon, The Lily of the Valley and Other Stories*, translated by Clara Bell and James Waring (Philadelphia: John D. Morris and Co., n.d.), p. 294.

23. After her return to Octave, Honorine writes to Maurice: "Je meurs pour la Société, pour la Famille, pour le Mariage, comme les premiers chrétiens mouraient pour Dieu. Je ne sais pas de quoi je meurs, je le cherche avec bonne foi, car je ne suis pas entêtée; mais je tiens à vous expliquer mon mal, à vous qui avez amené le chirurgien céleste" (I, 588).

24. Balzac, *Modeste Mignon, The Lily of the Valley and Other Stories*, p. 338.

25. Ironically, her sealed-off, self-supportive world shows up many cracks. It is precisely Honorine's act of creating flowers that provides the foothold Octave needs to sustain her world. He pays for the materials that produce the flowers and he buys her products for exorbitant prices—quite unbeknownst to her.

26. Ibid., p. 339.

27. Octave exclaims, for instance: "Et cette fleur se dessèche solitaire et cachée" (I, 574).

28. Franc Schuerewegen, one of the two critics to write about *Honorine*, also notes the importance of the "flower" in this récit, noting that Honorine is linked metaphorically and metonymically with flowers (p. 194).

Schuerewegen also notes the overdetermination of the floral motif and sees in it primarily a hidden allusion to the troubled relation between Honorine and Octave:

> Ainsi, les fleurs dissumulant une signification essentielle, il importe de lire *Honorine* avec tout le "génie du sous-entendu" (p. 525) que célèbre son incipit. L'opération herméneutique sollicitée par le texte est double: il incombe au lecteur d'effacer d'abord la thématique obturatrice pour remplir ensuite lui-même l'abîme en-dessous. (p. 196)

Franc Schuerewegen, "Pour effleurer le sexe. A propos d'*Honorine* de Balzac" in *Studia Neophilologica*, 1983, pp. 193–97.

29. For clarity's sake: Honorine conceived during her extramarital affair, but the child died before it was born at seven months. The role of maternity as an ambivalent form of productivity is also mapped out in an *étude philosophique* with the title *Massimilla Doni*.

We should also note that this child, the fruit of Honorine's erring, can be interpreted as the symbol of her quest for the *Idéal*, perhaps even as the figure of her search for her very own "story."

30. Balzac, *Modeste Mignon, The Lily of the Valley and Other Stories*, p. 370.

31. Ursule discusses with the priest, l'abbé Chaperon, the possibility of the dead returning to haunt the living. The priest provides a scientific, rather than purely religious, account in favor of the possibility of such reappearances:

> Il [le docteur Minoret] avait reconnu la possibilité de l'existence d'un monde spirituel, d'un monde des idées. Si les idées sont une création propre à l'homme, si elles subsistent en vivant d'une vie qui leur soit propre; elles doivent avoir des formes insaisissables à nos sens extérieurs, mais perceptibles à nos sens intérieurs quand ils sont dans certaines conditions. Ainsi les idées de votre parrain peuvent vous envelopper, et peut-être les avez-vous revêtues de son apparence. Puis, si Minoret [le faux héritier] a commis ces actions, elles se résolvent en idées; car toute action est le résultat de plusieurs idées. Or, si les idées se meuvent dans le monde spirituel, votre esprit a pu les apercevoir en y pénétrant. Ces phénomènes ne sont pas plus étranges que ceux de la mémoire, et ceux de la mémoire sont aussi surprenants et inexpli-

cables que ceux du parfum des plantes, qui sont peut-être les idées de la plante. (II, 530)

32. Professor Brombert's analysis of the narrative structure of *Le lys dans la vallée* stresses the figure of the hidden reader, who ultimately undermines the control of Félix over his subject matter. As a result of his telling his tale, Félix effectively loses in the narrative contract. He suffers a second loss; he is again prohibited from entering a sexual relation. He is debarred from a more vital form of life. Professor Brombert writes:

> Balzac's novel suggests throughout a poetry of silence, a poetry of repressed language which lends itself to "mysterious meanings" while serving the demands of modesty and the duplicities of hidden desire. . . . This dream of a language without words corresponds at another level to the incompatibilities between living and the act of telling. The word that says or describes is destined for the realms of absence and emptiness. (p. 28)

Victor Brombert, "Natalie, or Balzac's Hidden Reader" in *The Hidden Reader. Stendhal, Balzac, Hugo, Baudelaire, Flaubert* (Cambridge: Harvard University Press, 1988), pp. 23–36.

33. Stowe uses the "sequel" to *Le Lys dans la vallée* as an example of a hopeful narrative, where Felix is finally able to show tolerance to his new wife, because of his earlier suffering. In other words, *Une fille d'Eve* can be interpreted as a novel in which Felix, as one of the protagonists, has already experienced a form of symbolic death but must accept another form of his ego's death (this time caused by his own wife's naive infidelity) in order to assume a successful paternal role. William Stowe, *Balzac, James, and the Realistic Novel* (Princeton: Princeton University Press, 1983).

34. La Rabouilleuse's own death—as the excessive overdevelopment of the self—is torn in two directions. On the one hand, she suffers from alcoholism *(l'abus des liqueurs)*, but at the same time, her voracious desire for social grandeur leaves her own body devoured and consumed:

> Sous l'angle aigu d'un mansarde, sans papier de tenture, et sur un lit de sangle dont le maigre matelas était rempli de bourre peut-être, les trois jeunes gens aperçurent une femme, verte comme une noyée de deux jours, et maigre comme l'est une étique deux heures avant sa mort. Ce cadavre infect avait une méchante rouennerie à carreaux sur sa tête dépouillée de cheveux. Le tour des yeux caves était rouge et les paupières étaient comme des pellicules d'oeuf. Quant à ce corps, jadis si ravissant, il n'en restait qu'une ignoble ostéologie. (III, 188)

35. We should note here that Philippe Bridau, as the masterful decipherer, is the character who collects others' belongings successfully. He inherits the portraits meant for his brother, Joseph; he appropriates his uncle's wife, Flore Brazier; he buys his way into the social hierarchy, and although this final masterful plot is foiled by Bixiou's intervention, he maintains his powerful status within the hierarchy of the army as *colonel de l'Empire.*

36. Balzac's negative evaluation of bachelorhood is most clearly articulated in his *Un Curé de province*, in which he plays off three bachelors' frustrations against one

another. For Balzac, it seems, the inability to create or to produce generates a bitterness and destructiveness in the isolated self:

> Puis elles [les vieilles filles] deviennent âpres et chagrines, parce qu'un être qui a manqué sa vocation est malheureux; il souffre, et la souffrance engendre la méchanceté. En effet, avant de s'en prendre à elle-même de son isolement, une fille en accuse longtemps le monde. De l'accusation à un désir de vengeance, il n'y a qu'un pas. . . . Elles ne voient qu'elles en elles-mêmes. Ce sentiment les porte insensiblement à choisir les choses qui leur sont commodes, au détriment de celles qui peuvent être agréables à autrui. . . . Les vieilles filles sont donc jalouses à vide, et ne connaissent que les malheurs de la seule passion que les hommes pardonnent au beau sexe, parce qu'elle les flatte. (III, 70)

The masculine correlative of his critique of bachelorhood centers primarily on the (villainous) character of Troubert, who has entered into the Church as the means to succeed in society. His energy by not finding a place within the social structure becomes the bearer of a certain destructiveness typical of the nineteenth century:

> Nous vivons à une époque où le défaut des gouvernements est d'avoir moins fait la Société pour l'Homme, que l'Homme pour la Société. Il existe un combat perpétuel entre l'individu contre le système qui veut l'exploiter et qu'il tâche d'exploiter à son profit; tandis que jadis l'homme réellement plus libre se montrait plus généreux pour la chose publique. . . . L'histoire des Innocent III, des Pierre-le-Grand, et de tous les meneurs de siècle ou de nation prouverait au besoin, dans un ordre très élevé, cette immense pensée que Troubert représentait au fond du cloître Saint-Gatien. (III, 85)

37. In *Louis Lambert* the mathematical dimension of this narrative problem is explored as the condition for narration and thought. The passage occurs toward the end of the text, at a point where Lambert has already succumbed to a genial madness or mad genius, where his own language is already impregnated by the search for a truer fragment (rather than that of a masterful, continuous narrative). Here is the final fragment recorded of Lambert's "insights":

> TROIS est la formule des Mondes créés. Il est le signe *spirituel* de la création comme il est le signe *matériel* de la circonférence. En effet, Dieu n'a procédé que par des lignes circulaires. La ligne droite est l'attribut de l'infini; aussi l'homme qui pressent l'infini la reproduit-il dans ses oeuvres. DEUX est le Nombre de la génération. TROIS est le Nombre de l'existence, qui comprend la génération et le produit. Ajoutez le Quaternaire, vous avez le SEPT, qui est la formule du ciel. Dieu est au-dessus, il est l'Unité. (VII, 323)

38. Honoré de Balzac, *César Birotteau, Béatrix and Other Stories*, translated by Ellen Marriage and James Waring (Philadelphia: John D. Morris and Co., n.d.), pp. 55–56.

39. This "survival" of the plot is slightly reminiscent of Peter Brooks's analysis of *La Peau de chagrin*, although Brooks describes the "death" and "survival" of the plot in a more Freudian language:

> It is as if this novel had taken the desire that in various forms drives most novelistic plots and offered its full satisfaction halfway through the novel. . . .

> What Raphaël indeed discovers at the moment when his desire opens onto its full realization is death: "Il voyait la MORT" (p. 209). Desire realized through the magic skin *is* death, the diminishment of the life span. Hence realization must also mean the death of desire: as Raphaël discovers as a consequence of his vision of death, he can no longer desire." (p. 49)

Brooks goes on to make "narration" or the act of telling the means by which the death of the pleasure principle can be survived. He transforms "narration" into the "tenor" of the story. Peter Brooks, "Narrative Desire" in *Reading for the Plot, Design and Intention in Narrative* (New York: Random Books, 1984), pp. 57–61.

40. At the beginning of the final section of the novel, entitled "Triomphe de César," the anonymous narrator describes an ambiguous aspect of French, nineteenth-century Law, bound up with the naming of an individual as "legally dead."

> la Loi le déclare mineur et incapable de tout acte légal, civil et civique. Mais il n'en est rien. Avant de reparaître, il attend un sauf-conduit que jamais ni juge-commissaire ni créancier n'ont refusé, car s'il était rencontré sans cet *exeat*, il serait mis en prison, tandis que, muni de cette sauvegarde, il se promène en parlementaire dans le camp ennemi, non par curiosité, mais pour déjouer les mauvaises intentions de la loi relativement aux faillis. L'effet de toute loi qui touche à la fortune privée est de développer prodigieusement les fourberies de l'esprit. La pensée des faillis, comme de tous ceux dont les intérêts sont contrecarrés par une loi quelconque, est de l'annuler à leur égard. (IV, 217)

We note that the description, or metaphorical representation, of death in *César Birotteau* brings with it a confusion of the status of the Law. On the one hand, the Law protects the individual, even he who has transgressed it. But the status of each law is itself put into question, since it seems to act usually as the source of its own transgression.

41. Balzac, *César Birotteau*, translated by Ellen Marriage and James Waring, p. 55.

42. The formulation of these questions, and the consideration of their limitations for reading Balzac's *Comédie humaine* can emerge if we consider Lukàcs's attempt to appropriate Balzac into the corpus of "Marxist" writers. Lukàcs praises Balzac for his lucid irony and his damning criticism of his own age:

> The general is thus always concrete and real because it is based on a profound understanding of what is typical in each of the characters figuring in it—an understanding so deep that the particular is not eclipsed but on the contrary emphasized and concretized by the typical, and on the other hand the relationship between the individual and the social setting of which it is the product and in which—or against which—it acts, is always clearly discernible, however intricate this relationship may be. (pp. 54–55)

Lukàcs's analysis, however valuable, emphasizes Balzac's preoccupation with needing to motivate catastrophe. Lukàcs thus leaves aside the ambivalence associated with decline, where the terms *disaster* and *progress* no longer have necessarily fixed definitions. Lukàcs discusses Balzac's theory of social determinism in order to conclude:

> It is the wide sweep, the greatness itself of Balzac's realism which forms the sharpest contrast to the habits of thought and the experience of an age which is to an increasing degree turning away from objective reality and is content to regard either immediate experience, or experience inflated into a myth as the utmost that we can grasp of reality. (pp. 57–59)

Georg Lukàcs, "Balzac: Lost Illusions" in *Studies in European Realism* (New York: Grosset and Dunlop), pp. 47–64.

If we consider the plots of *Eugénie Grandet*, *Un Début dans la vie*, or even *Le Père Goriot* we can see that the analysis of progress and of decadence is not only prepared and explained analytically by Balzac. The trajectory and even separateness of progress and decline is put into question by the various novelistic protagonists.

43. The actual experience of dying is articulated, curiously enough, through a reference to Beethoven's symphony. César's experience of music becomes the trope to express the plenitude of experience and the passing from life into death. The linking of music and death can here remind us of Kleist's own preoccupation with a poetics of music.

44. Balzac, *César Birotteau*, translated by Ellen Marriage and James Waring, p. 55.

45. Roland LeHuenen at the University of Toronto provided many of these insights in his lectures on *Eugénie Grandet* (1978–79).

CHAPTER 4. *LA PENSÉE QUI TUE* BALZAC'S POETICS OF THOUGHT

1. Maurice Bardèche cites the famous anecdote of Balzac's death, where the author presumably calls upon the doctor Bianchon, a character from the *Comédie humaine*, to save him. Maurice Bardèche, "Les Romans philosophiques" in *Balzac Romancier* (Paris: Plon, 1940), pp. 373–91.

2. Although it is clear that the primacy of thought will be reflected upon in negative terms—as "death inducing"—the stress on the mastery of thought cannot be overlooked either. Here Albert Béguin's study of the visionary aspects of Balzac's *Etudes philosophiques* provides a useful formulation. He notes that each of the characters is caught in the struggle between "le désir au bonheur" and "l'ambition de la connaissance ou du pouvoir." He continues: "Le paradoxe demeure insoluble; l'éternité ne peut être possédée ni par la résignation à l'humble bonheur humain, ni par la conquête héroïque de l'intelligence. Elle est au delà de la mort" (p. 203). Albert Béguin, ". . . arracher des mots au silence, et des idées à la nuit" in *Balzac visionnaire* (Genève: Albert Skira, 1946), pp. 183–206.

3. Pierre Citron tends toward attributing the theories in the preface to Balzac. We should also note here that the chronology Balzac provides for the plan of the *Comédie humaine* is a doctored one.

4. Paul Robert, *Le Petit Robert, Dictionnaire alphabétique et analogique de la langue française*, rédaction dirigée par A. Rey et J. Rey-Debove (Paris: Le Robert, 1967/81).

5. Christopher Prendergast, "Narrative Contracts" in *The Order of Mimesis. Balzac, Stendhal, Nerval, Flaubert* (New York: Cambridge University Press, 1986), p. 95.

6. Balzac is quick to point out that he is not really following in the footsteps of Jean-Jacques Rousseau, when he is arguing for the importance of leaving untouched the natural simplicity of children. In his "Avant-Propos" of 1842 Balzac points in particular to Catholicism, but also to the Monarchy, as the two institutions meant to help individuals develop themselves properly and he denounces "interest" [greed or egotism] rather than social forces as the prime cause of decadence in individuals.

> L'homme n'est ni bon ni méchant, il naît avec des instincts et des aptitudes: la Société, loin de le dépraver, comme l'a prétendu Rousseau, le perfectionne, le rend meilleur; mais l'intérêt développe aussi ses penchants mauvais. . . . il en résulte cet enseignement que si la pensée, ou la passion, qui comprend la poussée et le sentiment, est l'élément social, elle en est aussi l'élément destructeur. (I, 53)

7. The description of the three ages of a thought is slightly lengthy, although wittily put. Here is a slightly abridged version of that portrayal:

> Une pensée a trois âges. Si vous l'exprimez dans toute la chaleur prolifique de sa conception, vous la produisez rapidement, par un jet. . . . Mais si vous ne saisissez pas ce premier bonheur de génération mentale . . . vous tombez soudain dans le gâchis des difficultés: . . . alors, ce sont vos idées qui vous brisent, vous lassent, vous sanglent des coups sifflants aux oreilles, et contre lesquels vous regimbez. . . . Vient le dernier âge de la pensée. Elle s'est implantée, elle a pris racine dans votre âme, elle y a mûri . . . [On aperçoit son idée] . . . dans toute la grâce de ses frondaisons, de ses floraisons, l'idée malicieuse, luxuriante, luxueuse, belle comme une femme magnifiquement belle, belle comme un cheval sans défaut! (VII, 582–83)

8. It is important to consider here Janet Beizer's claim, which resides in the fact that Balzac deliberately pursues a strategy of self-reflexivity in his *Comédie humaine*. Her point is that Balzac recognizes that "le langage ne peut imiter que le langage."

> Apprehensive of competing with reality, of constructing a mirror whose supplementarity can only result in loss, Balzac's narrators persistently attempt to isolate art from life, to abolish external referentiality. . . . Art's referent is fantasy, or illusion; mimesis becomes an internal aesthetic as art imitates art and fictional characters wander from narrative to narrative. (p. 176)

Although Janet Beizer's analysis of the structure of the *Comédie Humaine* is fascinating, we must concede that for the "Théorie" at least, even self-description is difficult, if not impossible, to sustain. Janet Beizer, *Family Plots. Balzac's Narrative Generations* (New Haven: Yale University Press, 1986).

9. Maurice Bardèche, p. 375.

10. Leuilliot's method is an interesting one. He juxtaposes Michelet's, Victor Hugo's, and Balzac's projects in order to conclude that all three make use of a retrospective "auto-contemplation" to transform "diverse digressions" into constituent elements of the "total work." Bernard Leuilliot, "Oeuvres complètes, oeuvres diverses" in Claude

Duchet and Jacques Neefs, *Balzac. L'Invention du roman* (Paris: Pierre Belfond, 1982), pp. 257–79.

11. Ibid., pp. 273–74.

12. Françoise Gaillard, "La Science: modèle ou vérité; Réflexions sur *l'Avant-propos à la Comédie humaine*" *in* Claude Duchet and Jacques Neefs, *Balzac: L'Invention du roman* (Paris: Pierre Belfond, 1982), pp. 57–83, cf. p. 74–75.

13. Ibid., p. 76.

14. Peter Brooks, "Narrative Desire" in *Reading for the Plot. Design and Intention in Narrative* (New York: Random Books, 1984), p. 61.

15. Ibid., p. 103.

16. Ibid., p. 61.

17. Janet Beizer, "Mirrors and Fatherhood: *Le Père Goriot*" in *Family Plots: Balzac's Narrative Generations* (New Haven: Yale University Press, 1986), p. 132.

18. Ibid., p. 137.

19. Roland Barthes, *S/Z* (Paris: Editions du Seuil, 1970), p. 221.

20. Ibid., pp. 118–20.

21. Christopher Prendergast, "Balzac: Narrative Contracts" in *The Order of Mimesis*, p. 117.

22. Balzac's *L'Auberge rouge* contains one passage that most clearly demonstrates Balzac's anxiety with a "democratic" procedure, one which does not allow straightforward ethical judgments, but rather disseminates and multiplies these in a contradictory manner. At the end of the récit the narrator calls upon representatives of his society to help him decide whether or not to marry the daughter of a murderer, and thereby to enrich himself of "stained money." His use of the ballot system—a rather striking symbol of a decentralized (perhaps even "shattered") society—only ends up augmenting his confusion:

> Messieurs, cet accident phénoménal de la nature intellectuelle est un de ceux qui sortent le plus vivement de l'état normal auquel est soumise la société, dit-il. Donc, la décision à prendre doit être un fait extemporané de notre conscience, un concept soudain, un jugement instructif, une nuance fugitive de notre appréhension intime assez semblable aux éclairs qui constituent le sentiment du goût. Votons. (VII, 140)

The narrator concludes from the findings: "... il y a unanimité secrète pour le mariage, et unanimité pour me l'interdire! Comment sortir d'embarras?" (VII, 140). The text leaves this question unanswered.

23. Cf. Prendergast, p. 116. Here Prendergast notes Balzac's rejection of "le bon mot" "... whose function is 'de mettre tout en question.'"

24. "'Devenir un autre que soi' signifie, pour le romancier, écrire autrement, admettre la relativité des points de vue.... Il s'agit d'inventer un langage, de chercher dans le livre du monde non des mots mais comme l'a dit Baudelaire, la génération des

mots." Martin Kanes, "Langage balzacien: Splendeurs et misères de la représentation" in Claude Duchet and Jacques Neefs, *Balzac: L'Invention du roman* (Paris: Pierre Belfond, 1982), pp. 281–95, cf. p. 289.

25. In his study of Balzac and Melodrama, Prendergast explains:

> In its feel for the euphoria of transgression, in its partial liquidation of the formal categories of the conventional 'character', *La Cousine Bette* is a text of negation challenging and subverting, not the values of social order as such (which would be crude and banal in the extreme), but the assumption by that order of its own unmovable security, a challenge that includes the novel itself in terms of its role as instrument of naturalization. (p. 170)

Christopher Prendergast, *Balzac: Fiction and Melodrama* (London: Edward Arnold, 1978).

26. Fredric Jameson, "The Ideology of Form: Partial Systems in *La Vieille fille*" in *Sub-stance* 1976, pp. 29–49, cf. p. 37.

27. Ibid., p. 37.

28. Compare Beizer's critique with Dällenbach's. Janet Beizer writes:

> Thus Balzac created, in *La Comédie humaine*, a strange hymn to language, whose primal and final objective is silence . . . The cry to flee, hide, and be silent, to preserve the ineffable, plaintively resounds through every novel, every story, every essay written by Balzac. But it is not unaccompanied. The call to silence is always doubled by a whispered fear that nothing but language separates the ineffable from the unmeaning, the absolute from the void.

Here the fragment can become simply a symbol of language's inadequacy to articulate a "vision" and reminds the reader of the threat to meaningful language. Beizer, *Family Plots*, p. 179.

The "ineffable" for Dällenbach beckons to be spoken—and respoken. The fragment shows the contours of a greater, as yet unrealized whole rather than symbolizing the unbridgeable gap between sign and "idea." Dällenbach uses *La Muse du département*—in which "fragmentation" is staged in order to develop his argument. In this text characters are attempting to reconstruct a novel from some (incomplete) pages. Dällenbach writes:

> The interest of this episode lies, on the one hand, in the ironic counterpoint which begins between a constant (the text of *Olympia* in ruins, objectified by its typography) and certain variables (the responses which the text elicits from a very heterogenous public) and, on the other hand, in the thematic scheme produced by a reading which succeeds in rewriting the fragments—in putting the pieces of the text together and making the whole intellible—by eliminating little by little all the factors of unreadability.

We see here, then, that Dällenbach ultimately tends to interpret the "fragment" as a symbol of the creativity implicit in reading rather than as a deathly limit of meaning and language. Lucien Dällenbach, "Reading as Suture (Problems of Reception of the Fragmentary Text: Balzac and Claude Simon)" in *Style* (18) 1984: 196–206, cf. p. 197.

29. Pierre Citron describes the complex genesis of *Louis Lambert*. The text carries traces of Balzac's early preoccupation with "supranormal" protagonists dating from 1828. He also incorporates qualities of many protagonists belonging to the *Etudes philosophiques*: Etienne d'Hérouville; Frenhofer; and Raphaël. Citron emphasizes Balzac's own qualities, presumably decipherable in the character of Louis:

> Balzac y a inséré nombre d'éléments personnels: la folie dont il s'est à plusieurs reprises senti menacé par excès de travail et de réflexion, les préoccupations philosophiques, le sentiment de l'importance qu'il y avait à utiliser la science mais à dépasser ses insuffisances, la double préoccupation de la synthèse et de l'analyse, la volonté d'être à la fois poète et logicien, le don de 'spécialité'... le désir d'appréhender tout l'univers en le réduisant à un principe d'unité, sont autant de traits balzaciens. (VII, 285–86)

Of equal significance is the realization that the fragmentary quality of the text is emphasized more and more in the later version. Again, Citron's information is useful here to explain the genesis of the narrative, spanning the years between 1833 and 1835:

> L'étendue de l'oeuvre avait presque doublé: Balzac avait gonflé les souvenirs de Vendôme et l'exposé du système de Lambert (ajoutant notamment le passage sur l'origine du langage, issu de Bonald, et le développement sur la source des mythes); surtout, il avait ajouté la lettre à l'oncle, une large part de la première série des pensées de Lambert et toute la seconde série, cette dernière conçue lors de son voyage à Vienne en mai 1835. (VII, 285)

The text is completed in 1835 but is only published in 1836. Its status within the context of Balzac's other works is equally uncertain. It belongs to the *Etudes philosophiques* but is then grouped separately as well with *Le Livre mystique*, composed of *Les Proscrits*, *Louis Lambert*, and *Séraphîta*. Only in 1846 does Balzac include *Lambert* in his *Comédie humaine*.

30. Honoré de Balzac, *Séraphîta*, *A Daughter of Eve*, *and Other Stories*, translated by Clara Bell and R. S. Scott (Philadelphia: John D. Morris and Co., n.d.), p. 273. All subsequent translations of *Louis Lambert* are from this edition and will be referred to as L, page no.

31. Most critics of *Louis Lambert* seem to note the interpretative dilemma posed by the protagonist, although they choose different terms for the antitheses present in the text. Here, for instance, is Michael Young's discussion of the potentially plural religious readings of the text: "If we choose to be believers, then *Louis Lambert* becomes a Mythic text, with a closure that has the qualities of *stans*, or eternity. As atheists, however, we will see *Louis Lambert* as a mythic text, for which historical-biographical closure—simply, the physical fact of death, a 'fake' *stans*—will be adequate. Or, we can be agnostics" (p. 347). Michael Young, "Beginnings, Endings, and Textual Identities in Balzac's *Louis Lambert*" in *Romanic Review* 77(4), 1986: 343–58.

32. As Madeleine Ambrière points out, such a refusal of communication in the domain of science (and presumably of thought in general) is in itself a form of radical death. Her evaluation is based on her study of Balthasar Claës's fate in the *Recherche de l'Absolu*. She writes: "Si la science, comme l'argent, comme le sang et l'énergie vitale, ne circulent pas, ils deviennent agents de mort, et le personnage représente un élément de

démonstration du système balzacien" (p. 52). Madeleine Ambrière, "Balzac, Homme de Science(s). Savoir scientifique, discours scientifique et système balzacien dans *La Recherche de l'absolu* in *Balzac. L'Invention du roman*, edited by Claude Duchet and Jacques Neefs (Paris: Pierre Belfond, 1982), pp. 45–54.

33. Citron writes: "Il songe plus nettement à grouper ses oeuvres en séries organisées; il invente l'idée des *Scènes de la vie de province*, et veut réunir toutes les séries de *Scènes* en *Etudes de moeurs au XIXe siècle*, pour lesquelles il signe un contrat" (I, 14).

34. The fragmented structure of the text can be perceived in the loss of control experienced by the anonymous narrator of *Gambara*. He is no longer simply recording the "true" facts of a biography, but succumbs rather to the fascination of one of the protagonist's (Andrea's) fiction. Andrea's (actantial) *raison d'être* in the narrative is to seduce Marianina, and in order to do so he must reconstruct Marianina's personal history simply by imagining it. Such a narrative is to prove the possible ideal of complete identification, and of the communicability of such an identification. His summing up of her life touches off Marianina's dismay over a life misspent.

> Aujourd'hui cette apparence si longtemps poursuivie est une ombre et non un corps. Une folie qui touche au génie de si près doit être incurable en ce monde. Frappée de cette pensée, vous avez songé à toute votre jeunesse, sinon perdue, au moins sacrifiée; vous avez alors amèrement reconnu l'erreur de la nature qui vous avait donné un père quand vous appeliez un époux. (VI, 599)

Andrea's account seduces Marianina to accept the undecidability of Gambara's madness as just another form of madness. But her decision to follow the seductive and intuitive "rationality" of Andrea leads her to an error that seems much more serious than her youth sacrificed to Gambara. This second erring, namely, remains unrepresented in the text. Marianina's adulterous abandonment of Gambara (and apparent betrayal by the captivating, identifying narrator, Andrea) remains an unacknowledged lacuna in the narrative and an enigma to the reader. The mastery of the narrator has been suspended, in effect, by the entire narrative structure, since he seems incapable of determining the true center of his text, preferring instead to dog Andrea's footsteps at the beginning of the text, only to fix on Gambara's destiny halfway through the story.

35. It is perhaps here that we can most clearly reject intoxication as the artist's "deathly" abandon of his self-consciousness that is represented by Andrea's cure. The appeal to sensation and sensationalism was, for Balzac, a great temptation, if we can use both Peter Brooks's and Christopher Prendergast's study of melodrama in Balzac's fiction. Prendergast, especially, notes Balzac's negative attraction to melodrama when he describes the rivalry between Balzac and his (inferior but successful) competitor of melodrama, Eugène Sue: "The problem (posed especially by *Splendeurs*) is whether or not Balzac achieved this belated popularity on his own terms or by providing, in part at least, simply a variation on the style and mode of Eugène Sue." Christopher Prendergast, *Balzac: Fiction and Melodrama* (London: Edward Arnold, 1978), pp.77–78.

What is at stake for Prendergast, who chooses to analyze *La Cousine Bette* and *Splendeurs et misères des courtisanes* is the question how Balzac ultimately adopts and transforms the iron "law of modern popular writing" in the style of the *roman-feuilleton* (Prendergast, p. 381).

36. In *Gambara* the narrator (sharing the two other, listening, characters' perspective) judges Gambara's musical composition: "Il n'y avait pas l'apparence d'une idée poétique ou musicale dans l'étourdissante cacophonie qui frappait les oreilles: les principes de l'harmonie, les premières règles de la composition étaient totalement étrangères à cette infirme création" (VI, 602).

37. This provisional cure, ironically, implicates the "analyst," since he is now caught in the no-man's land of having imposed his rationality upon Gambara and, simultaneously, of having lost the object of his game of seduction (Marianina, Gambara's wife).

38. Christopher Prendergast, *The Order of Mimesis*, p. 117.

39. Roland Barthes, *S/Z*, p. 47.

40. Ibid., p. 47.

41. "Balzac est le témoin et l'observateur passionné, . . . de pouvoir concevoir ces mêmes transformations comme un mouvement non orienté qui s'inscrit dans un continuum non marqué historiquement, et de nier ainsi l'irréversibilité des effets qu'impliquerait toute explication en terms de coupure ou de fracture." Françoise Gaillard, "La Science: modèle ou vérité," p. 76.

42. Janet Beizer, p. 183.

43. M. I. Sicard, "Ce qu'il n'a pu achever par l'épée, je l'accomplirai par la plume" in *Napoléon Balzac et l'empire de la Comédie humaine* (Paris: Albin Michel, 1979), p. 147.

44. Marthe Robert also discusses the importance of Napoleon to Balzac's own creative enterprise, although she focuses primarily on Napoleon as symbol of success and power: ". . . il fortifie le romancier virtuel dans l'idée que tout est possible; que l'Histoire elle-même s'incarne devant le mythe de toute-puissance infantile . . ." (p. 238). Her reading remains a powerful one, in that she notes Balzac's resemblance to the usurping "Bâtard" through his rewriting the world in order to subject it to his desires. Nevertheless, she does fail to take into account the destructive violence wreaked upon the authorial narrators in such varied texts as *Honorine*, *Louis Lambert*, *Facino Cane*, *L'Auberge rouge*, *Le Colonel Chabert*, and *Sarrasine*, to name but a few. This pattern seems to suggest a certain ambivalence toward the "Demiurgic" powers of the "Bâtard" figure. Marthe Robert, "La Recherche de l'absolu" in *Roman des origines et origines du roman* (Paris: Grasset, 1972), pp. 237–91.

BIBLIOGRAPHY

BALZAC BIBLIOGRAPHY

A. Primary Sources

Balzac, Honoré de. *La Comédie humaine, Tomes I–VII.* Préface de Pierre-Georges Castex; présentation et notes de Pierre Citron. Paris: Aux Editions du Seuil, 1965.

———. *César Birotteau, Béatrix and Other Stories.* Translated by Ellen Marriage and James Waring. Philadelphia: John D. Morris and Co., n.d.

———. *Modeste Mignon, The Lily of the Valley and Other Stories.* Translated by Clara Bell and James Waring. Philadelphia: John D. Morris and Co., n.d.

———. *Séraphîta, A Daughter of Eve and Other Stories.* Translated by Clara Bell and R. S. Scott. Philadelphia: John D. Morris and Co., n.d.

———. *The Works of Honoré de Balzac. Volume XI. Cousin Betty.* Freeport, N.Y.: Books for Libraries Press, 1971.

———. "A Study of M. Beyle" in *The Charterhouse of Parma.* Translated by C. K. Scott Moncrieff. New York: Liveright Publishing Corp., 1944.

Rousseau, Jean-Jacques. *Les Confessions.* Paris: Garnier-Flammarion, 1968.

B. Secondary Sources

Ambrière, Madeleine. "Balzac, Homme de Science(s). Savoir scientifique, discours scientifique et système balzacien dans *La Recherche de l'absolu* in Claude Duchet's and Jacques Neefs's *Balzac: L'Invention du roman.* Paris: Pierre Belfond, 1982., pp. 43–55.

Amossy, Ruth. "L'exploitation des contraintes génériques dans *La Comédie humaine.* L'exemple du récit licencieux" in Claude Duchet and Jacques Neefs, *Balzac: L'Invention du roman,* pp. 99–117.

Bardèche, Maurice. "Les romans philosophiques" and "Conclusion" in *Balzac romancier.* Paris: Plon, 1940, pp. 204–37, 373–91.

Barthes, Roland. *S/Z.* Paris: Editions du Seuil, 1970.

Béguin, Albert. *Balzac visionnaire.* Genève: Albert Skira, 1946, pp. 183–205.

Beizer, Janet L. *Family Plots: Balzac's Narrative Generations.* New Haven: Yale University Press, 1986.

Bernheimer, Charles. "Cashing in on Hearts of Gold: Balzac and Sue" in *Figures of Ill Repute. Representing Prostitution in Nineteenth-Century France.* Cambridge: Harvard University Press, 1989., pp. 34–68.

Brombert, Victor. *The Hidden Reader. Stendhal, Balzac, Hugo, Baudelaire, Flaubert.* Cambridge: Harvard University Press, 1988.

Brooks, Peter. *The Melodramatic Imagination. Balzac, Henry James, Melodrama and the Mode of Excess.* New Haven: Yale University Press, 1976.

Brooks, Peter. "Narrative Desire" in *Reading for the Plot: Design and Intention in Narrative.* New York: Random Books, 1984., pp. 37–61.

———. "Narrative Transaction and Transference (Unburying *Le Colonel Chabert*)" in *Novel: A Forum on Fiction,* pp. 101–10.

Butler, Ronnie. "Napoleon and the Revolution," "The July Revolution," "The Economic Expansion," "The 1848 Revolution," and "Conclusion" in *Balzac and the French Revolution.* Totowa: N.J.: Barnes and Noble, 1983.

Dällenbach, Lucien. "Reading as Suture (Problems of Reception of the Fragmentary Text: Balzac and Claude Simon)" in *Style* (18) Spring 1984, pp. 196–205.

Eagleton, Terry. *Literary Theory: An Introduction.* Minneapolis: University of Minnesota Press, 1983.

Fizaine, Jean-Claude. "Ironie et Fiction dans l'oeuvre de Balzac" in Claude Duchet and Jacques Neefs, *Balzac: L'Invention du roman,* pp. 159–80.

Frappier-Mazur, Lucienne. "Sémiotique du corps malade dans *La Comédie humaine*" in Claude Duchet and Jacques Neefs, *Balzac: L'Invention du roman,* pp. 15–41.

Gaillard, Françoise. "La science: modèle ou vérité. Réflexions sur l'Avant-Propos à *La Comédie humaine*" in Claude Duchet and Jacques Neefs, *Balzac: L'Invention du roman,* pp. 57–83.

Jameson, Fredric. "The Ideology of Form: Partial Systems" in *La Vieille fille* in *Substance* 1976, pp. 29–49.

Kanes, Martin. "Langage balzacien: Splendeurs et misères de la représentation" in Claude Duchet and Jacques Neefs, *Balzac: L'Invention du roman,* pp. 281–95.

Lepenies, Wolf. "Transformation and Storage of Scientific Traditions in Literature" in *Literature and History.* Edited by Leonard Schulze and Walter Wetzels. New York: University Press of America, 1983, pp. 37–63.

Leuilliot, Bernard. "Oeuvres complètes, oeuvres diverses" in Claude Duchet and Jacques Neefs, *Balzac: L'Invention du roman,* pp. 257–77.

Lock, Peter. "Origins, Desire, and Writing: Balzac's Louis Lambert" in *Stanford French Review* 1 (1977): 289–311.

Lukàcs, Georg. "Balzac: *Lost Illusions*" in *Studies in European Realism.* New York: Grosset and Dunlop, pp. 47–64.

———. "Balzac: *The Peasants*" in *Studies in European Realism.* London: Hillway Publishing Company, 1950, pp. 21–46.

Macherey, Pierre. "'Les Paysans' de Balzac: un texte disparat" in *Pour une théorie de la production littéraire*. Paris: Maspéro, 1966.

Nesci, Catherine. *La Femme mode d'emploi. Balzac, de la Physiologie du mariage à La Comédie humaine*. Lexington: French Forum, 1992.

Picon, Gaëtan. *Balzac*. Paris: écrivains de toujours/seuil, 1983.

Prendergast, Christopher. *Balzac: Fiction and Melodrama*. London: Edward Arnold, 1978.

———. "Balzac: Narrative Contracts" in *The Order of Mimesis. Balzac, Stendhal, Nerval, Flaubert*. New York: Cambridge University Press, 1986, pp. 83–118.

Richard, Jean-Pierre. *Etudes sur le romantisme*. Paris: Editions du Seuil, 1971.

Robert, Marthe. "Pourquoi le roman?," "Raconter des histoires," "La Recherche de l'absolu" in *Roman des origines et l'origine du roman*. Paris: Gallimard, 1972, pp. 11–39, 41–78, 237–91.

Rogers, Nancy. "The Wasting Away of Romantic Heroines" in *Nineteenth-Century French Studies* 11 (1983): 246–56.

Rose, Margaret A. "The Second Time as Farce": A Brief Survey of the Concept of History Understood as Fiction and Farce" in *Literature and History*. Edited by Leonard Schulze and Walter Wetzels. New York: University Press of America, 1983, pp. 27–35.

Schuerewegen, Franc. "Pour effleurer le sexe. A propos d'*Honorine* de Balzac" in *Studia Neophilologica* 1983: 193–97.

Sicard, M. I. "Ce qu'il n'a pu achever par l'épée, je l'accomplirai par la plume" in *Napoléon Balzac et l'empire de La Comédie humaine*. Paris: Albin Michel, 1979, pp. 145–75.

Smith, Bonnie. *Ladies of the Leisure Class*. Princeton: Princeton University Press, 1981.

Stowe, William. *Balzac, James, and the Realistic Novel*. Princeton: Princeton University Press, 1983.

Sussmann, Hava. "*Honorine*: Un Avatar du Mythe de Tristan et Yseut" in *L'année balzacienne* (1981): 296–99.

Weber, Samuel. *Unwrapping Balzac*. Toronto: University of Toronto Press, 1979.

Young, Michael. "Beginnings, Endings, and Textual Identities in Balzac's *Louis Lambert*" in *Romanic Review* 77, 4 (1986): 343–58.

KLEIST BIBLIOGRAPHY

A. Primary Sources

Goethe, Johann Wolfgang von. *Wilhelm Meisters Lehrjahre*. Berlin: Aufbau Verlag, 1962.

———. *Wilhelm Meisters Wanderjahre, oder die Entsagenden.* München: Wilhelm Goldmann Verlag, 1961.

Kleist, Heinrich von. *Sämtliche Werke und Briefe, Erster und Zweiter Band.* Edited by Helmut Sembdner. München: Carl Hanser Verlag, 1961.

———. *The Marquise of O—and Other Stories.* Translated by Martin Greenberg. New York: Frederick Ungar Publishing Co, 1973.

———. *Plays.* Edited by Walter Hinderer. New York: Continuum, 1982.

B. Secondary Sources

Altenhofer, Norbert. "Der erschütterte Sinn. Hermeneutische Überlegungen zu Kleists *Das Erdbeben in Chili*" in David Wellbery, *Positionen der Literaturwissenschaft. Acht Modellanalysen am Beispiel von Kleists "Das Erdbeben in Chili."* München: Beck'sche Elementarbücher, 1985, pp. 39–53.

Auerbach, Erich. *Mimesis: The Representation of Reality in Western Literature.* Translated by Willard Trask. Princeton: Princeton University Press, 1973.

Beaufret, Jean. "Martin Heidegger et le problème de la vérité." 1957, pp. 353–73.

Birault, Henri. "Le Problème de la mort dans la philosophie de Sartre" in *Autour de Jean-Paul Sartre. Littérature et philosophie.* Paris: Gallimard, 1981, pp. 183–215.

Brooks, Peter. *Reading for the Plot: Design and Intention in Narrative.* New York: Random Books, 1984.

Bürger, Christa. "Statt einer Interpretation. Anmerkungen zu Kleists Erzählen" in Wellbery, *Positionen der Literaturwissenschaft,* pp. 88–109.

Chase, Cynthia. "Mechanical Doll, Exploding Machine: Kleist's Models of Narrative in *Decomposing Figures: Rhetorical Readings in the Romantic Tradition.* Baltimore: Johns Hopkins University Press, 1986, pp. 141–56.

Conrady, Karl Otto. "Das Moralische in Kleists Erzählungen. Ein Kapitel vom Dichter ohne Gesellschaft" in *Wege der Forschung. Heinrich von Kleist,* pp. 709–35.

Derrida, Jacques. *Of Grammatology.* Translated by Gayatri Chakravorty Spivak. Baltimore: Johns Hopkins University Press, 1974.

Ellis, John. "Introduction: Theory and Interpretation" and "Kleist: 'Das Erdbeben in Chili,'" in *Narration in the German Novelle: Theory and Interpretation.* New York: Cambridge University Press, 1974, pp. 1–76.

Felman, Shoshana. *La Folie et la chose littéraire.* Paris: Editions du Seuil, 1978, pp. 11–31.

———. "Beyond Oedipus: The Specimen Story of Psychoanalysis" in *MLN 98* (1983): 1021–153.

Frank, Joseph. *The Widening Gyre: Crisis and Mastery in Modern Literature.* Bloomington: Indiana University Press, 1963.

Freud, Sigmund. *Drei Abhandlungen zur Sexualtheorie (1904-1905).* Frankfurt a.M.: Suhrkamp, 1983.

———. *Jenseits des Lustprinzips* in *Psychologie des Unbewußten. Band III.* Frankfurt a.M.: 1975, pp. 213–72.

———. *Totem and Taboo,* in *The Standard Edition of the Complete Psychological Works of Sigmund Freud. Volume XIII.* Translated by James Strachey. London: Hogarth Press, 1966–1974.

———. "Theme of the Three Caskets," pp. 67–75. London: Hogarth Press, 1966–1974.

———. "The Uncanny," pp. 394–406. London: Hogarth Press, 1966–1974.

Gallas, Helga. *Das Textbegehren des "Michael Kohlhaas." Die Sprache des Unbewußten und der Sinn der Literatur.* Renbek bei Hamburg: Rowohlt, 1981.

Girard, René. *La Violence et le sacré.* Paris: Grasset, 1972.

———. "Mythos und Gegenmythos: Zu Kleists 'Das Erdbeben in Chili,'" in Wellbery, *Positionen der Literaturwissenschaft,* pp. 130–48.

Hamacher, Werner. "Das Beben der Darstellung" in Wellbery, *Positionen der Literaturwissenschaft,* pp. 149–73.

Hermann, Hans-Peter. "Zufall und Ich. Zum Begriff der Situation in den Novellen Heinrich von Kleists" in *Wege der Forschung. Heinrich von Kleist,* pp. 367–411.

Hölderlin, Friedrich. "Anmerkungen zur Antigonae" in the *Stuttgarter Hölderlin-Ausgabe. 5. Band.* Edited by Friedrich Beissner. Stuttgart: Scheufele, 1952.

Hoffmann, E. T. A. "Beethovens Instrumental-Musik" and "Alte und Neue Kirchenmusik" in *Dichtungen und Schriften, sowie Briefe und Tagebücher. Gesamtausgabe.* Weimar: Erich Lichtenstein, 1924, pp. 14–25, 32–57.

Hohoff, Curt. *Heinrich von Kleist. Mit Selbstzeugnissen und Bilddokumenten.* Hamburg: Rowohlt, 1958/88.

Kayser, Wolfgang. "Kleist als Erzähler" in *Wege der Forschung. Heinrich von Kleist,* pp. 230–43.

Kittler, Friedrich. "Ein Erdbeben in Chili und Preußen" in Wellbery, *Positionen der Literaturwissenschaft,* pp. 24–38.

Koselleck, Reinhart. "Der Zufall als Motivationsrest in der Geschichtsschreibung" in *Vergangene Zukunft. Zur Semantik geschichtlicher Zeiten.* Frankfurt a.M.: 1979, pp. 158–75.

Lacan, Jacques. *Ecrits.* Paris: Editions du Seuil, 1966. [Especially "Le Stade du miroir" and "Le Séminaire sur 'La Lettre volée," pp. 11–61, 93–100].

———. *Le Séminaire. Livre I. Les Ecrits techniques de Freud.* Paris: Editions du Seuil, 1975. [Especially "La Topique de l'imaginaire," pp. 87–103.]

———. *Le Séminaire. Livre II. Le Moi dans la théorie de Freud et dans la technique de la psychanalyse.* Paris: Editions du Seuil, 1978. [Especially "Questions à celui qui enseigne" and "Le Désir, la vie et la mort," pp. 241–57 and pp. 259–74.]

Lacoue-Labarthe, Philippe. *Mimesis des articulations.* France: Aubier-Flammarion, 1975.

Lockemann, Fritz. *Gestalt und Wandlungen der deutschen Novelle.* München: Max Hueber Verlag, 1957.

Lützeler, Paul Michael. "Heinrich von Kleist: *Michael Kohlhaas* (1810)" in *Romane und Erzählungen der deutschen Romantik. Neue Interpretationen.* Edited by P. M. Lützeler. Stuttgart: Reclam, 1981, pp. 213–33.

Luther, Martin. *Schrift an den christlichen Adel deutscher Nation. Von des christlichen Standes Besserung.* (Juli 1520) in Luther's *Reformatorische Schriften. Band 3 and 4.* Edited by Otto v. Gerlach. Berlin: Eichler Verlag, pp. 159–94 [Band III]; pp. 5–64 [Band IV].

Müller-Salget, Klaus. "Das Prinzip der Doppeldeutigkeit" in *Wege der Forschung. Kleists Aktualität,* pp. 167–92.

Müller-Seidel, Walter. "Die Struktur des Widerspruchs in Kleists "Marquise von O . . . " in *Wege der Forschung. Heinrich von Kleist,* pp. 244–68.

———. "Todesarten und Todesstrafen. Eine Betrachtung über Heinrich von Kleist" in *Kleist-Jahrbuch 1985.* Edited by Hans Joachim Kreutzer. Berlin: Erich Schmidt Verlag, 1985, pp. 7–38.

M'Uzan, Michel de. *De l'art à la mort. Itinéraire psychoanalytique.* Paris: Gallimard, 1977.

Nancy, Jean-Luc and Philippe Lacoue-Labarthe. *L'Absolu littéraire.* Paris: Editions du Seuil, 1978.

Rousseau, Jean-Jacques. *Les Confessions.* Paris: Garnier-Flammarian, 1968.

Sauer, August. *Kleists Todeslitanei. Prager Deutsche Studien. Heft 7.* Prag: Carl Bellmann Verlag, 1907.

Schlegel, Friedrich. *Lucinde. Ein Roman. Erster Theil.* Berlin: bei Heinrich Frölich, 1799.

Schneider, Helmut. "Der Zusammensturz des Allgemeinen" in Wellbery, *Positionen der Literaturwissenschaft,* pp. 110–29.

Schneiderman, Stuart. *Jacques Lacan: The Death of an Intellectual Hero.* Cambridge, Mass.: Harvard University Press, 1983.

———. *Returning to Freud. Clinical Psychoanalysis in the School of Lacan.* New Haven: Yale University Press, 1980.

Schröder, Jürgen. "Kleists Novelle 'Der Findling'. Ein Plädoyer für Nicolo" in *Kleist-Jahrbuch 1985.* Edited by Hans Joachim Kreutzer. Berlin: Erich Schmidt Verlag, 1985, pp. 109–27.

Stewart, Garrett. *Death Sentences: Styles of Dying in British Fiction.* Cambridge, Mass.: Harvard University Press, 1984.

Stierle, Karlheinz. "Das Beben des Bewußtseins. Die narrative Struktur von Kleists *Das Erdbeben in Chili*" in Wellbery's *Positionen der Literaturwissenschaft,* pp. 54–68.

Szondi, Peter. *Schriften II.* Frankfurt a.M.: Suhrkamp, 1978.

Wellbery, David. "Semiotische Anmerkungen zu Kleists *Das Erdbeben in Chili*" in *Positionen der Literaturwissenschaft,* pp. 69–87.

GENERAL SOURCES

Alter, Robert. *Partial Magic. The Novel as a Self-Conscious Genre.* Berkeley: University of California Press, 1975.

Barthes, Roland. *Writing Degree Zero.* Translated by Annette Lavers and Colin Smith. New York: Hill and Wang, 1967.

Baudelaire, Charles. "La Mort des artistes" in *Les Fleurs du mal.* In *Oeuvres complètes, La Pléiade.* Paris: Gallimard, 1975.

Bernheimer, Charles. "Introduction" and "Parent-Duchâtelet: Engineer of Abjection" and "Conclusion" in *Figures of Ill Repute: Representing Prostitution in Nineteenth-Century France.* Cambridge: Harvard University Press, 1989.

Bersani, Leo. "Realism and the Fear of Desire" in *A Future for Astyanax: Character, Desire in Literature.* New York: Columbia University Press, 1984.

Bronhofen, Elizabeth, and Sarah Webster Goodwin. *Death and Representation.* Baltimore: Johns Hopkins University, 1993.

Corngold, Stanley. *Franz Kafka: The Necessity of Form.* Ithaca: Cornell University Press, 1988.

Culler, Jonathan. "Poetics of the Novel" in *Structuralist Poetics: Structuralism, Linguistics and the Study of Literature.* London: Routledge, Kegan, and Paul, 1980, pp. 189–237.

DeJean, Joan. "Introduction" and "*Les Liaisons dangereuses.* Writing under the Other's Name" in *Literary Fortifications: Rousseau, Laclos, Sade.* Princeton: Princeton University Press, 1984, pp. 3–19.

Durzak, Manfred. *Die deutsche Kurzgeschichte der Gegenwart.* Stuttgart: Reclam, 1980.

Frisch, Max. *Stiller.* Frankfurt a. M.: Suhrkamp, 1980.

Gaudon, Jean. "Eloge de la digression" in D. G. Charlston, J. Gaudon, and Anthony R. Pugh, *Balzac and the Nineteenth Century: Studies in French Literature Presented to Hubert L. Hunt by Pupils, Colleagues, and Friends.* Leicester: Leicester University Press, 1972.

Genette, Gérard. *Figures III.* Paris: Aux Editions du Seuil, 1972.

Heidegger, Martin. "Zweiter Abschnitt/Erstes Kapitel. Das mögliche Ganzsein des Daseins und das Sein zum Tode" in *Sein und Zeit.* Tübingen: Max Niemeyer Verlag, 1984, pp. 231–67.

Kafka, Franz. "In der Strafkolonie" in *Sämtliche Erzählungen.* Edited by Paul Raabe. Frankfurt a.M.: Fischer, 1980.

Kafka, Franz. *Tagebücher, 1910–1923.* Edited by Max Brod. Frankfurt a.M.: Fischer, 1984.

Kermode, Frank. *The Sense of an Ending. Studies in the Theory of Fiction.* New York: Oxford University Press, 1968.

Kristeva, Julia. *Black Sun: Depression and Melancholia.* New York: Columbia University Press, 1987/89.

Kurz, Gerhard. *Traum-Schrecken. Kafkas literarische Existenzanalyse.* Stuttgart: J. B. Metzlersche Verlagsbuchhandlung, 1980.

Lacapra, Dominick. "A Poetics of Historiography: Hayden White's *Tropics of Discourse*" in *Rethinking Intellectual History: Texts, Contexts, Language.* Ithaca: Cornell University Press, 1983, pp. 72–83.

Lacoue-Labarthe, Philippe, and J.-L. Nancy. "L'Exigence fragmentaire" and "Clôture" in *L'Absolu littéraire.* Paris: Seuil, 1978, pp. 57–81, 419–25.

Lacoue-Labarthe, Philippe. "Typographie" in S. Agacinski, J. Derrida, S. Kofman, J.-L. Nancy, and B. Pautrat, *Mimesis des articulations.* France: Aubier-Flammarion, 1975.

Miller, D. A. *The Novel and the Police.* Berkeley: University of California Press, 1988.

Montaigne, Michel de. *Essais, Tomes I-III.* Paris: Garnier-Flammarion, 1969.

Plato. *Phaedrus.* Translated by R. Hackforth, F.B.A. Cambridge: Cambridge University Press, 1979.

Reid, Roddey. *Families in Jeopardy: Regulating the Social Body in France, 1750–1910.* Stanford: Stanford University Press, 1993.

Selbmann, Rolf. *Der deutsche Bildungsroman.* Stuttgart: J. B. Metzler, 1984.

Tanner, Tony. *Adultery in the Novel. Contract and Transgression.* Baltimore: Johns Hopkins University Press, 1979.

Terdiman, Richard. *Discourse/Counter-Discourse. The Theory and Practice of Symbolic Resistance in Nineteenth-Century France.* Ithaca: Cornell University Press, 1985.

Todorov, Tzvetan. "Poetics and Criticism" in *The Poetics of Prose.* Ithaca: Cornell University Press.

Tolstoy, Leo. *The Death of Ivan Ilych and Other Great Stories.* Translated by Aylmer Maude. New York: Signet, 1960.

Vattimo, Gianni, "Etre-là et temporalité; L'être-pour-la-mort" in *Introduction à Heidegger,* 1971, pp. 55–63.

White, Hayden. "The Value of Narrativity in the Representation of Reality" in *The Content of the Form.* Baltimore: Johns Hopkins University Press, 1987, pp. 1–25.

Wolf, Christa. *Kassandra.* Darmstand: Luchterhand, 1984.

INDEX